Materializing Silence in Feminist Activism

Jessica Rose Corey

Materializing Silence in Feminist Activism

Jessica Rose Corey
Thompson Writing Program
Duke University
Durham, NC, USA

ISBN 978-3-030-81065-8   ISBN 978-3-030-81066-5 (eBook)
https://doi.org/10.1007/978-3-030-81066-5

© The Editor(s) (if applicable) and The Author(s), under exclusive license to Springer Nature Switzerland AG 2021
This work is subject to copyright. All rights are solely and exclusively licensed by the Publisher, whether the whole or part of the material is concerned, specifically the rights of translation, reprinting, reuse of illustrations, recitation, broadcasting, reproduction on microfilms or in any other physical way, and transmission or information storage and retrieval, electronic adaptation, computer software, or by similar or dissimilar methodology now known or hereafter developed.
The use of general descriptive names, registered names, trademarks, service marks, etc. in this publication does not imply, even in the absence of a specific statement, that such names are exempt from the relevant protective laws and regulations and therefore free for general use.
The publisher, the authors and the editors are safe to assume that the advice and information in this book are believed to be true and accurate at the date of publication. Neither the publisher nor the authors or the editors give a warranty, expressed or implied, with respect to the material contained herein or for any errors or omissions that may have been made. The publisher remains neutral with regard to jurisdictional claims in published maps and institutional affiliations.

Cover illustration: © Alex Linch shutterstock.com

This Palgrave Macmillan imprint is published by the registered company Springer Nature Switzerland AG
The registered company address is: Gewerbestrasse 11, 6330 Cham, Switzerland

To my husband, who challenges and supports me in my efforts to do more and do better

To Gram, Grandpa, and Jaybird, who loved me enough to support my dreams even when those dreams took me away from them

To my closest women friends, Barbara George and Lauren Esposito, who provide a constant source of inspiration and invention

To my former teachers and professors, whose work and encouragement made the world a magnificent mystery to be endlessly pursued

To every woman who uses her intelligence, wisdom, talent, and fortitude to fight for equity and justice—silently, quietly, or loudly

Acknowledgments

My undergraduate research assistant, Shernice Martin, contributed vital work to the research process. I greatly appreciate her insightfulness and work ethic.

My former student, Amber Smith, graciously allowed me to use her astute and creative work as an exemplar of what students can achieve. It has been a privilege to teach her and be taught by her.

My former colleague, T. Passwater, allowed me to share their teaching materials with readers, materials that have enriched my pedagogy and, therefore, my students' experiences with composing.

Pamela Takayoshi, Sara Newman, M. Karen Powers, and Nicole Rousseau, aside from responding to previous versions of this research, have served as models for the type of scholar and teacher I wish to be.

Jennifer (Jennie) O'Connell was invaluable to the organization of the Clothesline Project discussed in this book and to the data collection process. I could not have undertaken this work without her supportive involvement.

Patrick W. Berry provided guidance during the initial stages of navigating publication, during a time when Early Career Research felt vast and isolating. I am grateful for his generosity with "rhetorical listening."

Contents

1	Introduction	1
2	Rhetorics of Silence	51
3	Case Study of the CP Archive	89
4	"Making" Progress in the Classroom and Beyond	145
5	Future Directions	183

Appendix A: Mini Makerspace Scenarios (From T Passwater)	187
Appendix B: Public Scholarship Assignment Sheet	189
Appendix C: Amber Smith's Material Project Write-Up	193
Index	197

List of Figures

Fig. 1.1	Representation of the relationship among main variables discussed in the book	17
Fig. 1.2	Representation of the relationship among sub elements of Figure 1.1	18
Fig. 3.1	Shirts excluding designers' personal details	97
Fig. 3.2	Shirts with references to use of the body as active participation	100
Fig. 3.3	Shirts that include covert assertions of agency with characters (pronouns)	102
Fig. 3.4	Shirts that include covert assertions of agency with actions	103
Fig. 3.5	Shirts depicting personal experiences	108
Fig. 3.6	Shirts depicting socially constructed representations	108
Fig. 3.7	Shirts relying on the CP context for meaning	113
Fig. 3.8	Content of shirts providing commentary on cultural narratives	116

List of Tables

Table 1.1	Definitions of frequently used words	6
Table 1.2	Parallels between archives and the Clothesline Project	32
Table 3.1	"Bumper Sticker" messages in the CP (written as displayed on shirt)	106
Table 3.2	Visual representations on CP tee shirts	109
Table 3.3	Parallels between the CP and Danielson's (2010) conceptualization of archives	120

CHAPTER 1

Introduction

People have long valued activism as a way to "give voice" to minoritized and otherwise oppressed individuals and populations.[1] But these individuals and populations have always had a voice, albeit unheard and dismissed (Boo, n.d.; Buttry, 2016; Callahan, 2018). We must recognize, then, that embedded within activist opportunities are social, psychological, and political complexities of having, composing, "giving," and using voice through alternative means, such as material composition.[2] Through exploring the role of materiality, rhetoric, and silence in activism, this book illuminates how those in oppressed subject positions use literacy publicly and subversively in an attempt to create change, whether that change occurs on an individual level or a more collective scale. This work expands upon the long-standing feminist notion that "the personal is political" and explores the intricacies of blurred boundaries—how paradoxes like "silence speaks" allow for subversive communication in material forms.

---

[1] I use the term "minoritized," and many other terms throughout the book, because at the time of this writing, scholars and activists seem to widely accept the terms, and they encompass what I wish to communicate. I acknowledge, however, that language evolves and, therefore, the understanding and use of these terms may change.

[2] In this book, "material" refers to non-digital and non-electronic materials and tools, such as fabrics, markers and other drawing/writing utensils, paints, clay, wood, yarn, and materials involved in crafting (paper, pipe cleaners, pom poms, beads, etc.).

© The Author(s), under exclusive license to Springer Nature Switzerland AG 2021
J. R. Corey, *Materializing Silence in Feminist Activism*,
https://doi.org/10.1007/978-3-030-81066-5_1

Notions of active participation bombard us not only in activist spaces but within academic spaces (and in their intersections), from course syllabi to university mission statements that call for something often worded like "engaged citizens." People in many contexts commonly conceptualize active participation as extroverted participation (a noticeable public presence accompanied by verbal contributions to discussions). But such notions become increasingly complicated in a world with unfavorable, sometimes even dangerous, consequences to such displays of participation. One needs to look no further than Anita Hill, Monica Lewinski, and most recently, Dr. Christina Blasey Ford to see the physical and psychological threat of participation in America's justice system.

To address the complexities of participation, then, I conceptualize the subject matter of this book as consisting of two major elements: literate artifacts and psychosocial compositions. Literate artifacts refer to documents or materials, such as those produced during social action events (e.g., protest signs or other artifacts, listserv sign-up sheets, and exhibits). I use the term "psychosocial compositions" to refer to the metaphorical composing and revising of individual participants and society, and the contribution of alphabetic and visual texts (literate artifacts) as an input and output of the relationships between individuals and cultures. Psychosocial compositions include influences on one's ideologies and actions—for instance, ways in which literate practices and cultural discourse affect individuals' participation *in* and reception *of* civic engagement. The concept builds on Young's (1997) notion of "discursive activism," which involves action "directed at promoting new grammars, new social paradigms through which individuals, collectives, and institutions interpret social circumstances and devise responses to them" (p. 3). In other words, Young (1997) looks at a component of psychosocial composing—discourse as an input to people's understandings of a concept that creates a particular output/response. Through Young's (1997) discursive activism, change occurs via "reinterpretations of and, consequently, revised responses to sociopolitical situations...[so] language and society are co-constitutive" (Clark, 2016, p. 791).

If we conceive of psychosocial composing as such a process, it looks something like the following (written linearly for the sake of clarity, though the process occurs recursively):

1. Worldviews/schemas/social narratives/ideologies are constructed and sustained in society through circulation of texts (with "text"

broadly conceived as anything that communicates a message, locally or globally). These texts are outputs of the symbiosis between individuals' identities and existing worldviews/schemas/social narratives/ideologies (steps 2 and 3 below). These texts are also inputs to the symbiosis between sustaining and revising existing worldviews/schemas/social narratives/ideologies and composing new worldviews/schemas/social narratives/ideologies (steps 3, 4, and 5 below).
2. Individuals' identities are constructed (composed) in part *by*, in the context *of*, and in response *to* existing worldviews/schemas/social narratives/ideologies and circulating texts.
3. A person or group of people composes a text, within the context of, and in direct or indirect response to, existing worldviews/schemas/social narratives/ideologies and circulating texts.
4. Individuals' identities continue to be influenced (composed) by old and new circulating texts.
5. Existing worldviews/schemas/social narratives/ideologies are perpetuated and/or revised, and new worldviews/schemas/social narratives/ideologies are composed and circulated. Step 5, then, becomes step 1.

At least part of this process occurs subconsciously.

The concept of psychosocial compositions is inherent in the idea of storytelling, as "storytellers [are] story listeners" and narratives influence the very contexts that, in turn, shape narratives (Andersson et al., 2019, p. 6). Psychosocial compositions, then, guide literate practices such as writing therapy (Bolton, 2004). In fact, Almond (2012) stated: "literary endeavor has supplanted therapy as our dominant mode of personal investigation…the refuge of stories… remain the most reliable paths to meaning ever devised by our species" ("A Theory More or Less Guaranteed to Rankle Therapist and Writer Alike," para. 2; "A Word in Defense of the Writing Cure," para. 2). While one can question elevating stories to such a status, stories with personal and social significance can affect change. More specifically, life stories have had a significant role in creating a line of communication for marginalized and oppressed individuals and, as such, remain important to scholars in psychology, rhetoric and composition, women's studies, literacy studies, and pedagogy.

I further understand literate artifacts and psychosocial compositions in terms of how texts mediate trauma and recovery by allowing individuals to construct, deconstruct, and reconstruct narratives related to identity (Andersson & Conley, 2013; Fiandt, 2006; Lepore & Smith, 2002; Lieblich, 2013; Pennebaker, 1997; Rose, 1999; Smyth et al., 2001; Sharma-Patel et al., 2012). Psychological experiences become concrete through the use of narrative (Lieblich, 2013), so that composing allows us to become different, "othered" so to speak, thereby allowing us the advantages of perspective, relief, honesty, and growth. Language (and image) can help people break themselves apart and put themselves back together in impermanent and experimental ways, achieved with a sense of agency and safety (Frangos, 1997).

With these notions in mind, this book responds to the following overarching questions:

1. How do written and visual literacy embody and mediate lived experiences?
2. How can people use literate artifacts to revise social narratives?
3. In what ways do activists use silence in communicating their messages?
4. How does multimodal composition serve as a mediator between silence (imposed or un-imposed) and meaningful communication?

I use a case study of a Clothesline Project (CP) archive to respond to the above questions. The CP is an international event that invites survivors of gender violence, and families of victims,[3] to decorate tee shirts that get hung on clotheslines in public places; it began in Massachusetts in 1990 when a survivor of domestic violence and rape took the initiative to ask, "Where is our wall? Where is our memorial?…Where is the wall that commemorates the 51,000 women killed in the war against women?" (Hipple, 2000, p. 168). At that time, the Maryland Men's Anti-Rape Resources Center (MARS) had released information which estimated:

> During the 16 years of U.S. involvement in Vietnam, a war that claimed the lives of 58,000 men in Southeast Asia, more than 51,000 women were

---

[3] See Table 1.1 for a discussion of "survivor" and "victim" terminology.

murdered in this country [the U.S.] by their husbands, male friends, dates, and casual male acquaintances. (Hipple, 2000, p. 168)

Today, an estimated 500 CP projects exist globally (Walk a Mile in Her Shoes, n.d.). While CP organizers may most commonly offer fabric paints and markers during tee shirt-making sessions/workshops, some participants decorate tee shirts with felt, burlap, lace, pieces from childhood dresses; broken candles; and photographs (Rose, 2014, p. x). Rose (2014) further notes:

> Not everyone immediately understands the word 'clothesline' or will use T-shirts to break the silence. For example, in Venezuela, we needed to translate the word 'Clothesline,' and in Cameroon, we used traditional scarves as well as T-shirts; women there also felt more comfortable sewing or doing embroidery, a more familiar medium than drawing with paints and markers. But once explained, the concept resonates across cultures. (p. ix)

The CP, then, provides a rich site for critical examination of a variety of social dynamics and their complexities, which I address in the next section. Table 1.1 provides definitions of main terms critical to exploring those dynamics and complexities.

THEORETICAL CONSIDERATIONS

The research in this book takes up work regarding violence against women "beyond criminal justice and medical approaches" and examines "community-based transformational justice strategies," as arts and performing arts increasingly become part of activist efforts (Baker & Bevacqua, 2018, p. 371). This extended inquiry rests on a particular conceptualization of feminist activist work. I set forth this conceptualization with the understanding that others may perceive and define activism, and feminist activism, differently from the ways I define them for the purposes of this research. Certainly, other researchers have grappled with the complex issue of identifying criteria for engaging in feminist activism, as seen in Clover and Stalker (2008). Upon examining fabric arts projects created by women and used for raising awareness of particular social concerns, Clover and Stalker (2008) questioned the use of the

Table 1.1 Definitions of frequently used words

Survivor	Though not necessarily officially documented, common practice in activism is to refer to those who have experienced assault but not died at the hands of their assailant as "survivors." There is, however, some argument that such terminology denies living survivors their victimhood and is an inaccurate representation of their lived experiences during and after an act of violence/assault (Miller, 2019). Throughout the book, then, I often combine the terms as "survivor/victim" or use them interchangeably
Victim	Though not necessarily officially documented, common practice in activism is to refer to those who have been murdered by an assailant as "victims" of violence (see additional note above)
Composing	The written or graphic constructing and construing of representations of our recognitions (adapted from Berthoff's definition of "literacy") (Berthoff, 1990)
Psychosocial compositions	The metaphorical composing and revising of individual participants and society, and the contribution of written and visual texts as an input and output of the relationships between individuals and social culture
Literacy	Understanding knowledge and ideas in relation to context
Visual literacy	"the ability to understand and use images and to think and learn in terms of images" (Kaplan & Mifflin, 1996, p.107)
Literate practice	Response to context, audience, and purpose with consideration of content and form of a composition, regardless of medium. Writing or composing a particular product is a literate practice. The conscious or subconscious consideration of the social conditions under which one composes is also a literate practice. What audiences do with a particular composition can be considered another literate practice
Literate artifacts	Documents or materials, such as those produced during social action events (protest signs, listserv sign-up sheets, and exhibits)
Material/Materiality/Material Composing/Material Multimodal Composing	Non-digital and non-electronic materials and tools, such as fabrics, markers and other drawing/writing utensils, paints, clay, wood, yarn, and materials involved in crafting (paper, pipe cleaners, pom poms, beads, etc.). Any act of composing with these materials is material composing or material multimodal composing
Women's literate practices	Adoption, production, reproduction, or adaptation of textual or visual forms that respond to the needs of an individual or group of people in such a way that it advances personal and political positions within various forms of oppression

(continued)

Table 1.1 (continued)

Feminist	Relating to, or advocating for, rights, equality, and/or justice for all humans
Feminist activist work	The effort to bring about social change in regard to rights, equality and/or justice for people in oppressed positions
Silence	A "rhetorical art" (Glenn, 2004, p. 2), including an "absence of sound" and "absence with function" (Glenn, 2004, pp. 4-10)

term "feminist art," given that the works address more than just women's issues—though addressed "through the eyes of women" (p. 14).

Another definitional issue in regard to feminist activism comes in the question of whether people pay any mind to the work of women activists. Droogsma (2009) asks, "Do the persons who silenced woman abuse survivors, and therefore remain complicit in their oppression, listen to the Clothesline Project" (p. 494)? In other words, Droogsma (2009) questions whether those who dismiss, doubt, or blame sexual violence survivors pay mind to survivors' acts of resistance. While evidence may not support a definitive answer to this question, even if the CP fails to reach those who directly or indirectly oppress women, it has potential advantages for its participants, and may reach people experiencing oppression in various forms (e.g., systemic oppression, invalidation of feelings and experiences, marginalization in personal relationships or other social contexts).

We must determine whether we want to base definitions of activism on, or determine the success of activism by, measures of widespread reactions to activist efforts or overall behaviors and attitudes in society. To do so might oversimplify the objectives of activism. While we may desire to change cultural narratives on a large scale, we have little evidence to suggest that this actually occurs. As a case in point, sexism remains prevalent despite many efforts to achieve equity and equality among genders. That said, tracking and measuring changes in beliefs outside of tangible changes (such as those regarding policies) proves difficult to say the least. As I suggest earlier, however, activist efforts can help participants revise their own narratives and inspire fellow people in marginalized and oppressed positions to seek help or engage in composing about their own experiences. It seems, then, that activism must often have the objective of individual healing and satisfaction as much as that of societal or global change, especially if we seek evidence of the results of such efforts.

Moreover, activist efforts that focus on women, like the CP, have suffered criticism for their unintentional, and sometimes intentional, exclusion of men—because including men in shirt-making sessions or displaying shirts created by men may complicate participation by women whose perpetrators were male (Gregory et al., 2002) and because pervasive power dynamics between men and women may create tension. While some CP events do include male participants, we must question the extent to which we might encourage participation from males, non-binary individuals, and gender non-conforming individuals in the communication of experiences believed to affect women primarily, and determine how that communication influences activist efforts. This book, then, uses "feminist activist work" to mean *the effort to bring about social change in regard to rights, equity, equality, and/or justice for people in oppressed positions*.

As for the exclusion of men in many CP and other activist events, Julier (1994) considers whether all collaboration serves as "democratic good or whether it merely restructures the sites at which privilege and control are enacted, thus far silencing individual expression" (p. 258). Therefore, while feminist activists should advocate for the equal status of all people (regardless of race, gender, sexual orientation, physical abilities, and so forth), each of these groups, at times, needs its own space in which to speak for itself and communicate its unique struggles. My ability to speak on behalf of others, and for them to speak on behalf of me, remains limited by our differing experiences and by the different ways in which we experience similar circumstances. As Julier (1994) points out, having men participate in the CP (or any event addressing offences primarily documented as offenses committed against women) increases the risk that women's voices (or messages) will get lost among men's (especially since CP tee shirts themselves do not necessarily indicate gender). Furthermore, violence against men remains a unique experience for which I, as a woman, would fail to address justly (at least to some extent). Though we may have similar experiences, the social construction of our identities likely changes the way we experience differently the same acts. Similarly, while I advocate for self-identifying members of the LGBTQIA community, as a heterosexual and cis-gender woman, I would make appeals to ethos and pathos different from those that a participating member of that community could make. The same holds true for women of different races and from various socioeconomic groups.

All subject positions involve worldviews and social systems that influence responses to circumstances. In essence, while some activist events can and should achieve all-inclusiveness, all groups deserve their own space in society to express their own identities and the issues that surround those identities uniquely. We must remain cautious that in our altruistic attempt to be all-inclusive and speak on behalf of multiple groups, we avoid dominating, silencing, or misrepresenting the distinctive voices of those groups. In practice, inclusivity can be unclear.

To illustrate, around the time that I conducted my study, a fraternity on campus hosted its own shirt-making sessions and did not donate shirts made during those sessions to the main CP on campus or affiliate with the project in any other way. Perhaps some of the above factors contributed to this decision. I remember, too, that same year, a group of men wanting to accompany women during a Take Back the Night event, which raised discussion over whether accepting such a show of support would undermine the very argument of Take Back the Night that it should be safe for women to walk at all hours without male protection. Similarly, though not related to gender or activism directly, Blackwell (2018) argues for "black only" or "people of color only" spaces, pointing out that:

> In integrated spaces, patterns of white dominance are inevitable. These patterns include things like being legitimized for using academic language, an expectation of 'getting it right' (i.e., perfectionism), fear of open conflict, scapegoating those who cause discomfort, and a sense of urgency that takes precedence over inclusion… These patterns happen even when white people are doing the work of examining their privilege. They can happen even when facilitators design and model more inclusive ways of being together. Why? The values of whiteness are the water in which we all swim…It may be argued that to build an inclusive community, caucusing is actually necessary. In an article published by the American Political Science Association, citing her examination of intersectionality within women's movements, professor Laurel Weldon argues that inviting marginalized subgroups to hold their own spaces tends to strengthen broader movements. (paras 8–10 & para 28)

Because the CP does not collect identifying or demographic information on participants, we have no data on identities such as race or with which gender (if either) participants identify. But any time in activism that dominant groups attempt to advocate for nondominant groups, the risk of overshadowing the voice or presence of marginalized people remains. Dominant groups (determined by social structures) validating the message of nondominant groups may further a cause (such as when men recognize sexism and advocate for equality and equity for women); yet, such support may reaffirm the notion that reality is not real until men, white people, straight people, cisgender people, wealthy people (or people in other subject positions) say it is.

While some events and organizations focus on men's experiences with sexual violence (such as 1in6.org and malesurvivor.org), seemingly fewer exist for the LGBTQIA community. The work discussed in this book, then, does not take a trans-exclusionary radical feminist (TERF) approach. My focus on "women" rather than on "females," and my use of non-binary pronouns, attempt to communicate this. Additionally, as I previously state, if transgender participants created a portion of the shirts I studied, I had no way to account for that, given that (1) the CP does not collect identifying information on participants and (2) nobody responded to requests for interviews for my study.

Similar to the complexities faced in defining activism and feminist activism, we must sift through issues of defining literacy and "women's literate practices." In this book, I define "literacy" as *understanding knowledge and ideas in relation to context*. I define "women's literate practices" as *adoption, production, reproduction, or adaptation of textual or visual forms that respond to the needs of an individual or group of people in such a way that it advances personal and/or political positions within various forms of oppression*. The adoption, production, reproduction, and adaptation of literate practices and the ideas contained within them lead women to have fragmented identities (for better or worse). These literate practices also lead women, however, to defragment their personal identities, to put pieces together in new ways and learn about themselves as "whole" beyond dichotomies. These practices inherently include accepting and rejecting pieces of narratives from the larger social structures in which women find themselves. A connection exists among individual, local, national, and global experiences, and these connections get severed and reconfigured, sometimes from moment to moment. Luckily, the act of composing provides a way to make sense of, and give form to, the very chaotic experiences of these dynamics (Lieblich, 2013). The composition, though not final (Lieblich, 2013), gives us a shape, a framework within which we can start working (Daniell, 2003); it gives a text in which we can revise and re-imagine the possible (Julier, 1994).

Additionally, for the sake of clarity, I separate rhetoric from literate practices. Understanding and using rhetorical strategies remains a part of the invention, production, and reception of any literate artifact. Rhetoric (commonly thought of as implicit and explicit argument) influences the construction of literate practices, as literate practices influence the construction and dissemination of texts. But one can choose methods of textual analysis other than rhetorical analysis. Likewise, we can examine rhetorical situations (purpose, audience, context) without focusing on the literate artifacts within those situations. We can understand the distinction in terms of "interpenetration," described as "forg[ing] unities between subject and object, ultimately between all subjects and all objects, all subjects and all subjections, all objects and all objects, a total unity—without loss of individual identity" (Dolzani, 2012, pp. 27–28). In other words, rhetoric (or rhetorical strategy) remains embedded in composing processes and final products, as composing processes and final products remain embedded in rhetorical contexts. But we can have productive conversations about both of them separately.

Within these rhetorical considerations a symbiotic relationship exists between one's narrative, one's audience, and one's life (Rosenwald & Ochberg, 1992). As we find ourselves in constant tension with authoritative discourse and the discourse of all others we encounter, we must deal with persuasion and ideology as "not within us, but between us" (Warshauer & Ball, 2004, p. 29). Similarly, Kock and Villadsen (2012) use the term "rhetorical citizenship" to discuss the way in which discourse serves not as a precedent to action but as part of action itself (p. 1).

Davies (1992), in "Women's Subjectivity and Feminist Stories," points out that individuals use language and stories to understand themselves as "whole," as both sides of almost any duality. In addition, Jane Marcus (1988), in "Invincible Mediocrity: The Private Selves of Public Women," notes that a sense of double-consciousness makes any writing performed by or for an individual a collective construction. We see these dynamics displayed in Daniell's (2003) research with Mountain City women involved in Al-Anon (a support group for family members of people with alcohol addiction), which documents women using literacy to examine how other people dealt with adversity, seeking models to inform their own way of living. From there, the women from Mountain City turned to literacy as "practice," not solely in the sense of doing something repeatedly, but in the sense of aiming to reach a higher level of performance; they began to use literacy for political endeavors, like building community and creating empowerment (Daniell, 2003). Anne Ruggles Gere (1997) encountered similar dynamics in her studies of women's clubs and the ways in which women used writing to engage in personal development; but unlike the Mountain City women, the women in Gere's study felt it necessary to "appropriat[e] the ideology of selfless womanhood," thereby hiding motives for personal development behind humanitarian efforts (p. 12). Together, these scholars bring attention to "macro and micro practices" of literacy and deliberation (Kock & Villadsen, 2012, p. 6) and their implications for the status quo.

In contemporary culture, macro and micro literate practices have, of course, taken a multitude of forms, and led to many scholarly inquiries exploring multimodality as it intersects with social ideologies (Huang, 2015; Machin & van Leeuwen, 2016; Serafini, 2010). Clover and Stalker (2008), for example, present activists who feel the need to censor their art in order to avoid alienating their audience with the boldness of their message; these activists demonstrate knowledge of their compositions as they relate to audience and purpose. Furthermore, Hipple (2000) notes a CP tee shirt depicting a woman impaled by an oversized penis; the shirt reads, "Feel better now, Fucker?" Though the artist in Hipple's study certainly has a right to render their anger and agency however they feel compelled, it remains important to the issue of rhetoric and the objectives of activism to consider how an audience may receive such work. After all, rhetorical efforts are collectivist (to the extent that they involve interaction with an audience) and productive (to the extent that rhetoric leads to action) (Miller & Bowdern, 1999).

The issue of censorship in women's activism endures regardless of mode. Women and members of other marginalized groups, and their narratives, have traditionally been "silenced" (Benstock, 1988; Coleman, 1997), whether in the form of censorship or dismissal. Often, though, those who have been silenced find subversive ways to defy power structures. As a matter of fact, much feminist activist work takes place within silent spaces. Take Back the Night uses silence to create a tone of remembrance. LGBTQ's National Day of Silence stresses that the more people who join together in silence, the louder the message becomes ("Info + Resources"). And the CP advocates for the right of the survivor by allowing an alternative fashion of "speaking out" via decorating tee shirts. Making a material statement functions protectively; more specifically, it protects the marginalized individual from identifying their self when communicating their story. In this way, composing mediates the activist purpose of "speaking out" and the ethical dilemma of forcing one to be silent or to speak, or to reveal one's self. By using the clothesline and its connotations, image, space, and written words, CP participants defy dominant discourse, as Julier (1994) writes:

> The admonition not to hang dirty laundry in public defines public and private in ways which preserve the very power relationships that led to dirtying the laundry in the first place: To define incest, for instance, or wife-battering as a private matter is to isolate the experience from the social structures and relationships which give rise to the violence. To define it as private is to dictate the discursive context within which it may be spoken, and therefore understood. (p. 254)

Acknowledging the advantages of composing (discussed in greater depth in Chapter 4), one should note that all representations have limitations in their ability to reflect experiences (Kress, 2003). Kress (2003), for example, argues that images have supplanted the use of alphabetic text in communication; however, the results of my study of the CP reveal reliance on alphabetic text. In that case, trends in multimodal composition may have more to do with divides between digital and non-digital composing, rather than with divides between textual and visual composing (a problematic divide to begin with, as discussed in Chapter 4). Furthermore, as the New London Group (2014) asserts, design decisions and products are always historically interwoven with other texts. CP participants' design decisions suggest that the seemingly ubiquitous discourse of digital composition (composing with digital or electronic tools through digital media) influences understandings and use of composing practices in other modes.

Furthermore, Hocks and Balsamo (2003) raise questions about accessibility, power, and meaning in regards to tools and modes, questions echoed in the consideration of the tee shirt as a genre. Scholars have considered how the context of the CP gives new meaning to the tee shirt (Hipple, 2000; Julier, 1994), and how the physical space of the tee shirt might influence rhetorical invention, which then raises issues of how the tee shirt serves certain ends and not others. Wysocki's (2005) "awaywithwords: On the Possibilities of Unavailable Designs" takes up some of Hocks and Balsamo's (2003) questions by focusing on "how materials have acquired the constraints they have and hence why, often certain materials and designs are not considered available for certain uses"

(p. 55). As demonstrated in the CP, these constraints call for composers to understand the spaces *on* and *in* which they compose and, therefore, how they might use those spaces differently than an audience might expect(Wysocki, 2005).

Understanding how to use modes and spaces aligns with Jeffrey Grabill's (2010) focus on rhetoric as "work" that involves collaborating with others and learning to communicate effectively with writing, images, and information technology (p. 193). Grabill's work supports the discussion in this book of the value of linguistic text and image in modes beyond those that are digital. Jefferies (2001), moreover, observes the value of language and art in relation to activism and points out that all texts and images take their status as subversive (therefore gaining some of their value) only in relation to the dominant; in other words, activists must use the language of the dominant discourse even as they critique it. After all, social critique by those in oppressed positions almost always involves elements of disguise (Jefferies, 2001, p. 192). Certainly, disguise may come via use of many modes with various implicit arguments and ideologies.

Fiandt (2006) addresses the role of art in subversion, writing, "just as healing intentions spur art, socio political activist intentions spur art...Levins Morales writes, 'Every vital social movement immediately begins to generate art, songs, poetry, posters, murals, novels...' So, while writing demands action, action can, simultaneously demand art" (pp. 581–82). Previously, Edelmen (1995) connected art and literature, claiming that both forms of expression serve as examples of social action stemming from "personal or collective planning or plotting... psychopathology, or...emotion" (p. 9). From this view, writing and art (or writing *as an* art) provide illustrations of responses to social and personal experiences. Indeed, people adopt ideologies based, in part, on the visual representations they encounter (Felshin, 1995).

Weber (2008) noted how adoption of ideologies based on encounters with visual representations works with "mundane" images, which provide for a reconceptualization of their representations because people do not have their guard up in response to those images (p. 45). As a case in point, the AIDS quilt[4] exposes viewers to subtle yet transformative ways of thinking; the quilt raises awareness of a deadly disease and of associations of the disease with the home—in particular, the intimacy of a bed (Elsley, 1992). Those associations bridge the distance between the disease and people who perceive the disease as unrelated to them (Elsley, 1992). Similarly, some artists have used clothing to assert messages about gender, as empty clothing makes suggestions about androgyny and gendered stereotypes, and does so "visually, silently, continuously" (Felshin, 1995, pp. 20–24 & 29), yet with relatability.

The move from the use of literacy for personal growth or healing to the use of literacy for public commentary comes with complications, however. Nontraditional forms of communication can help activists make this move. One woman interviewed in Clover and Stalker's (2008) research suggested the use of fabric arts for private protest as a way for her to use her hands and "keep her tongue still," which she found safer than using her voice in a larger social arena; these arts, displayed anonymously and collectively, get to say what their creators could not say without negative consequence (p. 7). Here again, we see the construction of the individual, of her self-understanding as it relates to a particular social structure, of an idea, of artwork, and of a movement. The above examples demonstrate women adopting and using literate practices to produce their own ideas and responses, to reproduce cultural ideas, and to attempt to modify ideas. Skinner (2009) shows this dynamic when she recounts her experience of sexual assault as an undergraduate; specifically, when confiding in a friend, Skinner received the advice that, if it happened again, she should try to relax so that it would not hurt as badly (p. 178). Her participation in events like "Take Back the Night," and her act of writing a book, aided the internalization of her new identity as a survivor and kept her experiences from consuming her (Skinner, 2009).

Some people, however, find such comfort in composing only if done anonymously. Disclosure of identity opens composers to critiques of their multiple subject positions, perhaps even unjustly placing focus on the wrong aspect of a composer's experience. The use of traditionally trivial artifacts, like art, allows for social commentary that protects the composer

---

[4] A product of The NAMES Project Foundation, the Names Quilt originated in 1987 and consists of panels dedicated to victims of the AIDS virus ("The AIDS Memorial Quilt"). "Today there are NAMES Project chapters across the United States and independent Quilt affiliates around the world" ("The AIDS Memorial Quilt").

yet maintains the rhetorical nature of the literate act. Women using fabric arts in Clover and Stalker's (2008) study reported struggling with internal and external censorship, or determining what they felt comfortable disclosing even anonymously and how the public would receive the disclosure.

These struggles illustrate how literacy includes an understanding of audience, meaning-making, and process; composing activism and its literate artifacts demonstrates and teaches how text, image, and spoken words mediate disclosure and enclosure. Writing or creating artwork about sexual assault can lead to personal and political awareness, even if external circumstances change very little or not at all. Activism involves composing ourselves. Metaphorically speaking, dressing our wounds with words, and letting others dress our wounds with their experiences, still leaves us wounded but with lessons and resources to offer others—and ourselves. We compose activism when we seek meaning from our experiences, seek investment from others in our cause, and act accordingly. The call for attention to how alphabetic texts and, increasingly, visuals get enacted (or not) to make arguments about justice remains crucial. Once again, these words and visuals, as activists choose, avoid, and use them, and as audiences receive them, relate to rhetorics of silence. As with the examples of Take Back the Night, Day of Silence, and the CP briefly presented earlier, Michel Foucault points out that the historically silenced culture of women has often used silence to resist the traditional hierarchies in which society has placed them (Ferguson, 2011).

Silence as a choice and a right related to "individual freedom of mind" (Bosmajian, 1999, p. 180) is a conceptualization of silence less recognized than the idea of silence as oppressive. But the right to refrain from speaking aloud publicly can become an issue of dignity, personal autonomy, and integrity; calls to speak, just like calls to remain silent, may interfere with self-fulfillment (Bosmajian, 1999, pp. 186 & 195). In a society where people may still judge women by, or reduce them to, their status as survivors of sexual violence, Audre Lorde's (1984) proclamation that "your silence will not protect you" (p. 41) falls short of realizing that, in many ways, silence *does* protect. Silence, in some situations, protects one from self-incrimination, vulnerability, humiliation, pain, and responsibility. Glenn (2004) asserts, "The question is not whether speech or silence is better, more effective, more appropriate. Instead, the question is whether our use of silence is our choice (whether conscious or [sub]conscious) or that of someone else" (p. 13).

To aid in synthesizing the ideas presented in these theoretical considerations and, therefore, enhance understanding of the line of inquiry this book takes up, I offer the graphic representations in Figs. 1.1 and 1.2. Figure 1.1 depicts the relationship among cultural narratives, literate practices, and psychosocial compositions; as each gear shifts and rotates, it influences the movement of the others. In addition, we see psychosocial compositions represented as the largest gear because psychosocial compositions constitute the main component, in that they consist of various functions of cultural narratives and literate practices. We can conceptualize a subset of processes, driven by the processes in Fig. 1.1, as represented in Fig. 1.2. Various understandings and amalgamations of cultural narratives, literate practices, and psychosocial compositions lead to the production of alphabetic and visual texts; these texts then attempt to change the status

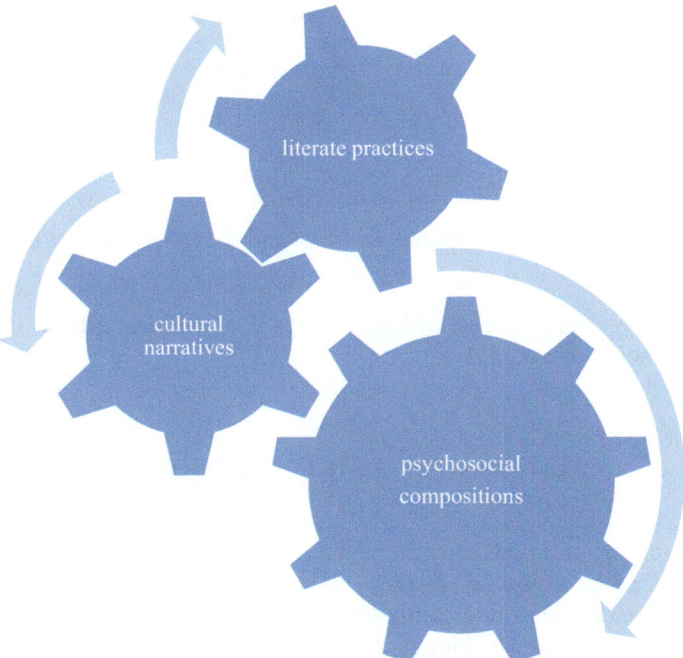

Fig. 1.1 Representation of the relationship among main variables discussed in the book

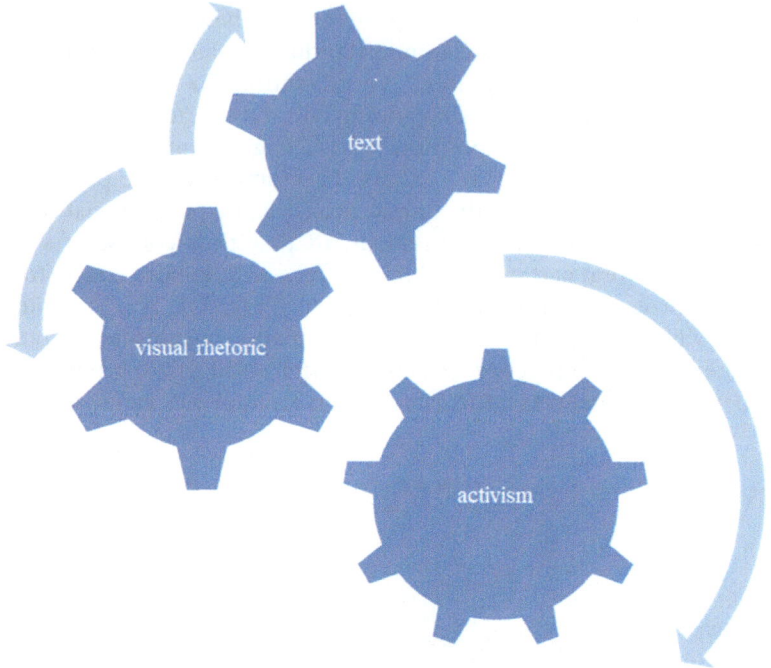

Fig. 1.2 Representation of the relationship among sub elements of Figure 1.1

quo, or change some of the understandings and resulting actions involved in the elements in Fig. 1.1.

MATERIALITY AND PSYCHOSOCIAL ACTIVIST RESEARCH: THE TEE SHIRT

Understanding the tee shirt as a literate object begins with considering the psychology of clothes in general. First printed in 1930, *Psychology of Clothes* asserts three functions of clothing: decoration, modesty, and protection (Flugel, 1950, p. 16). Whereas decoration serves to enhance one's attractiveness and draw attention to the individual, modesty provides social boundaries for decoration (Flugel, 1950). Perceptions of attractiveness relate, in part, to the features of the decoration, such as fit and color of clothing, as well as to the degree of bodily exposure permitted by particular garments. Clothing may also decorate one with references to their identity (Cornwell, 1990). CP participants, for instance, decorated tee shirts with words and images depicting physical and psychological scars associated with experiences of violence and participants' understanding of their identity at various points in dealing with these experiences. Hipple (2000) further recognizes CP shirts as "a uniform that confers legitimacy, decorates casualties of this 'war against women'" (p. 174).

Clothing, moreover, offers protection from cold, heat, enemies, accidents, animals, psychological dangers, moral danger, and "the general unfriendliness of the world as a whole" (Flugel, 1950, p. 77). People perceive unfriendly environments as "cold" environments and wrap themselves in warm or comfortable clothing in response to distress or sadness (Flugel, 1950, pp. 77–80). In the case of CP participants, the use of clothing to protect them from enemies, as well as from psychological and moral danger, has failed. Interestingly, the CP uses clothing to comment on these dangers while protecting participants from direct re-victimization, at least within the context of this event.

Women artists, in fact, have long depicted or used empty clothing to oppose the objectification of women (Julier, 1994) that "deform[s] [women's] experiences" (Hipple, 2000, p. 174) and may lead to psychological issues, such as eating disorders, depression, and sexual dysfunction (Szymanski et al., 2011). Objectification, then, may alter one's body and sense of self. With their decorated tee shirts, CP participants aim to reclaim such experiences and perhaps transform the experiences of other women. Julier (1994) notes clothing as "that which stands for the disembodied self" (p. 255); she points out that the use of disembodied shirts represents women's general "invisibility" and the disembodiment that many women experience during acts of gender violence, particularly sexual assault (p. 171). In regards to the CP, tee shirts represent disembodied bodies of evidence of the physical, emotional, and psychological trauma suffered by participants; and the tee shirts respond to the ways in which perpetrators objectified participants' bodies during acts of violence. We can think of these disembodied bodies of evidence as similar to Black's (1988) notion of a judge's robe as a form of synecdoche, a class of metonymy, which proclaims the judge synonymous with justice. The tee shirts, pieces of evidence of an attack, and pieces of an activist event, likewise, constitute parts of a whole synonymous with a sense of justice.

Further described, "Each shirt is a voice, a story" (Julier, 2000, p. 378). To some extent, the shirt voices what perpetrators prevented participants from voicing during an attack, or what they did voice but was ignored. CP participants, of course, lack full control over how an audience receives their messages; but as an activist event, the CP allows for more deliberately thoughtful and empowering communication than that which can probably take place during the chaos, violence, and oppression of an attack. Still, as discussed in Chapter 3, the tee shirt, as a disembodied entity, remains incapable of "speaking," and the content of shirts remains dictated by the unjust experiences of the CP participant (caused by offenders and members of society who perpetuate re-victimization) and the cultural attitudes that may have contributed to such acts of violence in the first place. Empty tee shirts, then, both reveal and conceal women's identities, their experiences, and the communication of those experiences.

A more direct understanding of the tee shirt as a literate and psychosocial object comes in studies like those conducted by Hamilton (2000), Cornwell (1990), England (England, 2008), and McNair (in Cockrell, 2014). Hamilton (2000) studied photographs in newspaper articles about education, politics, sports, and neighborhood and bureaucratic conflict. More specifically, she examined how these photographs depicted literacy practices, discovering themes of literacy as threat ("'paperwork stress' associated with money, exam results or legal proceedings"), defiance (use in opposition, as in graffiti and protests), evidence (use in "legal and bureaucratic power structures"), accessory (signifiers of professional status), display (signifiers of identity), and ritual public gesture (use of one's signature in social transactions) (Hamilton, 2000, pp. 20–21). Like the photographs in Hamilton's (2000) study, CP shirts may represent literacy as threat, defiance, evidence, accessory, and display. Specifically, CP shirts may pose a threat to the extent that they can "out" flawed social and institutional structures that perpetuate gender violence, and "out" perpetrators (by name if the perpetrator has been convicted). CP shirts represent literacy as defiance by violating social norms to avoid *airing one's dirty laundry* (Julier, 1994, p. 254). As noted earlier, CP shirts demonstrate literate objects as forms of criminal evidence. In terms of accessory, CP shirts serve, rather than as signifiers of professional status, as signifiers of tee shirt creators as experts, those with firsthand knowledge unobtainable by those without firsthand experience. Finally, literacy as display refers to images in which literacy relates to individual or collective identity, with this theme recognized primarily on tee shirts and hats (Hamilton, 2000). CP shirts assert the individual and collective identity of survivors or allies associated with gender violence. Hamilton (2000) notes that 28% of the images collected in her study constituted "literacy on the body" (clothing, tattoos, body painting) and that this form of literacy served as "decorating the human body with a variety of visual semiotics" (p. 30). The themes of literacy Hamilton (2000) identifies, and the notion of decorating the body with visual semiotics, share notions of CP tee shirts as literate objects and disembodied bodies of evidence. These findings also align with Cornwell's (1990) work.

Cornwell (1990), in her article, "T-Shirts as Wearable Diary: An Examination of Artifact Consumption and Garnering Related to Life Events," examined tee shirts according to cultural meaning, ritual behavior, primitive behavior, and consumption symbolism. Her work suggests the cultural value of the tee shirt as representative of people's pursuit of meaning, rather than pursuit of material objects; tee shirts' pervasive presence in society and their (often) low cost and depreciating value over time suggest they have greater significance than materiality (Introduction, para. 6). According to Cornwell (1990), tee shirts function in people's lives as a form of identification. With regard to cultural categories, tee shirts label people in terms of their relational identity (affiliation with political party, sport or sports team, geographic region, university or organization, or religious group); indicated on tee shirts, people can remove or change any one of these identities, and at almost any time (Cornwell, 1990, Introduction para. 9). In addition, tee shirts represent rites of passage rituals (such as high school shirts that list everyone's name in a graduating class), and serve as trophies (tee shirts received for participating in sporting clubs or events); tee shirts, then, can attract people with whom we have commonalities (Cornwell, 1990).

In a closer analysis, Cornwell (1990) examined five "tee shirt diaries," or entire tee shirt collections of five individuals, and coded symbols, slogans, meanings, acquisition, and grouping. Using data collected via lists, field notes, and photographs, Cornwell (1990) concluded that diarists "psychic investment ranged from organizing T-shirts by color (a low psychic investment) to T-shirt coordination and integration with specific life events for the explicit intention of evoking a response from a subset of the community (a high psychic investment)" (Conclusions, para. 1). All diarists thought of tee shirts as trophies and labels of cultural category, but not as representations of rites of passage (perhaps related to the age of participants) or as means of attracting like-minded people; however, participants reported tee shirts as "useful in self expression which may indirectly function in the same capacity" (Cornwell, 1990, Conclusions, para. 1). Certainly, activists using tee shirts for their cause hope to attract people with similar interests, though activists use clothing to draw attention from those in support and opposition alike. Though Cornwell (1990) theorized themes outside of the framework of literacy and Hamilton (2000) focused their work on photographs rather than on clothing, both studies provide grounds for building an argument that tee shirts significantly involve literacy as display, ritual, and identity and are, therefore, psychosocial compositions.

Similarly, England's 1994 study of lesbian culture and social geography focused on the "spatial fabric of everyday life" (England, 2008, p. 241).[5] In her work, she highlighted sexual identity as constructed, challenged, and defended—processes in which public protest plays a significant role (England, 2008, p. 246). Tee shirts printed with sayings like "DYKE" or "I'm so queer I can't even think straight" "reclaim meanings [and lead to] disrupting and challenging the very process of categorizing and labelling" (England, 1994, p. 246). In other words, social constructs lead to structuring public spaces that privilege heterosexuals; protests (even on tee shirts) infiltrate that space and tacitly implicate connections among identity, space, and subversion (England, 2008).

McNair provided another examination of the social activist "work" tee shirts can do (Cockrell, 2014). Her inquiry involved asking the following questions about tee shirts used in Black protest: "Was a T-shirt created by a grassroots organization to raise consciousness or funds, or was it offered by a strictly commercial venture? When worn in public, does it serve to start a conversation? To preserve history, articulate a struggle or memorialize a martyr?" (Cockrell, 2014, para. 5). McNair observes a shift in the content of shirts; while shirts used to feature images of well-known activists, they now feature images of Black people like Trayvon Martin, Renisha McBride, Michael Brown, and a host of

---

[5] This work was originally published in 1994 in *The Professional Geographer* 46 (1), pages 80–89. The work was reprinted in 2008, in *Critical Geographies: A collection of readings*.

other Black people murdered since McNair's observations.[6] In this way, McNair proclaims, "a moment becomes a movement" (Cockrell, 2014, para. 11). Julier (1994) further points out that tee shirts support such activist efforts, given their status as a common, low-cost item in American culture; their availability makes them suitable for public messages such as those involved in advertising, identifying with particular groups, and expressing ideological beliefs.

Clifford (1992), moreover, describes the tee shirt as "that blank sheet, mystic writing pad, so close to the body" (p. 114), a writing pad some teachers have used to teach "T-shirt literacy" by asking students to research social issues and create persuasive tee shirts related to those issues (Shankar-Brown, 2014, p. 366). Such projects serve the teaching of multiliteracies. To illustrate, Shankar-Brown (2014) discusses her favorite tee shirt, decorated with the *Schoolhouse Rock* logo, arguing for the shirt as a conversation piece that engages people in the literacies of viewing, speaking, and listening (p. 366). After all, "The words textile and text both derive from the Latin *texere*, which means 'to weave,' either through cloth or story" (Hipple, 2000, p. 164); the CP tee shirts themselves come from weaving together cloth, while the CP event illustrates the weaving together of personal stories with a collective narrative about gender violence.

Finally, understanding CP tee shirts as literate objects and psychosocial compositions collected and re-displayed in the years subsequent to their initial creation has implications for understanding the CP as a potential archive, a collection of artifacts that documents and preserves personal experiences, while attempting to modify understandings of cultural narratives. I explore these concepts in the next section.

---

[6] In February 2012, unarmed 17-year-old, Trayvon Martin, was shot and killed by a Caucasian neighborhood watchmen who claimed the shooting as self-defense ("Trayvon Martin shooting fast facts"). Renisha McBride was fatally shot (at the age of 19) after seeking help in regards to a car accident; the white homeowner claimed that he mistook McBride for a possible intruder (Hanna & Sanchez, 2014). Eighteen-year-old Michael Brown was fatally shot by police officers while being placed under arrest; circumstances and the justification of the shooting have been debated (McLaughlin, 2014).

The Clothesline Project as a Case Study

The CP provides an illustration of how women's literate practices remain embedded in a reciprocal relationship with cultural and individual narratives. Events like the September 2017 rescinding of the "Dear Colleague" letter by the United States Department of Education (Saul & Taylor, 2017) bring particular relevance to the work carried out in and through the CP. Originally released by the Office of Civil Rights in 2011, the "Dear Colleague" letter had provided guidance to institutions of higher education in handling reported cases of sexual violence in accordance with Title IX of the Education Amendments of 1972 (Ali, 2011). The rescinding of the letter came from concern that the guidelines led to unfair treatment of individuals accused of sexual violence (Saul & Taylor, 2017).

Three years after the letter's release, in 2014, President Obama created a task force to investigate the issue of sexual violence on college campuses, revealing the finding that 20% of female college students had been assaulted, though only 12% of those students reported the crime (Steinhauer, 2014). As a result of these findings, The White House issued guidelines that would "increase the pressure on universities to more aggressively combat sexual assaults on campus" (Steinhauer, 2014). As Tal (1996) states:

> the American woman lives in fear of an enemy who stalks her today. Her enemy is free to assault her on the street, in her place of work, or in her own home. He may attack her once or repeatedly. If she tries to hide from him, he may find her...If she tries to press charges, he [may] be protected by a legal, political and social system that is biased against her. (p. 20)

Tal's statement seemed particularly pertinent under the Trump administration, whereby threats to women went beyond rescinding efforts to reduce sexual violence (Frothingham & Phadke, 2017).

In response to issues such as these, this book grounds arguments about the role of material multimodality in feminist activism in a case study of the CP. Therefore, while an estimated 500 CP projects exist globally (Walk A Mile In Her Shoes, n.d.), I look at tee shirts collected for only one of those events, totaling 74 shirts. The coding of these shirts (which I detail in Chapter 3) yielded 897 data points from which I draw some of the conclusions and arguments in this book; I also establish applicability of the data to a social context beyond the single CP archive I examined for my work. Data collection and analysis spanned the years 2013–2015, with additional research and updates to the context of the analysis taking place throughout 2018, 2019, and 2020. Though no official record of when the CP began on the campus where I conducted my study exists, some administrators in the Women's Center guessed around 2008; as of 2020, the University continues to display the archive annually. As I will discuss in Chapter 3, the results of my study align with studies of the CP completed about a decade before my research and with a CP study that occurred after my research. This strengthens the arguments made in Chapter 3 about the influence of cultural narratives and psychosocial composing/compositions. Finally, while the CP provides an accessible demonstration of notions of silence, composition, and social narratives, this book's discussion of the Project does not intend to prioritize sexual violence over other feminist social issues. Now is a Kairotic moment to explore the communicative acts of any and all activists.

Previous studies of the CP have aimed to understand rhetorical functions of the event through analysis of linguistic and visual patterns in tee shirt messages (Bex Lempert, 2003; Droogsma, 2009; Goodnow, 2005; Gregory et al., 2002; Hipple, 2000; Julier, 1994, 2000; Ostrowski, 1996). This collection of studies establishes the CP as a feminist, activist text itself that illustrates writing in general as a socially embedded practice and provides rich data sets for further exploration of women's rhetorical communicative acts as both influenced by, and influencing, political ideologies (see explanation of psychosocial compositions discussed earlier).

In 1994, just four years after the CP's inception, Julier compared the CP, The Vietnam Veterans Memorial, and the NAMES Project as texts and events. As the CP invites witnesses to contribute to the Project, it "is a witness to healing and a means of healing, a private act and a work of social activism" (Julier, 1994, p. 255). The CP, then, redefines the discursive space in which people understand violence; and it achieves such redefinition by employing the following: voicing what has been silenced, creating a paradox whereby participants assert individuality as a means of creating community, and using the tension between "airing dirty laundry" as a form of empowering defiance and rethinking the spaces of oppression and liberation (doing the laundry as a "home" task and clothing as "both intimacy and violation") (Julier, 1994, p. 255). Julier (1994) also made the leap to pedagogical implications as she argued for allowing private texts in academic settings, questioning when calls for the use of "personal voice" and calls for collaboration both lead to the silencing of students. Julier (1994), therefore, established the CP as a text and asserts its value to scholarly and pedagogical inquiry in a variety of fields mentioned earlier in the book.

Two years later, Ostrowski (1996) wrote about the CP as a consciousness-raising (CR) experience for participants, but one that speaks against criticism of CR as focusing on the individual without implicating social and political influences on—or even causes of—individual experiences. More explicitly, the CP focuses on individual participants and implicates social and political influences on violent experiences in that: (1) the CP is public and (2) though a national office offers guidance and support to groups wanting to organize CP events, "there is no central authority figure" controlling the narratives women share (Ostrowski, 1996, p. 3). Each CP event consists of the individual story told on each shirt; the collective story told by displaying the shirts together; the story told through the addition of new shirts and particular ordering of the shirts by CP organizers, which changes with each display of a CP; and the meanings of the stories that audience members (viewers) construe via cognitive and emotional responses to the CP—all of which comprise an overall coping narrative (Ostrowski, 1996, p. 5).

Two years after Ostrowski's study, and six years after Julier's initial research, Julier (2000) built on her previous work by honing in on the rhetoric of CP tee shirt messages, specifically examining how rhetoric represented notions of women's therapeutic processes. She aimed to determine how women communicate their identities during the healing process, and in what "senses they talk about writing as healing" (2000, p. 362). She discovered that women tended to disclose what happened to them in "abbreviated elliptical forms," that they spoke of themselves as "wounded," that they referred to an effort to heal, and that they indicated "the move from private language into public discourse…as an act of healing" (2000, p. 378). Many shirts suggested the inefficiency of language to communicate traumatic experiences, while others suggested that language aided individuals' ability to see their experiences in new ways, which aids the healing process (Julier, 2000).

That same year, Hipple examined how the use of tee shirts in and of themselves functioned rhetorically, and how CP participants adapted shirts for the purpose of communication (e.g., using the two sides of the shirt for "before" and "after" narratives). She argued for the disembodiedness of the tee shirts as protection for participants' identities that "emboldens their speech" and provides evidence of trauma (Hipple, 2000, p. 174). For example, in her study, a red shirt reads, "Sweet 16 and never been kissed, but anally raped." An orange shirt depicts a tiny-bodied, nude, blue, and lifeless woman impaled by an oversized penis; it reads "Feel better now, Fucker?" (Hipple, 2000, p. 167). Hipple (2000) further found that the front of shirts often addressed cultural narratives about violence against women, while the backs of shirts responded to those cultural narratives; she argued that this represented the notion of every storing having two sides (Hipple, 2000).

Gregory and her colleagues (2002) built on prior understandings of the rhetoric of the CP by taking the first interdisciplinary approach to the CP, focusing on the political theory of "faces of power." Faces of power include "explicit, observable uses of power"; "unobservable uses of power," such as threats and control of political agendas; manipulation of "people's self-understandings and perceptions of their own interests" (p. 435); and the "creation of subjects" (people's identities) (p. 436). Gregory and her colleagues (2002) asserted that the CP addresses these faces of power by "creating a public space for political action, offering an alternative communicative medium, educating in a context of dismissal and silence, and contributing to social and cultural transformation" (p. 433). They used the CP to further argue that a relationship exists between emotion and rational discourse, as too much of one without the other will likely fail to motivate and mobilize people to act on behalf of those experiencing (or those who have experienced) injustice (Gregory et al., 2002).

Bex Lempert (2003) then combined elements of rhetoric, politics, and pedagogy to introduce the CP in a "Family Violence" course. She had students create a tee shirt as a tribute to a woman who had experienced violence (whether themselves, someone they knew, or someone in the news). With this project, she argued, the CP "challenges student passivity and disengagement with the learning process while simultaneously focusing attention on the experiences of victims of intimate, interpersonal violence" (Bex Lempert, 2003, p. 483). She made the point that engaging students in the CP allows them to gain both awareness of their own narratives and awareness of how cultural narratives shape personal narratives. Finally, allowing students to compose anonymously permitted disclosure with some sense of control over how they subjected themselves to responses to their stories, and shed light on the possibility of choosing to not disclose as an assertion of authority (Bex Lempert, 2003).

A few years later, Goodnow (2005) became one of the first people to focus on the CP's visual rhetoric. She observed the presence of "before" and "after" narratives; the "before" narratives included the following pentadic terms: "act: the abuse; agent: the perpetrator; agency: dependent on act; scene: places of previous safe harbor; purpose: to expose the abuse" (Goodnow, 2005, p. 183). Meanwhile, "after" narratives include: "act: surviving; agent: survivor; agency: empowerment; scene: any place; purpose: to reclaim control of the survivor's life" (Goodnow, 2005, p. 185). In other words, the "after" narratives exhibit a sense of control and agency on the part of the survivor, whereas "before" narratives tend to place the survivor in a position of vulnerability, taking much of the focus off of themselves altogether (Goodnow, 2005). Goodnow (2005) further concluded that words and images function differently, with words depicting details, and images depicting overall attitudes of participants.

Droogsma's (2009) content analysis of CP shirts sheds light on the relationship between social narratives and textual and visual rhetoric. Results from her study revealed several themes: society contributing to violence against women, women experiencing double victimization, and survivors being silenced and voicing opposition. Using feminist standpoint theory,[7] Droogsma (2009) drew attention to how women's experiences of oppression influence their worldviews and to how they use their personal lives to comment on social structures and "form a collective experience" (p. 496). She noted, "That society plays a role in the epidemic of woman abuse emerged as the strongest theme in this rhetorical analysis" (p. 487). While Goodnow (2005) looked at the visual rhetoric of the CP, Droogsma (2009) also asserted the CP as activist art because it remains collaborative, encourages creative expression, and welcomes community members to get involved. The visuals in the CP aim to change participants and viewers alike.

Several years later, Rose (2014) published her book, *Challenging Global Gender Violence: The Global Clothesline Project*, in which she details

---

[7] "Feminist standpoint theory calls attention to the knowledge that arises from conditions and experiences that are common to girls and women. This focus on experiences draws on Marxist theory's claim that the work we do— the concrete activity in which we engage—shapes what we know and how we behave" (Wood, 2009, p. 396).

her study of 700 CP shirts, and interviews with 200 participants, across cultures. She found similarities in expression of experiences—in terms of words, images, and colors—regardless of the cultural context in which women experienced violence (Rose, 2014). In particular, she found the use of hearts on CP shirts common; "hearts—black, bruised, broken, and torn—were one of the most frequent images women and children used to express pain and betrayal," (p. 15), though some represented feelings like "strength and hope" (p. 27). Additionally, interviews with college counselors revealed that college students may feel "more embarrassed and thus afraid to run out into the dorm hallway half-naked and screaming in order to save [themselves] from being raped than to endure the rape and its consequences" (Rose, 2014, p. 44). My work differs from Rose's (2014) and the work of scholars discussed earlier by focusing on materiality as it intersects with silence in the CP, by conceptualizing the CP as an archive, and by more deeply considering implications of CP research in composition pedagogy.

One of the most important issues related to conceptualizing CP shirts as an archive involves modifying common ideas of archives as "print records and ephemera" (Schultz, 2008, p. ix) available in a particular location and time. Indeed, archives may consist of "catalogs, yearbooks, literary journals, newspapers, diaries, student essays, letters, class notes, crush notes, census records, board of regents reports, recipes, receipts, photographs, oral histories, magazine advertisements, napkin scrawls, gossip, and Google searches" ("Interview..." 2010). I argue, then, that archives can include materials such as tee shirts. The everyday provides a significant window into the past, as the shift in time and culture shifts the meanings of objects.

Furthermore, authors in *Beyond the Archives: Research as a Lived Process*, understand "cultural memory" as archived in theater performances, festivals, monuments, and even city streets (Schultz, 2008, p. ix). Archives, then, may be somewhat fleeting, displayed at intervals over time, and organized atypically. Though often not catalogued or organized, saving CP shirts as a collection and re-displaying them annually suggests their value as objects worth archiving. Davy (2008) writes of her experience researching women's lesbian theater and her resort to the Lesbian Herstory Archives:

> Lacking the resources to properly catalogue its holdings, the staff could do little but point me in the direction of a few boxes marked 'WOW'

> [Women's One World][8] or 'women's theater.' Into these boxes had been tossed, in no particular order, press releases, programs, scripts, copies of opening night reviews, videotapes of some productions, and a smattering of photographs. Archival work in my case resembled more of an archeological dig—mining memories and boxes of stuff, carefully examining disparate bits and pieces of a whole, widely scattered and deeply buried. (p. 130)

Like the Brooklyn Herstory archive, CP shirts from the event I studied, when not displayed, get placed in plastic bins, in no particular order but neatly folded, and stored in the Women's Center garage at Kent State University (at least at the time of my study). The Kent State Women's Center, housed (literally) in an old carriage house, has a foyer that serves as an office space for two employees, two private offices, one public restroom, a small kitchen, and a conference room that holds a maximum of 15 people. Such limited space prevents organizing and displaying artifacts in the way we might typically think of the structure of an archive. Schultz (2008) and Davy (2008) emphasize, though, that limitations on space or other resources should not dismiss that a collection of artifacts has archival value. Likewise, Myers (2013) asserts that "the value and authenticity of a document does not depend on its form" (p. 458). I, therefore, argue that we can consider "form" not only in terms of material and condition, but in terms of organization and permanent versus temporary display.

Mason and Zanish-Belcher (2013), additionally, argue for documenting "how 'ordinary' people lived their lives and how their everyday actions affected and were affected by the world around them" (p. 293). "Microcollecting" refers to their focus on local rather than state and national collections (Myers, 2013, p. 442). Archivists' microcollecting aids women in creating their memories and provides opportunity for women to re-create and assert authority over their memories (Mason & Zanish-Belcher, 2013, p. 300). The CP demonstrates microcollecting in that it invites "ordinary" women with a shared (though still individual) experience to document that experience. The CP provides a space (on the tee shirt and on campus) to share memories in a way that may make

---

[8] "WOW, or Women's One World, began as an international women's theatre festival in 1980. Soon after, the group moved into its own space and began its tenure as an East Village arts institution dedicated to presenting women's performance year-round. In 1984, WOW moved to the black box theatre it inhabits today at 59–61 East 4th Street" ("WOW Café Theatre").

them more bearable, at least for a time; to create new memories in relation to their experiences by associating trauma with an act of creativity or activism; and to gain a sense of control over their experience that they lacked during acts of gender violence.

The Women's Center, some sororities, and Inter-Hall Council at Kent State University all host shirt-making sessions in various locations on campus. Covered windows at these locations offer privacy, though fliers and website advertising inform potential participants that they can create their shirts elsewhere and drop them off at the Women's Center. Hosts of shirt-making sessions collect participants' shirts and donate them to the Women's Center for the event. Though the CP takes place once a year and, as mentioned, the Women's Center stores shirts in their garage when not in use, anyone can have access to them at any point. I requested access to, and went through, the collection of shirts on multiple occasions. This access further contributes to the effort to reach "ordinary" people, even with restraints on physical space. These intentions align with the notion of the CP as an archive and an event related to social justice.

Harris (2007) wrote extensively about archives as they relate to social justice. He asserts that archivists remain, to some extent, products of and contributors to politics; and because of the socially filtered nature of experience and information, information is always under construction. So too, then, are justice and the records associated with it. Harris (2007) states that "records are always in the process of being made, they open into (and out of) the future" (p. 254). Archivists, as record makers, should engage in analysis and in justice, moving beyond "disciplinary and professional boundaries" (Harris, 2007, p. 256). After all, narratives of archivists and users interconnect with the narratives of larger society, an interconnection between local and much broader contexts. Context, therefore, remains dynamic and "infinite," and raises the issue for archivists of which contexts to seek meaning in and from, especially as text and context infiltrate one another but remain impossible to understand exhaustively (Harris, 2007, p. 260).

Furthermore, the CP archive changes with the yearly addition of shirts, while the event changes with the changing of artists and audience. Past and current personal and cultural narratives modify the context of the CP. The documentation of the past, the growth of the collection, and the collection's influence on an understanding of the present allow the CP to be considered a potential archive. Table 1.2 communicates the elements and processes involved in archiving, as set forth by Danielson (2010);

Table 1.2 Parallels between archives and the Clothesline Project

Term/process involved in archives	Definition/criteria	How the CP meets the definition/criteria
Appraisal	The process of "determining which documents have permanent historical or evidentiary value" (p. 48)	I argue that CP artists and writers do this when determining the design of their shirts. In addition, though rare, CP administrators or planners sometimes call the inclusion of particular tee shirts into question
Solicitation, collection development, and documentation strategy	The process of "proactively seeking appropriate collections" (p. 48)	This occurs when planning committee members advertise the Clothesline Project and shirt-making sessions leading up to the event and determine the most promising sites to acquire additions to the collection of shirts. For example, they reach out to particular campus organizations (Inter-Hall Council, the Health Center, Psychological Services, Sororities) and strategically schedule shirt-making sessions based on student behavior and campus events
Loans and deposits	Loaned or donated artifacts attained from individuals/institutions	CP writers and artists donate their work for the sake of a humanitarian effort. They give full authority over the work to an individual CP event
Accretion, accrual, and increment	The process of adding, or objects added, to a collection	As an annual event that features shirts made for prior events and the current year's event, the CP archive continuously accrues new artifacts
Research Value	The contribution the artifact can make to scholarship	Though CP organizers may not think of "research" per se, the CP shirts, and the purposes of the project, contribute to research value within the notion of research as "creative work undertaken on a systematic basis in order to increase the stock of knowledge, including knowledge of man, culture and society, and the use of this stock of knowledge to devise new applications" (The Organisation for Economic Co-Operation and Development). Shirt-making sessions and the CP event are planned, and tee shirts are acquired, in a systematic manner for the purpose of increasing knowledge of the individual, humanity, culture and society and contributing to new applications of such knowledge (such as policy development or civic engagement)

(continued)

Table 1.2 (continued)

Term/process involved in archives	Definition/criteria	How the CP meets the definition/criteria
Artifactual Value	The monetary worth of the artifact	CP organizers assess the monetary value of artifacts to be acquired only to the extent that tee shirts and materials must be purchased. The CP itself, and the value of the writing/art on each tee shirt, is not assessed in terms of monetary value

their definitions/criteria; and how the CP aligns with these elements and processes.

Danielson (2010) additionally argues for the formation and management of archives to align with the mission of the organization housing the archive. The CP event and archive, in a general sense, has the mission "to address the issue of violence against women" ("History of the Clothesline Project"), which aligns with the mission of the Kent State University Women's Center (the organization housing the CP discussed in this book) in 2013 through 2015:

> Kent State University's Women [sic] Center exists to facilitate the advancement of and to enhance the quality of educational experience and professional life for women students, faculty and staff of all campuses.
>
> The Women's Center serves as a resource for advocacy by providing education, information and referral programs and services.
>
> The Center is dedicated to promoting dialogue and interaction with all campus constituencies concerned with the pursuit of equity and equality. The Women's Center also provides collaborative outreach and support services to women in Kent's larger educational and geographical communities.[9]

In 2020, the mission statement looks different, though still speaks to notions of inclusion, awareness, and support:

---

[9] Due to the revision of the Women's Center Mission Statement, this version is no longer accessible.

The Kent State University Women's Center leads and supports efforts for equity for female/female identifying students, faculty and staff, through alliances of advocacy and care.

Value Statements
The work of the Women's Center is grounded in, and demonstrated by, the values we cherish most, which are:
- Promoting the pursuit of higher education and knowledge for female students as a source of power, economic independence, and self-actualization
- Honoring diversity and inclusiveness in all we do
- Supporting the rights of women to pursue safety and dignity in all aspects of their lives
- Engaging in vibrant dialogue, strong collaborations, and purposeful action in working toward a just and inclusive community where people of all genders, orientations, classes, races, ages, and abilities can thrive
- Honoring the dignity of all individuals and productively challenging them to be their best selves
- Valuing and encouraging women's ways of learning and expression and the importance of engaging those voices to shape our community.

Core Commitments
The work of the Women's Center is guided by the value we place on action, community, mentorship, and growth:
- We work to empower female/female-identifying students to pursue and achieve their potential in the higher education setting
- We work to foster community and collaboration among those with diverse experiences and aspirations
- We work for the elimination of barriers to gender equity
- We work to facilitate dialogue which actively resists sexism, racism, homophobia, transphobia, and discrimination in all forms within our community
- We hold commitments to gender, reproductive, economic, and social justice
- We actively engage in action which supports the prevention of sexual, physical, and verbal violence.
- The Women's Center staff strives to treat all community members with kind, welcoming, and non-judgmental service. ("Women's Center Mission Statement")

In other words, the missions of the CP and the Women's Center both include addressing quality of life for women/women- identifying individuals and providing a space for advocacy and collaboration. The shared mission enhances the integrity of the archive and brings us back to the discussion of social narratives contained *in* and produced *by* the CP.

Archives construct narratives (Lerner, 2010), just as narratives construct the artifacts of the archive. For example, the CP both responds to and creates a narrative about sexual violence. Additionally, each tee shirt contains a piece of the individual writer's or artist's story, whether that piece addresses the story of healing, reaching out to other survivors, losing a loved one, or navigating structures and discourses of power. Because we understand individuals and their stories within a particular social context, discourse mediates society's actions and one's comprehension of their own identity (Rosenwald & Ochberg, 1992). Therefore, my study of the CP explores how archival artifacts adopt and revise (or try to revise) social narratives, as evidenced in the discourse of the Clothesline tee shirts. Bloom's (2010) account of engaging in archival work aligns with my understanding of the CP archive:

> The deep sea diver, a.k.a. the archivist, is looking for buried treasure. At 'full fathom five' [Shakespeare's *The Tempest*]—or even deeper—lie the coral and the pearls and whatever else may have survived life's tempests. These relics, shards, fragments constitute the body of evidence necessary for the research at hand. Much has been lost, forgotten, completely washed away. The rest is in danger of disappearing. Everything that survives has suffered 'a sea change' and as a consequence of the catalytic action of time, has become transfigured 'into something rich and strange,' more valuable and more beautiful than it was in its original incarnation. It is up to the archivist to search out these materials, convey them to the surface, pluck the valuable materials from the detritus, enriched and enhanced by juxtaposition with other materials in the collection. (p. 278)

Considered in some of Bloom's (2010) terms, the CP commemorates those who have "survived life's tempests." Each tee shirt serves as a "body of evidence." Survivors of sexual violence, and their identity as depicted in their tee shirts, have "suffered 'a sea change'" and, through "time," have changed "into something rich." Dealing with their assault has led participants to the CP and its mission. Researchers must "search out these materials," the tee shirts, "enhanced by juxtaposition with other materials in the collection."

When we talk about juxtaposing fragments or materials, we talk about composition, the composition of texts and individual and cultural identities. Likewise, Lerner (2010) refers to archival materials as "testimonies" given birth to by their creators (p. 196) and says that we must ask: "Who are the people who have played a potential role in the narrative that might be constructed from archival evidence" (p. 204). After all, personal accounts imply an understanding of one's self in relation to an audience; "In telling our story to another we establish who that other is...as the telling of the tale turns the listener into the audience required by the teller, the storyteller's identity is reaffirmed or even altered" (Rosenwald & Ochberg, 1992, p. 9). The social and the personal remain inherently intertwined, as the texts we produce remain intertwined with those that came before us and our texts, a term Tilden (2004) refers to as "literary thrifting" (p. 710). In essence, we must question the social narratives of the past and present: what the narratives were, how they are represented currently, and how they have been and might be revised.

Again, while people commonly consider archives as physical collections of materials, scholars like Schultz (2008) and Davy (2008) characterize temporary and unconventional mediums (e.g. theater and city streets) as possible archives. Not all collections of materials, however, form an archive. The way in which the CP aligns with archivists' ideologies and criteria for formation moves the CP beyond being just a collection of tee shirts. First, the CP purposefully and strategically seeks artifacts that contribute to a particular mission (providing commentary on gender violence and supporting the Women's Center in providing educational, outreach, and support services). Second, CP organizers and participants strategically collect and use tee shirts. Third, though perhaps not deliberately organized on the clothesline itself or in storage, CP organizers strategically display tee shirts in terms of the time and location of the CP event itself. At Kent State in particular, the CP planning committee decided to move the event once held outside of KSU's Women's Center to the Student Center; further deliberations came about when considering University policies, inclement weather, ramifications of indoor placement, and resources available at the event.

Seeing the CP as an archive allows for a more systematic understanding of the event as a cultural artifact (composed of material literate artifacts), which sheds further light on patterns of a whole, a collective and purposeful narrative. Such a view also yields information about social change over time by situating the CP event in narratives of contemporary culture (government initiatives to combat sexual assault on university campuses; lack of government support for victims/survivors; cases such as those involving Steubenville High School football players, Penn State University fraternities, and the events at Stanford University; the documentation that men feel they have a right to women's bodies and, in fact, lack fear over potential consequences of violating women's bodies; and popular music like Robin Thicke's "Blurred Lines").[10] Additionally, investigations of particular CP events provide insight into local composing practices and considerations of feminism and feminist practices. Initial moves toward understanding the CP as an archive, then, allow for an understanding of cultural psychosocial compositions, not just the psychosocial compositions of individuals. Looking at the CP as a whole, and at the way it documents women's experiences with the same issue across time, allows us to better understand influences on the content and form of women's responses to social yet personal experiences and reveals information about effective outreach efforts for survivors of trauma. The CP as an archive provides a collection and a location for nonconventional, multimodal forms of expression.

---

[10] In 2014, President Obama launched the "It's On Us" campaign to combat sexual assault on college campuses (Somanader, 2014).

In 2012, politician Todd Akin claimed abortion in cases of "legitimate rape" would be unnecessary because in "legitimate rape" "the female body has ways to try to shut the whole thing down" (Alter, 2014).

In 2012, a high school girl from Steubenville, Ohio was raped; the attack was recorded and disseminated on social media. Two teens were convicted of the rape, but at least one was released and returned to his position on the Steubenville High School football team (Augustine, 2014).

In May 2015, Penn State suspended the fraternity, Kappa Delta Rho, for a period of three years. The suspension came after it was revealed that the fraternity had posted photos of naked women on Facebook; some of the women appeared to be unconscious (Johnson, 2015).

In 2015, Brock Turner sexually assaulted who we know now as Chanel Miller, but who was known as Emily Doe at the time. The legal case made international headlines, and Miller's 2016 victim impact statement went viral upon release to the media (Miller, 2019).

In 2016, Keller, Mendes, and Ringrose (2016) noted the focus of scholarly work on "the role of entitlement in rape culture" (p. 27).

In 2013, Robin Thicke released his hit song, "Blurred Lines," which was criticized for its glorification of rape. The music video was at one point pulled from YouTube (Mosbergen, 2013).

Finally, some may reasonably wonder how I accommodate a psychosocial approach to an archive when I have not spoken to CP participants themselves. In the interest of obtaining first-hand accounts from at least recent CP participants, the original design of this study sought CP participants willing to complete a survey and engage in a follow-up interview. I surmise the discomfort and vulnerability of revealing one's identity and discussing such personal experiences kept participants from volunteering (though I cannot definitively argue for particular reasons). Keller et al. (2016) also experienced difficulty obtaining interviews from women engaging in online activism about harassment and assault, even given anonymity and the mediation of digital space (though they suggest that digital spaces may make people feel safer when sharing experiences). I modified my research questions and redesigned the study to account for a lack of survey and interview data. Given this modification and re-design, I cannot—and I do not—argue that the CP participants made particular design decisions for particular reasons. Instead, I identify the patterns in the content and designs of the sample and argue for the ways in which social narratives are embedded, implicitly and explicitly, in the content and designs. Even interview data would fail to deliver definitive information about the internalizing of social narratives and the process of psychosocial composing, since, arguably, the internalizing of social narratives and, in turn, the process of psychosocial composing, happens, at least to some extent, subconsciously.

I articulate in my discussion of the results in Chapter 4 that the data suggest that larger social narratives inform the narratives of women's experiences of assault and, therefore, call for continuing efforts to serve survivors, activists, and the broader public. The field of rhetoric and composition long ago established the premise that "writing is a social practice" informed by audience, purpose, and context. My research, however, looks at what in the broader context of American culture and writing studies gets communicated in participants' compositions and what the implications of that could be for a variety of stakeholders. Finally, while I refer to CP participants as activists in this book, without talking to participants, I do not know if they would label themselves as such; however, I conceive of the work of the CP (to provide a place for women to express themselves without putting themselves on the line and to draw attention to individual and collective narratives of violence against women) as activist work. Bobel (2007) argues that to be an activist, one must "'live the issue,' demonstrate relentless dedication, and contribute to a sustained effort to duly merit the label" and, therefore, not all "social movement actors" conceive of themselves as activists or could engage in such efforts even if desired (p. 147). Therefore, engaging in activist work, even just through participation in one form or event, merits the label in this text.

Takeaways

I wish to make clear that while much of the introduction, and all of Chapter 3, examines the CP as a rich site of rhetoric and composition research, it serves as a case study that sheds light on activism; political science; writing studies; multimodal composition pedagogy; art and design; and perhaps even fields that respond to victims and survivors such as psychology, social work, and criminology. Specifically, the case study of material multimodality in the CP empirically examines emerging narratives in tee shirt content and design as well as patterns in both alphabetic and visual representations of those narratives. This analysis provides a foundation for making arguments about the implicit and explicit presence of cultural narratives in composers' messages and how composers and their products are inputs and outputs of cultural narratives that circulate about sexism; feminism; political policy; victimization and the justice system; and expectations for, and practices in, communication that may oppress or empower people. The book in its entirety, then, takes up the notion of psychosocial compositions and the ways in which texts (broadly conceived) construct, deconstruct, and reconstruct narratives related to identity.

Also, given the shift to a society navigated via technology, much research takes up the exploration of digital texts or digital and electronic multimodality in terms of gender (e.g., Blair & Takayoshi, 1999; Bray, 2007; De Hertough et al., 2019; Hocks & Balsamo, 2003; Shepherd, 2016), and more recently, technology and activism (e.g. Fileborn, 2017; Loney-Howes, 2015; McNutt, 2018; Powell, 2015). But fewer works explore materiality, especially in regards to its applicability to such a variety of stakeholders (as previously mentioned). Those interested in activism and the dynamics of re-victimization can learn about the ways in which people communicate experiences with gender violence, and the potential role of materiality and silence in those communications. This, then, could inform future activist efforts and approaches to victims and survivors by police officers, detectives, survivor/victim advocates, social workers, and therapists. Understanding the rhetorical effectiveness of communicative practices and products, and the circulation of those practices and products, ultimately determines social awareness, empathy, and implementation of just social policies and practices. The issues discussed in this book, then, have particular relevance to writing studies and composition pedagogy; the discussion questions at the end of each chapter can aid researchers' own thinking about such topics as well as aid discussions with students about subject positions, ethics, form and content, rhetorical effectiveness, and implications of compositions.

In sum, consideration of psychosocial compositions, literate practices, rhetorics of silence, materiality, and activism makes connections among the disciplines of composition and rhetoric, psychology, sociology, political science, women's and gender studies, art and design, pedagogy, and history, therefore demonstrating possible interdisciplinary approaches to writing studies. Along with these connections, findings related to relationships between textual and visual rhetoric suggest the opportunity to teach more sophisticated understandings of multimodal composing, especially regarding digital versus material composing. In particular, some findings discussed in this book shed light on students' conceptualizations of rhetorical relationships between image and alphabetic text; the symbiotic relationship between cultural narratives and individual identities; and ways that activists navigate dissent and mediation. Survivors' communication practices might influence how members of the legal system and non-profit organizations communicate to or with survivors, and ways in which mental health professionals might deal with survivors of gender violence (particularly with creative therapies). The notion of psychosocial compositions may inform how activists and policy-makers attempt to change cultural attitudes and enact concrete results stemming from activist movements. Finally, those in art and design may find activist events rich sites for exploring implications of theories and practices related to their field.

What's Next?

The next chapter provides an introduction to the definition of "rhetorics of silence" and explores understandings and uses of silence from a variety of global cultures; the chapter therefore argues for broader acceptance of silence in American culture. The discussion addresses the following questions: How do people typically frame silence in relation to activism? What forms do rhetorics of silence take in activism and why do they take those forms? What do rhetorics of silence "look" like in activism? How does composition, including multimodal composition, modify the presence or appearance of silence in activism? What does this mean for people wanting to become involved in social causes?

From there, Chapter 3 moves to the case study of a CP event, which empirically examines emerging narratives in tee shirt content and design, and patterns in both alphabetic and visual representations of those narratives. The chapter responds to questions such as: What do patterns suggest about how silence may have been imposed and how it may have been "broken"? How are composers and their products both inputs and outputs of narratives regarding silence, feminism, and activism? In responding to these questions, the chapter argues that despite living in a visual culture, many activists rely heavily on alphabetic text, and that activists' messages suggest composers as inputs and outputs of cultural narratives.

Chapter 4 discusses the implications of findings in regards to the history of making, materiality, and pedagogy. This chapter explores the questions: What do patterns in textual and visual representations suggest about openings for rhetorical multimodal composition pedagogy? What are some practical strategies for teaching multimodality as rhetorical and innovative in discursive spaces other than those that are digital or electronic? This chapter, then, argues for a multimodal composition pedagogy that includes materiality.

The final chapter, Chapter 5, acknowledges limitations of my work and addresses potential inquiries for the future work of researchers.

In its entirety, the book argues for psychosocial composing as a different lens through which to examine composing practices; a conceptualization of events and the products that come out of those events as archives that create historical records of cultural experiences and that have potential to inform future communicative acts; the validation of silence as a medium through which power gets displayed or exercised, even in activism; and activists' communicative acts as those that inform what and how we teach students about effective rhetorical communication and resourcefulness.

Discussion Questions

1. At what point does composers' consideration of the rhetorical context become censorship of the composer? What criteria might you use to determine this?
2. Where can we identify complex notions of, and relationships between, seeing (and/or visualizing) and speaking? What do these relationships mean for rhetorical efforts to create positive social change?
3. How do you define/understand feminism and/or activism. Where does that understanding come from and how is similar to or different from how this book discusses these terms?

References

Ali, R. (2011). *Dear colleague*. United States Department of Education Office for Civil Rights. https://www2.ed.gov/about/offices/list/ocr/letters/colleague-201104.pdf

Almond, S. (2012, March 23). *Why talk therapy is on the wane and writing workshops are on the rise*. The New York Times. http://www.nytimes.com/2012/03/25/magazine/why-talk-therapy-is-on-the-wane-and-writing-workshops-are-on-the-rise.html?r=0

Alter, C. (2014, July 17). *Todd Akin still doesn't get what's wrong with saying 'Legitimate Rape.'* TIME. https://time.com/3001785/todd-akin-legitimate-rape-msnbc-child-of-rape/

Andersson, M. A., & Conley, C. S. (2013). Optimizing the perceived benefits and health outcomes of writing about traumatic life events. *Stress and Health, 29*(1), 40–49. https://doi.org/10.1002/smi.2423

Andersson, U., Edgren, M., Karlsson, L., & Nilsson, G. (2019). Introductory chapter: Rape narratives in motion. In U. Andersson, M. Edgren, L. Karlsson, & G. Nilsson (Eds.), *Rape Narratives in Motion* (pp. 1–16). Palgrave Macmillan. https://doi.org/10.1007/978-3-030-13852-3

Augustine, B. (2014, August 12). *Ma'Lik Richmond, convicted in Steubenville rape case, returns to football team*. New York Daily News. http://www.nydailynews.com/news/national/ma-lik-richmond-convicted-steubenville-rape-case-returns-football-team-article-1.1900655

Baker, C. N., & Bevacqua, M. (2018). Challenging narratives of the anti-rape movement's decline. *Violence against Women, 24*(3), 350–376. https://doi.org/10.1177/1077801216689164

Benstock, S. (1988). *The private self: Theory and practice of women's autobiographical writings*. The University of North Carolina Press.
Berthoff, A. E. (1990). I.A. Richards and the concept of literacy. In *The sense of learning* (pp. 136–149). Boynton/Cook.
Bex Lempert, L. (2003). The clothesline project as student production: Creativity, voice, and action. *Teaching Sociology, 31*(4), 478–484. https://doi.org/10.2307/3211371
Black, E. (1988). Secrecy and disclosure as rhetorical forms. *Quarterly Journal of Speech, 74*(2), 133–150. https://doi.org/10.1080/00335638809383833
Blackwell, K. (2018). Why people of color need spaces without white people. *The Arrow: A Journal of Wakeful Society, Culture, & Politics*. https://arrow-journal.org/why-people-of-color-need-spaces-without-white-people/
Blair, K. & Takayoshi, P. (1999). *Feminist cyberscapes: Mapping gendered academic spaces*. Ablex Publishing.
Bloom, L. Z. (2010). Deep sea diving: Building an archive as the basis for composition studies research. In A. E. Ramsey, W. B. Sharer, B. L'Eplattenier, & L. S. Mastrangelo (Eds.), *Working in the archives: Practical research methods for rhetoric and composition* (pp. 278–289). Southern Illinois University Press.
Bobel, C. (2007). "I'm not an activist, though I've done a lot of it": Doing activism, being activist and the "perfect standard" in a contemporary movement. *Social Movement Studies, 6*(2), 147–159. https://doi.org/10.1080/14742830701497277
Bolton, G. (2004). *Writing cures: An introductory handbook of writing in counselling and psychotherapy*. Brunner-Routledge.
Boo, K. (n.d.). *On not 'giving voice to the voiceless.'* The Pulitzer Prizes. https://www.pulitzer.org/article/not-giving-voice-voiceless
Bosmajian, H. A. (1999). *The Freedom not to speak*. New York University Press.
Bray, F. (2007). Gender and technology. *Annual Review of Anthropology, 36*, 37–53. https://doi.org/10.1146/annurev.anthro.36.081406.094328
Buttry, S. (2016, May 18). *The voiceless have a voice. A journalist's job is to amplify it*. Columbia Journalism Review. https://www.cjr.org/first_person/buttry_story.php
Callahan, M. (2018, April 17). *The power of 'voice,' and empowering the voiceless*. News@Northeastern. https://news.northeastern.edu/2018/04/17/the-power-of-voice-and-empowering-the-voiceless/
Clark, R. (2016). "Hope in a hashtag": The discursive activism of #WhyIStayed. *Feminist Media Studies, 16*(5), 788–804. https://doi.org/10.1080/14680777.2016.1138235
Clifford, J. (1992). Traveling cultures. In L. Grossberg, C. Nelson, & P. A. Treichler (Eds.), *Cultural studies* (pp. 96–116). Routledge.
Clover, D. E., & Stalker, J. (2008). Feisty fabrics: Women's education, learning and activism through fabric arts in Canada and Aotearoa New Zealand. *Studies*

in the Education of Adults, *40*(1), 80–95. https://doi.org/10.1080/02660830.2008.11661557

Cockrell, C. (2014, September 8). *Where T-shirt culture meets the black protest tradition*. https://news.berkeley.edu/2014/09/08/where-t-shirt-culture-meets-the-black-protest-tradition/

Coleman, L. S. (1997). *Women's life-writing: Finding voice, building community*. Bowling Green State University Popular Press.

Cornwell, T. (1990). T-Shirts as wearable diary: An examination of artifact consumption and garnering related to life events. *Advances in Consumer Research, 17*, 375–379.

Daniell, B. (2003). *A Communion of friendship: Literacy, spiritual practice, and women in recovery*. Southern Illinois University Press.

Danielson, E. S. (2010). *The ethical archivist*. Society of American Archivists.

Davies, B. (1992). Women's subjectivity and feminist stories. In C. Ellis & M. G. Flaherty (Eds.), *Investigating subjectivity: Research on lived experience* (pp. 53–78). SAGE Publications.

Davy, K. (2008). Cultural memory and the lesbian archive. In G. Kirsch & L. Rohan (Eds.), *Beyond the archives: Research as a lived process* (pp. 128–135). Southern Illinois University Press.

De Hertough, L. B., Lane, L., & Ouellette, J. (2019). "Feminist leanings": Tracing technofeminist and intersectional practices and values in three decades of Computers and Composition. *Computers and Composition, 51*, 4–13. https://doi.org/10.1016/j.compcom.2018.11.004

Dolzani, M. (2012). Blazing with artifice: Light from the Northrop Frye notebooks. *University of Toronto Quarterly, 81*(1), 17–28. https://doi.org/10.1353/utq.2012.0006

Droogsma, R. A. (2009). "I am the woman next door": The Clothesline Project as woman abuse survivors' societal critique. *Communication, Culture & Critique, 2*, 480–502. https://doi.org/10.1111/j.1753-9137.2009.01049.x

Edelmen, M. (1995). *From art to politics: How artistic creations shape political conceptions*. University of Chicago Press.

Elsley, J. (1992). The rhetoric of the NAMES Project AIDS quilt: Reading the text(ile). In E. S. Nelson (Ed.), *AIDS: The literary response* (pp. 187–196). Twayne.

England, K. V. L. (2008). Getting personal: Reflexivity, positionality, and feminist research. In H. Bauder & S. Engel-Di Mauro (Eds.), *Critical geographies: A collection of readings* (pp. 241–256). Praxis.

Felshin, N. (1995). Clothing as subject. *Art Journal, 54*(1), 20–29.

Ferguson, K. (2011). Silence: A politics. In C. Glenn & K. Ratcliffe (Eds.), *Silence and listening as rhetorical arts* (pp. 1–22). Southern Illinois University Press. https://doi.org/10.1080/07350198.2011.604613

Fiandt, J. (2006). Autobiographical activism in the Americas: Narratives of personal and cultural healing by Aurora Levins Morales and Linda Hogan. *Women's Studies*, *35*(6), 567–584. https://doi.org/10.1080/00497870600809772

Fileborn, B. (2017). Justice 2.0: Street harassment victims' use of social media and online activism as sites of informal justice. *British Journal of Criminology*, *57*(6) 1482–1501. https://doi.org/10.1093/bjc/azw093

Flugel, J. C. (1950). *The psychology of clothes* (3rd ed.). Hogarth Press.

Frangos, J. (1997). "I love and only love the fairer sex": The writing of a lesbian identity in the diaries of Anne Lister (1791–1840). In L. S. Coleman (Ed.), *Women's life writing: Finding voice/building community* (pp. 43–62). Bowling Green State University Popular Press.

Frothingham, S., & Phadke, S. (2017). *100 days, 100 ways the Trump administration is harming women and families*. American Progress. https://www.americanprogress.org/issues/women/reports/2017/04/25/430969/100-days-100-ways-trump-administration-harming-women-families/

Glenn, C. (2004). *Unspoken: A rhetoric of silence*. Southern Illinois University Press. https://doi.org/10.5860/choice.42-4476

Goodnow, T. (2005). Empowerment through shifting agents: The rhetoric of the Clothesline Project. In K. Smith, S. Moriarty, G. Barbatsis, & K. Kenney (Eds.), *Handbook of visual communication: Theory, methods, and media* (pp. 179–192). L. Erlbaum.

Grabill, J. T. (2010). On being useful: Rhetoric and the work of engagement. In J. Ackerman & D. Coogan (Eds.), *The public work of rhetoric: Citizen-scholars and civic engagement* (pp. 193–208). University of South Carolina Press. https://doi.org/10.2307/j.ctv6wghr9

Gregory, J., Lewton, A., Schmidt, S., Smith, D., & Mattern, M. (2002). Body politics with feeling: The power of the Clothesline Project. *New Political Science*, *24*(3), 433–448. https://doi.org/10.1080/0739314022000005455

Hanna, J., & Sanchez, R. (2014, September 4). *Man gets 15–30 years for shooting Michigan teen on his porch*. Retrieved April 3, 2020, from https://www.cnn.com/2014/09/03/justice/michigan-porch-shooting-sentencing/index.html

Hamilton, M. (2000). Expanding the new literacy studies: Using photographs to explore literacy as social practice. In D. Barton, M. Hamilton, & R. Ivanič (Eds.), *Situated literacies: Reading and writing in context* (pp. 16–34). Routledge.

Harris, V. (2007). *Archives and justice: A South African perspective*. The Society of American Archivists.

Hipple, P. C. (2000). Clothing their resistance in hegemonic dress: The Clothesline Project's response to violence against women. *Clothing and Textiles*

Research Journal, 18(3), 163–177. https://doi.org/10.1177/0887302X0 001800305

History of the Clothesline Project. (n.d.). http://www.clotheslineproject.org/history.htm

Hocks, M. E., & Balsamo, A. (2003). Women making multimedia: Possibilities for feminist activism. In B. E. Kolko (Ed.), *Virtual publics: Policy and community in an electronic age* (pp. 192–214). Columbia University Press.

Huang, S. (2015). The intersection of multimodality and critical perspective: Multimodality as subversion. *Language Learning & Technology,* 19(2), 21–37. https://doi.org/10125/44428.

Info + Resources. (2015). http://www.dayofsilence.org/resources/

Interview: David Gold--on keeping a beginner's mind. (2010). In A. E. Ramsey, W. B. Sharer, B. L'Eplattenier, & L. Mastrangelo (Eds.), *Working in the archives: Practical research methods for rhetoric and composition* (pp. 42–44). Southern Illinois University Press.

Jefferies, J. (2001). Textiles. In F. Carson & C. Pajaczkowska (Eds.), *Feminist visual culture* (pp. 189–205). Routledge.

Johnson, M. (2015, May 26). *Penn State suspends Kappa Delta Rho fraternity for three years.* NBC News. http://www.nbcnews.com/news/us-news/penn-state-suspends-kappa-delta-rho-fraternity-three-years-n365066

Julier, L. (1994). Private texts and social activism: Reading the Clothesline Project. *English Education,* 26(4), 249–259.

Julier, L. (2000). Voices from the line: The Clothesline Project as healing text. In C. M. Anderson & M. M. MacCurdy (Eds.), *Writing and healing: Toward an informed practice* (pp. 357–384). National Council of Teachers of English.

Kaplan, E., & Mifflin, J. (1996). "Mind and sight": Visual literacy and the archivist. *Archival Issues,* 21, 107–127.

Keller, J., Mendes, K., & Ringrose, J. (2016). Speaking 'unspeakable things': Documenting digital feminist responses to rape culture. *Indian Journal of Gender Studies,* 27(1), 22–36. https://doi.org/10.1080/09589236.2016. 1211511

Kock, C., & Villadsen, L. S. (2012). Introduction: Citizenship as a rhetorical practice. In C. Kock & L. S. Villadsen (Eds.), *Rhetorical citizenship and public deliberation* (pp. 1–10). Pennsylvania State University Press.

Kress, G. R. (2003). Literacy in the new media age. *Routledge.* https://doi.org/10.4324/9780203299234

Lepore, S.J. & Smyth, J.M. (Eds.). (2002). *The writing cure: How expressive writing promotes health and emotional well-being.* American Psychological Association. https://doi.org/10.1037/10451-000

Lerner, N. (2010). Archival research as a social process. In A. E. Ramsey, W. B. Sharer, B. L'Eplattenier, & L. S. Mastrangelo (Eds.), *Working in the archives: Practical research methods for rhetoric and composition* (pp. 195–205). Southern Illinois University Press.

Lieblich, A. (2013). Healing plots: Writing and reading in life-stories groups. *Qualitative Inquiry, 19*(1), 46–52. https://doi.org/10.1177/1077800412462982

Loney-Howes, R. (2015). Beyond the spectacle of suffering: Representations of rape in online anti-rape activism. *Outskirts: Feminism Along the Edges, 33*, 1–17.

Lorde, A. (1984). The transformation of silence into language and action. In *Sister outsider: Essays and speeches* (pp. 40–44). Crossing Press.

Machin, D., & van Leeuwen, T. (2016). Multimodality, politics and ideology. *Journal of Language and Politics Multimodality, Politics and Ideology, 15*(3), 243–258. https://doi.org/10.1075/jlp.15.3.01mac

Marcus, J. (1988). Invincible mediocrity: The private selves of public women. In S. Benstock (Ed.), *The private self: Theory and practice of women's autobiographical writings* (pp. 114–146). University of North Carolina Press.

Mason, K. M., & Zanish-Belcher, T. (2013). Raising the archival consciousness: How women's archives challenge traditional approaches to collecting and use, or, what's in a name? In T. Zanish-Belcher & A. Voss (Eds.), *Perspectives on women's archives* (pp. 283–303). Society of American Archivists.

McNutt, J. G. (2018). *Technology, activism, + social justice in a digital age.* Oxford University Press.

Miller, C. (2019) *Know my name: A memoir.* Viking.

Miller, T. P., & Bowdon, M. (1999). Archivists with an attitude: A rhetorical stance on the archives of civic action. *College English, 61*(5), 591–598. https://doi.org/10.2307/378977

Mosbergen, D. (2013, July 11). *Robin Thicke's 'Blurred Lines' dubbed 'Rapey,' hit song under fire from critics.* Huffington Post. http://www.huffingtonpost.com/2013/06/18/robin-thicke-blurred-lines-rapey_n_3461215.html

Myers, E. A. (2013). I am my sister's keeper: Women's archives, a reflection. In T. Zanish-Belcher & A. Voss (Eds.), *Perspectives on women's archives* (pp. 433–461). Society of American Archivists.

New London Group. (2014). A pedagogy of multiliteracies: Designing social futures. In C. Lutkewitte (Ed.), *Multimodal composition: A critical sourcebook* (pp. 193–210). Bedford/St Martin's.

Ostrowski, C.J. (1996). The clothesline project: Women's stories of gender-related violence. *Women and Language, 19*(1), 37+.

Pennebaker, J. W. (1997). Writing about emotional experiences as a therapeutic process. *Psychological Science, 8*(3), 162–166. https://doi.org/10.1111/j.1467-9280.1997.tb00403.x

Powell, A. (2015). Seeking rape justice: Formal and informal responses to sexual violence through technosocial counter-publics. *Theoretical Criminology, 19*(4), 571–588. https://doi.org/10.1177/1362480615576271

Rose, S. (1999). Naming and claiming: The integration of traumatic experience and the reconstruction of self in survivors' stories of sexual abuse. In K. L. Rogers, S. Leydesdorff, & G. Dawson (Eds.), *Trauma and life stories: International perspectives* (pp. 160–179). Routledge.

Rose, S. D. (2014). Challenging global gender violence: The global clothesline project. *Palgrave Macmillan.* https://doi.org/10.1057/9781137388483

Rosenwald, G. C., & Ochberg, R. L. (1992). Introduction: Life stories, cultural politics, and self-understanding. In G. C. Rosenwald & R. L. Ochberg (Eds.), *Storied lives: The cultural politics of self-understanding* (pp. 1–18). Yale University Press.

Ruggles Gere, A. (1997). Introduction. In *Intimate practices: Literacy and cultural work in U.S. women's clubs, 1880–1920* (pp. 1 16). University of Illinois Press.

Saul, S. & Taylor, K. (2017, Sep 22). *Besty DeVos reverses Obama-era policy on campus sexual assault investigations.* The New York Times. https://www.nytimes.com/2017/09/22/us/devos-colleges-sex-assault.html

Schultz, L. M. (2008). Foreward. In G. Kirsch & L. Rohan (Eds.), *Beyond the archives: Research as a lived process* (pp. vii–x). Southern Illinois University Press.

Serafini, F. (2010). Reading multimodal texts: Perceptual, structural and ideological perspectives. *Children's Literature in Education, 41*(2), 85–104. https://doi.org/10.1007/s10583-010-9100-5

Shankar-Brown, R. (2014). Wearing language: Celebrating multiliteracies through graphic tees. *Journal of Adolescent & Adult Literacy, 57*(5), 366–366. https://doi.org/10.1002/jaal.257

Sharma-Patel, K., Brown, E. J., & Chaplin, W. F. (2012). Emotional and cognitive processing in sexual assault survivors' narratives. *Journal of Aggression, Maltreatment & Trauma, 21*(2), 149–170. https://doi.org/10.1080/10926771.2012.639053

Shepherd, R. P. (2016). Men, women and web 2.0 writing: Gender difference in Facebook composing. *Computers and Composition, 39*, 14–26. https://doi.org/10.1016/j.compcom.2015.11.002

Skinner, J. (2009). Recovery from trauma: A Look into the process of healing from sexual assault. *Journal of Loss and Trauma, 14*(3), 170–180. https://doi.org/10.1080/15325020902724537

Smyth, J., True, N., & Souto, J. (2001). Effects of writing about traumatic experiences: The necessity for narrative structuring. *Journal of Social and Clinical Psychology, 20*(2), 161–172. https://doi.org/10.1521/jscp.20.2.161.22266

Somanader, T. (2014, September 19). *President Obama launches the "It's On Us" Campaign to end sexual assault on campus*. https://www.whitehouse.gov/blog/2014/09/19/president-obama-launches-its-us-campaign-end-sexual-assault-campus

Steinhauer, J. (2014, April 28). *White House to press colleges to do more to combat rape*. The New York Times. http://www.nytimes.com/2014/04/29/us/tougher-battle-on-sex-assault-on-campus-urged.html

Szymanski, D. M., Moffitt, L. B., & Carr, E. R. (2011). Sexual objectification of women: Advances to theory and research. *The Counseling Psychologist, 39*(1), 6–38. https://doi.org/10.1177/0011000010378402

Tal, K. (1996). *Worlds of hurt: Reading the literatures of trauma*. Cambridge University Press.

Tilden, N. (2017). Nothing quite your own: Reflection on creative nonfiction. *Women's Studies, 33*(6), 707–718. https://doi.org/10.1080/00497870490480181

Walk A Mile In Her Shoes. (n.d.). *Clothesline Project*. https://www.walkamileinhershoes.org/clothesline-project

Warshauer Freedman, S. & Ball, A.F. (2004). Ideological becoming: Bakhtinian concepts to guide the study of language, literacy, and learning. In A.F. Ball and S. Warshauer Freedman (Eds.), *Bakhtinian perspectives on language, literacy, and learning* (pp. 3–33). Cambridge University Press. https://doi.org/10.1017/CBO9780511755002

Weber, S. (2008). Visual images in research. In J. G. Knowles & A. L. Cole (Eds.), *Handbook of the arts in qualitative research: Perspectives, methodologies, examples, and issues* (pp. 41–54). SAGE Publications.

Women's Center Mission Statement. (n.d.). Kent State University Women's Center.https://www.kent.edu/womenscenter/womens-center-mission-statement

Wood, J. T. (2009). Feminist standpoint theory. In S. W. Littlejohn, & K. A. Foss (Eds.), *Encyclopedia of communication theory* (Vol. 1, pp. 396–398). SAGE Publications.

WOW Café Theatre. (2011). FAB NYC. http://www.fabnyc.org/members/wow-caf%C3%A9-theatre

Wysocki, A. (2005). awaywithwords: On the possibilities in unavailable designs. *Computers & Composition, 22*(1), 55–62. https://doi.org/10.1016/j.compcom.2004.12.011

Young, S. (1997). *Changing the wor(l)d: Discourse, politics, and the feminist movement*. Routledge.

CHAPTER 2

Rhetorics of Silence

The conceptualizations and implications of silence in feminist activism can only be understood through an examination of historical definitions and cultural uses of silence. Despite scholars' past neglect of the critical study of silence as a form of rhetoric, or a rhetorical technique, a multitude of theories about the uses of silence currently exist. This chapter first presents conceptualizations and categorizations of silence before examining values and roles of silence in particular cultural contexts, and then ending with a general discussion of how silence can positively impact pedagogy and activism.

CONCEPTUALIZATIONS AND CATEGORIZATIONS OF SILENCE

While a chronological presentation of the scholarly literature on silence would show the development of rhetorics of silence as a legitimate area of study, the intersections among many of the theories would create a disjointed and repetitive reading experience. Therefore, I have tackled the discussion thematically, from general theories (including negative and positive stereotypes) to those that pertain to religion and meditation, politics, art, pedagogy, and sexual violence and activism.

To begin, then, Reinharz (1994) understands voice as more than sound, noting that in order to *not* be silenced, one needs the ability, the means, and right to self-expression; this notion focuses on liberties regarding *what* one says rather than on the ability to say *something*. Likewise, Solnit (2017) differentiates quietness from silence, with the former associated with peace and the latter associated with oppression, acknowledging that having a voice includes the right not to speak. Talking in and of itself, therefore, does not indicate voice (Fivush, 2010; Jungkunz, 2012). In light of these arguments, Keating (2013) separates "enforced silences…from silent refusal, silent witness, and deliberative silence" (p. 25). Silent refusal takes the form of refusing to speak, despite demands and requests to do so; Keating (2013) gives the example of a woman who refused to speak about her involvement in the Indian Independence movement because she wanted to "resist a particular narrative about both herself and the nation" (p. 26). Therefore, those in power can use silent refusal as a way of slowing the perpetuation of certain problematic narratives (Keating, 2013). Rather than highlighting the ways in which *voice* gets enforced, such as with silent refusal, silent witness highlights the ways in which *silence* gets enforced (e.g., the silence used in some activist events); people often enact the role of silent witness in an "organized and collective" manner (Keating, 2013, p. 27). Lastly, "deliberative silence" (a type also discussed by Lynch, 2001) involves silencing one's own "problematic" beliefs by examining and resisting our own dominant subject positions (e.g., confronting white fragility) (Keating, 2013, p. 28).

Silence as Keating (2013) describes it aligns with Donofrio's (2020) idea of "tactical silence," which "mediate[s]" power by "directing audiences' attentions toward silence with a function" (p. 551), therefore creating opportunities for change. Donofrio (2020) notes that in public meetings, hearings, and debates, speakers receive approximately equal time to talk, and going beyond the time granted may negatively impact the effectiveness of the message. In such a case, as a speaker, silencing one's self may prove beneficial. What is more, using the time typically allocated to speak instead to remain silent "magnifies whatever time [tactical silence] steals from dominated space" (Donofrio, 2020, p. 554). According to Donofrio (2020), tactical silence has:

> seven primary characteristics, which are overlapping and independent: (1) it emerges from the dominated; (2) it points to an irony about choice; (3) it is amplified by aesthetic appeals [such as signs, gestures, etc.]; (4) it relies on opportune timing to create a disruption; (5) it requires cooperation; (6) it magnifies whatever time it steals from a dominated space; and (7) it invites the (re)creation of dialogue. (p. 552)

As I discuss later in the chapter with regards to Jeffco student protests, tactical silence employs the irony of remaining silent even when one has the right (or expectation) to speak (Donofrio, 2020, p. 552).

Donofrio's (2020) tactical silence suggests that remaining silent may prove more powerful than saying what could be said (hence, speaking nonverbally), while hooks (2015) asserts that "who is speaking is never as important as what is being said" (p. x). If we take the position that "silence speaks," Donofrio (2020) and hooks (2015) make similar arguments. Likewise, Barringer (1992) writes:

> In the introduction to *Voices in the Night*, editors McNaron and Morgan state: 'This book is about breaking silence. It is true that there are many kinds of silence, some of them eloquent, but the most eloquent silence of all can be shut out by the closed ear.' The same is true of speaking: the most powerful speech can be rendered into silence by the 'closed ears' of one's listeners. (p. 18)

In other words, what is being said, and by who, is interdependent with who listens, why they listen, and what they hear.

Dobson (2014) further argues that silence should facilitate dialogue rather than shut it down (though this dismisses silence as a form of communication itself). For instance, in *Politicus*, moments of silence between Socrates and the stranger invite the reader into the dialectic and, therefore, involve Plato showing silence as that which invites "a multiplicity of voices" (Eades, 1996, p. 253). Relatedly, Glenn (2004) pushes against Aristotle's assertion that "rhetoric is the counterpart to dialectic," noting that rhetoric and dialectic are both spoken, and so "the true counterpart of verbal rhetoric can only be nonverbal—silence" (p. 13). Therefore, verbal and nonverbal rhetoric remain complements to each other. Meanwhile, we see Bakhtin (1986) assert silence as a complement to action, pushing against the idea of silence as inaction, with the notion of "active responsive understanding" as "silent responsive understanding" (p. 134). Intensifying Bakhtin's (1986) message, Geoffrey Sirc (2002) goes so far as to say that, "Only those who don't listen to silence think it's silence" (p. 47).

The differentiation between literal (not speaking) and more philosophical understandings of silence (as oppression and empowerment) gets further illustrated in van Manen's (1990) organization of silence into three categories: literal, epistemological, and ontological. Literal approaches consider silence as "the space between words"; epistemological approaches view silence as "knowing without being able to articulate what we know" (tacit knowledge) (Clair, 1998, p. 6); ontological approaches view silence as "the silence of Being or Life itself...the 'dumb'-founding sense of silence that fulfills yet craves fulfillment" (van Manen, 1990, p. 114), resembling Plato's notion of "divine madness" discussed later (Greene, 1940, p. 182). Clair (1998) adds to van Manen's (1990) list with an ideological approach, which views silence as "a powerful aspect of oppression and possible means to emancipation" (Clair, 1998, p. 6).

Of course, much research exists regarding the more obvious consideration of silence in direct relation to speech. As one of the earliest researchers to take up this topic, Picard (1963) pointed out the necessity of silence *to* speech, thereby making space for listening. A decade later, Bruneau (1973) defined three major forms of silence in terms of linguistics: Psycholinguistic (divided into fast-time and slow-time), Interactive, and Sociocultural Silence. Fast-time Psycholinguistic silences are mental silences related to the processing of speech, while slow-time Psycholinguistic silences are mental silences associated with "semantic processes of decoding speech" (p. 26); Interactive silences exist as "pausal interruptions in dialogue, conversation, discussions, debate, etc." (p. 28); "Socio-cultural silences relate to the characteristic manner in which entire social and cultural orders refrain from speech and manipulate both psycholinguistic and interactive silences" (Bruneau, 1973, p. 36). Ephratt (2011), too, presents silence through the lens of linguistics, with notions of extralinguistic silence (silence as an icon, an anomaly, e.g., experiencing a loss for words when overcome by emotion), paralinguistic/"eloquent silence" (silence as part of speech), and linguistic silence (silence that symbolically replaces speech). Oliveros (2012) further acknowledges silence in regards to saying one thing versus another and choosing to remain silent for an extended period of time for personal or social reasons (as in remembrance). Samovar et al. (2017), then, document additional reasons for silence as taking "time to think, encode a lengthy response or inaugurate another line of thought" (p. 331).

Also within the realm of conversation, Carolyn Cusick categorizes intentional, incidental (lack of need for response), indirect (misunderstanding), and selective silence (intentional omission or selection of content based on audience awareness) (Dobson, 2014). Related to selective silence, Fivush (2010) points out that our narrations are always partial, that we include and exclude details based on a variety of rhetorical factors. Additionally, silence may indicate that "(1) the speaker is disinclined to talk; (2) the speaker does not know what to say next; (3) the speaker cannot speak due to amazement; (4) the speaker has nothing to say; (5) the speaker forgets what [they have] to say; (6) the speaker is silent because other people are talking; (7) the speaker is hiding something; (8) the speaker is indifferent" (Vershueren, 1985 in Hao, 2010, p. 294).

Mirroring some of these reasons for silence, we might think of silence as a commodity, such as in Black's (1988) observation of our referring to silence as, "keep[ing] the secret" or not "giv[ing] someone away" (p. 141). Kurzon (2007) echoes and builds on Black's (1988) observation by asserting silence as thematic (remaining silent about a particular topic) and situational (remaining silent under certain circumstances). (Like theories already discussed, Kurzon also refers to textual silence (reading in silence) and conversational silence.) But while the aforementioned understandings of silence shy away from oversimplifying silence as inherently and ultimately oppressive, many negative stereotypes of silence exist and circulate.

Covarrubias (2007) points to one such stereotype as the idea of "consumptive silence," characterized as an "interpersonal malfunction" (p. 268). Jung (2017) further notes the perception of silent protesters as a threat for their potential to suddenly become violent. Similarly, Price's (2011) *Mad at School* discusses how society perceives and/or represents quiet people as dangerous and/or mentally ill. For these reasons, Cain (2012) makes a clear distinction among introverts, shy people, anti-social people, and people who have autism, calling out the common conflation of these labels (and misunderstanding of people in any of these groups. Indeed, silence, according to many people, may "hide evil intentions" and remains an indication of deeper disturbance (Saunders, 1985, p. 181).

Another common (and often immediate) negative meaning ascribed to silence pertains to oppression, by which *only* speaking demonstrates one's power and agency (Ahrens, 2006). Within this understanding, silence signifies "apathy, indifference, ignorance, or general accepting of the status quo" (Jungkunz, 2012, p. 127). As a matter of fact, *Women's Ways of Knowing* cites silence as one of five perspectives of knowing, in which women understand themselves as "mindless" and "voiceless"; for the women discussed in that text, "growth" meant "gaining a voice" (Field Belenky et al., 1997, pp. 15–16). The authors write:

> In describing their lives, women commonly talked about voice and silence: 'speaking up, speaking out, being silenced, not being heard, really listening, really talking, words as weapons, feeling deaf and dumb, having no words, saying what you mean, listening to be heard, and so on...[Authors] found that women repeatedly use the metaphor of voice to depict their intellectual and ethical development; and that the development of a sense of voice, mind, and self were intricately intertwined. (Field Belenky et al., 1997, p. 18)

In *Women's Ways of Knowing*, we see women internalize common tropes of power as voice/speaking. Yet we also see the problematic entwining of power, speaking, and ethics. As discussed in the previous pages of this chapter, speaking, remaining silent, or even asking someone else to remain silent (as we will see in Chapter 4) is not inherently oppressive or unethical. Context and social dynamics determine oppression, not silence itself. Therefore, who speaks, what they say, how they speak and/or enact silence, and who constitutes one's audience determine the ethical nature of verbal and nonverbal expression, not speech and silence themselves.

Still, Horsman's (2009) *Too Sacred to Learn: Women, Violence, and Education* raises questions of oppression and responsibility. Specifically, Horsman (2009) uses a study of counselors and educators in Canada to argue that silence makes violence appear uncommon; this appearance of violence as uncommon suppresses the reality of the situation and perpetuates the idea that the problem of violence lies with individuals and not with social systems. Even more extreme, as Olson (1997) writes in "On the Margins of Rhetoric: Audre Lorde Transforming Silence into Language and Action," Audre Lorde posited cancer as an analogy for silence that results from shame; she argued that breaking silence can "[entail] a complex sequence of self-naming through reference to demographic groupings...human, but not male; woman, but not white; black, but not straight; lesbian, but not childless; living with cancer, but not a passive victim" (Olson, 1997, p. 66). In Lorde's view, "voicing" ourselves and the complexities in our identities strips others of the power to "name" us, to reduce us to their particular notions of any subject position.

As many feminists and activists have advocated, and continue to advocate, for "breaking silence," Brown (2012) writes about silence as "social technology," particularly in commemorative events in which the silence "perform[s] the psychological," and is used with the intent of breaking silence. He further notes that without other forms of commemoration, people easily dismiss silence (Brown, 2012, p. 234) and fail to engage in meaningful individual reflection or collective interaction. More specifically, Brown (2012) argues that, beginning with Armistice Day in 1919, coming together for two minutes of silence fostered personal contemplation of our place in society and reflection on our differences; it provided a means of gaining a sense of camaraderie. Over time, however, without more dedication to remembrance, after two minutes, the silence breaks and we return to our own agendas. In this way, silence may actually suppress difference and camaraderie (Brown, 2012). Even when used intentionally, then, we often intend to undermine silence.

Without denying the validity of these conceptualizations, we can recognize positive aspects of silence. Hesford's (2004) exploration of patterns in Sattler's *Teaching to Transcend: Educating Women Against Violence* revealed women's use of silence in a Florida shelter as a means to protect themselves and others, pertinent to their escape from violence. Motsemme (2004) noted the importance of silence in "deny[ing] and acknowledge[ing]" the realities of living through apartheid (pp. 924–925). And McIntyre (2013) noted silence used by incarcerated women in order to shield loved ones from their experiences. Therefore, silence in some circumstances ensures privacy, protection, and even survival.

Amidst protecting and surviving, silence may yield an opportunity for reflection and a sense of peace, or communicate respect for a person or situation (Fivush, 2010), especially given the plethora of emotions that shape what constitutes appropriate rhetorical responses to others' experiences. Greene (1940) argues that even Plato accounted for silence experienced in moments of awe with his notion of "divine madness" (p. 182). Greek rhetorical theory additionally accounts for silence in terms of aposiopesis, or stopping mid-sentence due to emotion or effect (Bokser, 2006). Of course, silence can additionally demonstrate one's responsibility to hold back emotion, to refrain from hurting others with our words or from saying what we might later regret (Greene, 1940).

In increasing awareness of one's actions and surroundings, such as described in the previous paragraph, silence may lead to or demonstrate creativity (Glasby, 2016; Hull, 2001). Responses to creativity may involve silence as a means of showing engagement with, or contemplation of, a work of art (St. Clair, 2003). In fact, initial responses to creativity often involve silence and/or stillness (Bruneau, 1973). Voegelin (2010) explores a series of works of art that involve silence in some way, arguing that each work of art draws his attention to his experience of his own body and what he chooses to hear. Sontag (1969) further argues that artists' attempt to connect material reality with other realms of existence have made art less concrete; the artist falls silent through the "unintelligibility" of the work; "behind the appeals for silence lies the wish for a perceptual and cultural clean slate," (p. 17) and the artist experiences more satisfaction through this than through using art to "find a voice" (p. 6). In other words, "Silence is the artist's ultimate other-worldly gesture: by silence, he frees himself from servile bondage to the world, which appears as patron, client, consumer, antagonist, arbiter, and distorter of his work" (Sontag, 1969, p. 6). Silence used in these ways takes the form of both resistance and conformity.

Just as artists connect silence to their lived experiences, Voegelin (2010) refers to silence as an opportunity in which she "start[s] to build [her] own narrative between the heard and the anticipation of what there is to hear next" (p. 89). Thus, Voegelin establishes harmony among past, present, and future. Indeed, both silence and language play a role in *creating* and *expressing* our narratives (Clair, 1998), which, as argued in Chapter 1, occurs recursively. Ben-Ze'ev et al. (2010) explore the connection of silence and narratives through memory in particular. Specifically, they argue that the opposite of memory is not amnesia: trauma may be suppressed (forgotten), remembered (expressed), or remembered but not expressed; the authors feature such dynamics through a collection of works on national "historical memory" regarding war trauma in Spain, Africa, Turkey, and Israel (Ben-Ze'ev et al., 2010). Greene (1940) sees the power of silence in our narratives so much that she capitalizes the word in acknowledgment of its ability to allow us to create and foster knowledge. Silence goes beyond a lack of words to become "stillness that means great activity" (Greene, 1940, Prefatory Note).

Some people believe this great activity occurs within religious practices. Despite religions' strong association with language and being (e.g., "In the beginning was the Word, and the Word was with God, and the Word was God") (Glenn, 2004, p. 3), practices such as prayer and self-reflection often rely on silence. Greene (1940), however, argues for a "mature" and "disciplined" silence that allows one to cultivate spiritual connection, and even notes warnings by Quaker leader, John Rowntree, that young and inexperienced worshipers should avoid practicing silence (pp. 20, 30). The power of silence makes it potentially dangerous; the awakenings it produces can lead to the questioning of authority, and undisciplined silence can lead to "fruitless" fantasy or a false sense of spiritual growth (Greene, 1940, p. 153). The Quietists, a Protestant sect, taught that God communicates through silence, but that silence must pertain to words and to one's mind, creating stillness (Greene, 1940). According to Greene (1940), Professor Rudolf Otto, a follower of the Quaker method, distinguished three forms of silence that lead to genuine spiritual experience:

> The terms he used for these in his church service are (1) the silence of waiting; (2) the Silence of Union or Fellowship; and (3) the numinous Silence of Sacrament. The first aims at the subsidence of activity in the congregation, the withdrawal of attention from outer concerns and distractions. It has the value of preparing the soul to becoming receptive. The second, that of Union or Communion, signifies the approach by the individual to 'the larger.' These two earlier stages of silence prepare for the third—that profound Silence in the presence of God suggested in the Old Testament. (pp. 48–49)

Similarly, practitioners of Zen Buddhism believe that silence shows one's inner strength (which external realities often hide) and brings about a sense of rejuvenation (Greene, 1940); in Buddhism, silence exists as an internal state of being (Carrillo Rowe & Malhotra, 2013). Motsemme (2004) specifically draws attention to the role of silence and prayer in women sufferers of apartheid who experience silence as "an alternative sanctuary...to retreat to and reclaim their sense of self" (p. 924). Silence, then, sometimes offers a space in which to heal (Ahrens, 2006) from emotional pain and deal with physical pain, as speaking of pain brings it to the forefront of experience and prevents opportunity for relief (Pollock, 2013).

Practitioners of yoga (Carrillo Rowe & Malhotra, 2013) and meditation also spout the affordances of silence in creating a sense of oneness among intellectual, emotional, and spiritual experiences (Kalamaras, 1994). Rather than naming the Word discussed in religious contexts, meditation allows one to become the Word (Kalamaras, 1994). Hindus' practice of yoga serves as a particular example of using silence to create a sense of unity with God (Jandt, 2017).

While religious, meditative, and therapeutic uses of silence may emphasize individual development and spiritual connection, political uses of silence emphasize community development and interpersonal connection.

Though people often conceptualize political spaces as spaces in which voices must be heard, silence plays a key role in ensuring representative voices *are* heard—and considered.

Of course, politicians themselves often use silence negatively, such as with "agenda control," in which politicians attempt to avoid certain matters by leaving them off the public agenda (St. Clair, 2003, p. 3). However, as has occurred historically, citizens might use silence to withhold acclimations from rulers or leaders (Jung, 2017). An old saying asserts that "the silence of the people is the lesson of kings" (or one of the greatest "resources" of kings, depending upon the source); such instances illustrates silence as "political action with a rhetoric of its own" (Jung, 2017, p. 440). While some may argue that a lack of verbal acclimation without including verbal disapproval leaves the meaning of silence open to interpretation and, therefore, to people perceiving the silence as approval (Jung, 2017), all forms of communication are open to interpretation. We may struggle to decipher differences between what one says and what one believes or means.

Brummet (1980) extends the discussion of silence in politics with the notion of "political strategic silence"—a leader's use of silence that (1) "violates expectations," (2) is easily explained by the public in common ways, and (3) "seems intentional and directed at an audience" (p. 289). Brummet (1980), however, also asserts arguments potentially controversial for some scholars; explicitly, he asserts strategic silence as accompanied by common tropes regarding its meaning—"mystery, uncertainty, passivity, and relinquishment"—and that these commonly ascribed meanings remain "independent from the contexts in which strategic silence occurs" (p. 290). Whereas I might argue that the context determines *which* of the common meanings people ascribe to the silence, Brummet (1980) understands silence as somewhat reflexive, with strategic silence "encourag[ing]" particular meanings to be ascribed "to itself and to its context" (p. 291). According to Brummet (1980), then, political strategic silence, in part, determines the meaning of itself and the context in which people use it. It ultimately "violates expectations, encourages the attribution of specific meanings, is often directional, goes largely unexplained, replaces verbal discourse that plays a unique political role, seems intentional, and is of an appropriate type" (Brummet, 1980, p. 296). Still, the question remains of how one would determine an appropriate type of silence without having an understanding of the context.

Whatever the strategies behind the use of silence in the political arena, effective politics require silence in the sense of providing room for all stakeholders to speak and a space for reflection upon what others have communicated (Dobson, 2014). In this sense, and often contradictory to narratives that circulate around political involvement, "discursive democracy requires less speech and more silence" (Dobson, 2014, p. 105). Silence in politics, on local and global scales, becomes a matter of ethics and efficiency, making sure that what people say gets heard and responded to sensitively and justly (Glenn & Ratcliffe, 2011). Spivak (1988) famously made this argument in "Can the Subaltern Speak?" by pointing out the dangers of re-enforcing silence through misinterpretation of actions carried out by people in subaltern groups. One must listen to the various ways in which subaltern groups speak, and listen in a manner that does not solely rely on dominant narratives (Spivak, 1988) (further discussed in Chapters 3 and 4). Such ethical construction of silence and listening involves acknowledging and questioning one's emotional responses to others' ideas (Jung in Glenn & Ratcliffe, 2011).

So far, this chapter has established that silence serves a variety of purposes, such as "intimacy, assertiveness, focus of attention, complex social routines and etiquette, failure and rejection, pain,... loss and bereavement" (Argyle et al., 1981 in Hao, 2010, pp. 293–294), and communication of agreement, apathy, awe, confusion, disagreement, embarrassment, obligation, regret, repressed hostility, respect, sadness, thoughtfulness (Jandt, 2017, p. 117), affirmation (Covarrubias, 2007), grief, disappointment, shame, love, and even joy (Bruneau, 1973). Overuse of silence, though, runs the risk of it losing its power to convey critical messages; it becomes mundane rather than "disruptive" (Hatzisavvidou, 2015, p. 516)—though we can argue the same of overusing speech. Meanwhile, Bokser (2006) claims that silence makes an impact only if explained; otherwise, people will perceive it as meaningless. On the contrary, Brummet (1980) and Jungkunz (2012) argue that people should not explain silence (for Junkunz, this is for silences that refuse), as the explanation undermines the act of remaining silent. I contextualize such complexities within specific cultural values and uses of silence in the next section.

Values and Roles of Silence in Cultural Contexts

Context determines all understandings and functions of silence. As people communicate, they "construct, reflect, recount, and even judge a particular code of cultural communicative conduct" (Covarrubias, 2007, p. 267). While this chapter provides an overview of a variety of cultures and the ways in which people understand and use silence within them, this research proved difficult to come by. As a matter of fact, the most in-depth coverage of the topic seemed to come from Tannen and Saville-Troike's (1985), *Perspectives on Silence*. Though now decades old and unable to necessarily shed light on current practices within some of the cultures explored in this chapter, it shows the various ways people *have used*, and may *still use* silence within many cultural contexts. Therefore, this portion of the manuscript follows through on the intent to examine the complexities of silence and further denounce the dichotomy of silence as detrimental and speech as advantageous. It provides an overview rather than an in-depth examination of the use of silence for different purposes and accounts for cultural practices related to race and ethnicity. The subsequent section on activism accounts for cultural uses of silence related to other facets of identity, such as in Deaf and LGBTQ(IA) cultures.

Basso's (1970) research with a Western Apache population serves as one of the earliest and most cited studies of cultural silence. He spent sixteen months with the population in Arizona, discovering that the Western Apache feel no obligation to introduce people to one another, leaving such introductions to take place between the parties involved when they feel comfortable (which could take days) (Basso, 1970). Talking to strangers too quickly, in fact, may lead one to conclude that that person only has interest in gaining something from the conversation (such as money, a ride, or a favor) (Basso, 1970, p. 219). Also in American Indian culture, speaking too quickly may suggest a lack of forethought and, therefore, lack of substantial knowledge on a topic (Samovar et al., 2017). In addition to approaching eager speech with hesitation, the Apaches in Basso's (1970) study encountered angry people with uncertainty and silence, since anger could create danger.

Ceremonies, such as curing ceremonies, provided another potentially dangerous experience that required silence (Basso, 1970). Ceremonial practices made participants more powerful and, therefore, more menacing; and given the significance of the occasion, after ceremony attendees communicated well wishes and the medicine man had begun his work—and until a period of time thereafter—all attendees were required to remain silent (Basso, 1970). Afterward, as a result of gaining increased power and superiority, limited conversation transpired between the individual who had been the focus of the ceremony and other citizens (Basso, 1970). Glenn's (2004) research with American Indians additionally documented silence while meeting strangers, during courtship, on homecoming, as an effect of criticism, when in mourning, and during ceremonies.

While many of these uses and expectations of silence seem grounded in hesitation or fear, participants in subsequent studies on the use of silence by American Indians have noted ways in which silence allows for the opportunity to "simply be...and enjoy the connectedness that being in unrestricted timing afford[s] (in contrast to the Eurocentric fascination for doing measurable achievements by unyielding deadlines)" (Covarrubias, 2007, p. 269). For the Western Apaches, silence embodied effective means of learning to "just be" with individuals in their grieving process in particular, recognizing the effort it takes to speak under the weight of such emotion (Basso, 1970, p. 222); members of this population further believed that talking about loss only brings attention to it and its resulting grief (Basso, 1970). In American culture more generally, the notion of sitting quietly with people in their grief remains a common approach to, and goal within, psychotherapy (Bravesmith, 2012).

Similar to ceremonial silences and those used in regards to loss, a study of the Igbo population in Nigeria revealed the necessity of using silence in sacrificial practices (including the transport of sacrifices); that study revealed that silence preserved the sanctity of the act of sacrificing and protected those involved in making sacrifices from evil spirits (Nwoye, 1985). Moreover, it was customary for fellow mourners to approach family members of the deceased only after a period of four days following the death of a loved one (Nwoye, 1985). Interestingly, this silent appearance occurred, in part, to assert one's innocence in the death of the deceased; Nwoye (1985) notes, "it is believed that someone with magical powers that can cause death cannot stand before the spirit of the deceased" (p. 186). Members of the Igbo population considered silence as a means to clear one's name of wrongdoing, and as a last-resort punishment for someone who had committed an offense; cutting off all communication with the offender, including that which would allow the offender to earn a livelihood, aimed to encourage repentance and admission back into society (Nwoye, 1985).

Though unrelated to wrongdoing, silence among some Italian people may have also preserved social connections, but within family units more than within larger society. Saunders (1985) studied a group of Italians in the village of Valbella in northwestern Italy, the results of which countered stereotypes of Italian people as loud and expressive, and instead showed frequent uses of silence to avoid conflict or navigate situations in which one was uncertain of how to act. In Valbellan culture at that time, both silence and the expression of emotion aided formulating and identifying the emotion—or masking more honest emotions (Saunders, 1985). The expression or suppression of emotion often served the goal of maintaining positive family dynamics; and in instances of people going silent during a disagreement, bystanders encouraged participants in the conversation to drop the matter (Saunders, 1985).

Similarly, many people in Asian cultures might still utilize silence to evade conflict when they disagree with another's position on an issue (Samovar et al., 2017), or when navigating subject positions associated with stigma (Bondy, 2015). Bondy (2015) explored Burakumin[1] communities in Japan, specifically in the towns of Kuromatsu and Takagawa, in regards to what he terms "the protective cocoon" around Burakumin children. He found that in Kuromatsu, policies actually forbid talk of Buraku issues, while Takagawa encourages such discussion and even recognizes Burakumin history through building signage and school curricula (Bondy, 2015). Furthermore, "Burakumin" and "Buraku" terminology remains problematic and is sometimes avoided, which may hinder confronting the issues surrounding marginalization; as a result of such stigma, children in Kuromatsu are physically separated from their non-Burakumin peers in certain educational contexts like after-school study spaces (Bondy, 2015). Bondy (2015) argues that both approaches (silencing and encouraging discussion) lead adolescents to employ agency by determining when to reveal their identity and when to remain silent about their identity.

In broader Asian contexts, Confucianism and Taoism, which hold silence in high esteem, may make Chinese people less likely to initiate speech, especially in the presence of authority figures (Yuan, 2015). Confucian silence rests on the premise of actions speaking louder than

---

[1] "Burakumin, meaning 'hamlet people', dates back to the feudal era. It originally referred to the segregated communities made up of labourers working in occupations that were considered impure or tainted by death, such as executioners, butchers and undertakers" (Sunda, 2015, para 9).

words and, therefore, promotes being a student of the universe, engaging in self-development and "finding the way" without being instructed by others (Lyon, 2004, p. 138). Confucius, in fact, rejected the notion of talking about "what was over and done with," perceiving such discussion as a waste of time (Lyon, 2004) or unproductive.

The association of silence with action and productivity also marginally exists in notions of "administrative silence," which "occurs when administrative authority does not reply to an application in the legally prescribed time or does not take action when such action is legally prescribed" (Kovač et al., 2020, p. 4). Within administrative silence, silence as rejection constitutes negative silence and silence as approval constitutes positive silence (Kovač et al., 2020, p. 5). In Europe, France, Spain, Portugal, Italy, Netherlands, Slovenia, Serbia, and Croatia have strict policies about administrative silence, while Germany has largely neglected the topic of administrative silence (Kovač et al., 2020).

Of course, rhetorical understandings of the "action" associated with silence could take the form of listening to enhance insight or understanding. In many Eastern cultures, such as those in India, silence serves as a means to enlightenment and happiness (Jandt, 2017). And in Japanese culture, silence indicates sophistication and ethos, as evidenced by the Japanese proverb, "The silent man is the best to listen to" (Samovar et al., 2017). Lehtonen and Sajavaara's (1985) study of Finnish people echoes the role of silence in active, meaningful communication, though differently from the ways discussed previously. Specifically, Lehtonen and Sajavaara (1985) found that Finnish people used silent cues such as head nods over vocalized responses such as "mmhmm." Observed more recently in Finland, Sweden, Denmark, and Norway, silence communicates engagement in what a speaker says, even encouraging the speaker to continue talking (Samovar et al., 2017).

Across cultures in general, silence also historically resulted from fear over the spread of smallpox (Nwoye, 1985). Conversing with another without knowing about the person's whereabouts and possible exposure could pose a particular risk of contracting the virus (Nwoye, 1985). This historical use of silence, of course, has new meaning for a world struggling through the COVID-19 pandemic.

Globally, gendered expectations for silence exist as well. Western Apache culture taught women and girls to use silence as a form of modesty, and couples often avoided engaging in substantial conversation until well into their relationship (Basso, 1970). But, as noted earlier in the chapter, contrary to traditional thought in Western cultures, expectations for silence are not always directly associated with oppression, and voice may not indicate personal agency. In Chinese culture, for example, silence in response to a marriage proposal typically indicates acceptance rather than refusal (Yuan, 2015). In the Igbo population of Nigeria, women met marriage proposals with silence and the physical leaving of the premises; to reject the proposal required a woman to remain physically present and silent until the would-be suitor decided that enough time had passed to accept the action as a rejection (Nwoye, 1985). The expectation of silence from women in these scenarios relates to the expectation for feeling overcome with emotion when being proposed to by a significant other (Nwoye, 1985). This expectation for silence may both play into stereotypes of women as more emotional beings than men—and who highly prioritize romantic relationships—and break the stereotype of silence as suppressing women's desires.

In American culture, bell hooks (2015) wrote about silence and women in Black culture specifically, noting that society considers outspokenness among girls as a sign of empowerment, but that it signifies something different for black girls themselves.[2] hooks (2015) writes of her own gendered experiences of being punished for being too expressive, noting:

> Had I been a boy, they might have encouraged me to speak believing that I might someday be called to preach. There was no 'calling' for talking girls, no legitimized rewarded speech. The punishments I received for 'talking back' were intended to suppress all possibility that I would create my own speech. That speech was to be suppressed so that the 'right speech of womanhood' would emerge. (p. 6)

Yet, hooks (2015) notes witnessing black women speaking out quite regularly, and though men may have dismissed or ignored them, they received great attention from fellow women; in other words, hooks's outspokenness was simply a result of her cultural upbringing, not a symbol of defying patriarchy (though it also speaks to the expectation of women to do or be, but to not do or be too much or in certain ways). We cannot make assumptions about how speech and silence work in service

---

[2] I use the lowercase "b" because hooks chose not to capitalize "Black."

or in opposition to feminism, though our tendency to categorize and dichotomize leads to such an oversimplified notion (Kalamaras, 1994).

Also deviating from such oversimplified ideas of verbal expression and silence, research with Jewish women immigrants concluded that their use of silence and fragmented speech indicated a "complex act of forging a new sense of self whereby hegemonic narratives are adopted and resisted and appropriated and refashioned," a use not needing to be "overcome" in the way we often talk about silence (Nagar-Ron & Motzafi-Haller, 2011, p. 661). As briefly discussed earlier, however, Western cultures often view silence as a detriment and as associated with mental health issues (Cain, 2012; Jandt, 2017). Talking earns one a label of "civilized," at least for men (Glenn, 2002). These cultures may encourage a perception of women as talking too much, which may often get incorrectly attributed to notions of women's emotional or psychological instability. Kalamaras (1994) discusses the misunderstandings of silence and speech in Western cultures at length and reminds us of the use of silence in gaining introspection and empathy.

In sum, while cultural practices regarding speaking and silence exist, people use silence (or not) based on a variety of local and global factors (Jaworski, 2005). Learning the cultural uses of silence can be one of the most difficult aspects of learning a language (St. Clair, 2003), though rhetorical uses of silence and listeningcan help us navigate cultural differences and power structures (Glenn & Ratcliffe, 2011). Thus, when it comes to cultural research that relies on primary accounts, we must acknowledge that we are limited to interpretation, and therefore limited in what we can argue about the rhetorical nature of artifacts and practices (Gries, 2015). Regardless of the situation, Lyons's (2000) notion of "rhetorical sovereignty," or "the right to speak or not on our own terms," remains important (Glenn, 2004, p. 108). Yet educational institutions across the United States have struggled to promote the notion of rhetorical sovereignty.

SILENCE IN CLASSROOMS

Cultural comparisons between Eastern and Western values of silence have included ideas that in China and Japan, academic experiences might differ from those of North American students (Samovar et al., 2017). Specifically, North American teachers often expect students to speak in class and interact with both peers and the instructor, while Chinese and Japanese teachers expect students to not only remain quiet but to remain disciplined even in their body language (Samovar et al., 2017). These expectations for quietness persist even when students struggle with course material, under the assumption that if students improve their listening, they will come to grasp course concepts (Hao, 2010). While some researchers have rightly pushed against an oversimplification of differences between Asian students and non-Asian students, we must note that cultural differences in education *do* exist (King, 2013), and not just between Asian and American (or Asian American) cultures.

King (2013) examined classroom behavior of 924 English language learners across 9 Japanese universities, finding that students accounted for less than 1% of initiated talk in classes, and 1/4 of all class time remained silent (no talking by students or staff). King's (2013) research also revealed that classes relied heavily on an "Initiation Response Feedback" pattern that required single-word or brief responses from students, though students remained appropriately silent during particular classroom activities or during cognitive processing of course material. Some students, however, stayed silent due to confusion or self-consciousness (fear of embarrassment); King (2013) states, "If we consider these two malevolent influences, coupled to the Japanese enculturated notion of an ever-watching 'other' which results in an egocentric concern for presenting the self in an acceptable light...yet another route through which silence becomes apparent emerges" (pp. 338–339). In the local and national context, then, administrators, teachers, and students find lack of oral class participation acceptable; though we should acknowledge that the reasons for lack of oral participation vary, ranging from language ability, pedagogical techniques, cultural norms, or even tiredness (King, 2013).

King and Atsuko (2017) explored differences in the tolerance of silence between students in Japan and students in the United Kingdom while meeting one-on-one with their teachers. In this study, teachers stopped talking at a set point in the meeting and researchers documented how long the silence remained before students spoke, later interviewing students regarding their thoughts and feelings about the silence (King & Atsuko, 2017). Researchers found no significant difference in tolerance of silence by students from Japan and the United Kingdom, and both groups reported unease in response to the silence, though the research revealed no correlation between length of silence and degree of emotion (King & Atsuko, 2017). Across interviews, students reported anxiety as the primary feeling experienced, with King and Atsuko (2017) naming this phenomenon "situational silence anxiety," or "feelings of apprehension during situated encounters in which talk is expected but does not occur" (p. 489). In addition to the self-reported feelings of anxiety, for 73.33% of UK students and 80% of Japanese students, researchers documented physical signs of anxiety during silence, such as "self-touching, postural rigidity, closed body positions and gaze aversion" (King & Atsuko, 2017, p. 494). That Japanese students reported a desire to understand the teacher's silence emerged as one difference (King & Atsuko, 2017).

A need to understand silence should exist on the part of students and instructors, and in all cultures. Given that American classrooms often strive to remain somewhat democratic and encourage participation and sharing of ideas, teachers often use silence in the classroom not only to command attention (or acknowledge students' undesirable conduct) but to encourage students' verbal participation (Hao, 2010) as a means of inclusivity. Again, though, silence does not necessarily indicate a feeling of exclusion or an inability to communicate effectively (Hao, 2010). In fact, the expectation to speak often privileges white and Western students (Hao, 2011). And while teachers and administrators sometimes favor quiet students over overly talkative students (Hao, 2010), Li (2005) suggests:

> [e]ducators must not deliberately silence silence…Instead, it is essential for educators to question the polarization of silence and speech and to challenge the primacy of speech in current discourse on multicultural education. Beyond reclaiming silenced voices, educators also need to inquire into silence as a source of pedagogical knowledge. (pp. 70–71)

Course requirements for verbal participation can actually leave students feeling violated (Hao, 2011, p. 281). Farmer (2001) further argues that students' "imitation" of composing—instead of critical engagement with ideas, argument construction, and the rhetorical situation—is "the worse form of silencing" (p. 7). Arguably, teaching writing "rules" rather than "conventions," and limiting students' experiences with genres and rhetorical situations, silences students' ideas and opportunities for intellectual development.

Though I personally rarely felt my intellectual development stifled by rigid requirements, as a student, I never became comfortable speaking in class. It took time, and a lot of cognitive and emotional processing on my part, to obtain the status of "someone who participates." When, if at all, I began to appease teachers with my verbal participation, they may have already categorized me as a substandard participant—and, possibly, as a second-rate student altogether. (Yes, I had a few final grades lowered due to my lack of verbal participation.) Therefore, the anxiety of proving myself to my teachers and professors perpetuated from class to class, semester to semester. The marginalization of "the quiet student," regardless of cause, frequently yields value-laden judgments of one's ability and willingness to learn. Restructuring the way in which teachers call upon students to "actively participate" creates an environment less rigid, and therefore more conducive to the exploration in which we strive to engage.

We should, moreover, remember that students enter our classrooms with a variety of mental health issues and personal struggles that may affect students' feelings about speaking in class. While speaking more frequently may address some of these reservations (as in the case of Cognitive Behavior Therapy (CBT) for certain anxiety disorders) (Alden & Taylor, 2010), individuals should determine whether they engage in a form of treatment, not course requirements. The clinical setting respects introverts but academic settings often assert that engaging in extroverted tendencies, under any circumstances, remains best for *all* students.

Nancy Poling (1997), in *Accommodations—Or Just Good Teaching?: Strategies for Teaching College Students with Disabilities*, offers her discovery of how opportunity for dialogue validated socially marginalized students, primarily those with behavior and physical disorders. She writes, "I picture Paula successfully trying to be invisible, all the while her head full of questions and observations. Now, in the privacy of my office, she could discuss those wonderful ideas swirling in her head" (Poling, 1997, p. 104). In this example, Poling (1997) demonstrates that quiet students engage in critical thinking even though they may express such engagement differently. But, Poling (1997) goes on to say that, "The developmental educator can lessen social isolation by initiating discussion and by creating forums where education and social interaction converge" (p. 104). This statement, along with the note in the margin that reads, "Good teaching practices including verbal interactions among all students may be the key to actively involving the student with a disability in the learning environment" (Poling, 1997, p. 104) fails to consider that the effect Poling experienced in the office may not exist in the larger classroom. We must ask, "social interaction" to what extent, or by what definition? In addition, Poling's (1997) writing limits social interaction to verbal dialogue and suggests that lack of verbal expression complicates her teaching

Though not in opposition to Poling and other educators who advocate verbal dialogue, Mary M. Reda (2009), in *Between Speaking and Silence: A Study of Quiet Students*, asserts that teachers often view silence as "the inability to speak, an unwillingness to 'participate,' resistance, hostility, lack of preparation or engagement, disempowerment or alienation, [and] unwillingness to 'go along' with the teacher" (pp. 25–26). Kennan Ferguson, in *Silence: A Politics* (2011), adds to the list teachers' perception of students' silence as an indication of distraction or a hangover. Reda (2009) challenged such notions when she studied her own College Writing students with the intent of finding out the criteria quiet students use when deliberating about speaking; she concluded that silent students, "conscious of their own ethos and authority, and the demands of the audience as it invites, shapes, or limits their voices… make active conscious choices about speaking and silence in the oral and written texts they produce" (p. 121).

Silence, in fact, often serves the individual, whether it leads to further inquiry, insight, or action; we can liken it to the speech, prose, or creative work we create but, in the end, crumple up and abandon. We must sometimes respect silence as a process in which students have the right to engage without producing evidence that such engagement occurred. All people should have the right to experience themselves in, or by way of, silence. Teachers often assume that silence restricts potential when, in fact, their demand for students to speak may restrict students' potential to experience the classroom—or the course as a whole—positively, or to engage with opportunities for personal development (Coleman, 2006) in a multitude of ways. Duffey (2011) points out that speaking constitutes *one* way of participating in discussion; some students prefer, and require, longer periods of internal reflection, leading to diverse ways of expression—such as writing, having significant conversation in conferences with teachers, and making infrequent but stimulating comments in class. Additionally, I make clear to my students that I consider "active" participation to include "coming to class prepared, with annotated reading materials and assignments; engaging in discussion (this includes remaining attentive if you do not feel comfortable speaking); remaining focused and productive during workshop periods; taking notes; asking relevant questions in class, via email, or in online forums; sharing sources; visiting the Writing Studio; and attending office hours."

Though some individuals may reveal themselves in smaller circles, in more introverted ways, and with greater anxiety than others, effective communication does not cease to exist in their lives. Furthermore, communicative behavior varies not only with context but with the individual communicating. A. H. Maslow (1993), in *The Farther Reaches of Human Nature*, points out that:

> Counseling is not concerned with training or with molding or with teaching in the ordinary sense of telling people what to do and how to do it...It is a Taoistic uncovering *then* 'letting be'...Taoism is not a laissez-faire philosophy or neglect or refusal to help or care. As a kind of model of this process we might think of a therapist who, if he is a decent therapist and also a decent human being, would never dream of imposing himself upon his patients or propagandizing in any way or trying to make a patient into an imitation of himself. What the good clinical therapist does is to help his particular client to unfold, to break through the defenses against his own self-knowledge, to recover himself, and to get to know himself...The job is, if we are to take this model seriously, to help them be more perfectly what they already are.... (pp. 50–51)

Maslow (despite only using male pronouns) presents an interaction between change and constancy, one that perhaps the field of education should allow for in terms of its participation requirements. Glenn (2004) notes, "The question is not whether speech or silence is better, more effective, more appropriate. Instead, the question is whether our use of silence is our choice (whether conscious or unconscious) or that of someone else" (p. 13). In other words, silence is sometimes a matter of social justice in our classrooms, in more ways than we perceive or discuss.

Silence in Activism

Much research has examined the ways in which silence oppresses women and other subaltern groups (Anzaldúa, 1981/1983; Kohrs Campbell, 1989; Lorde, 1984; Moraga & Anzaldua, 1981/1983; Olsen, 1978; Rakow & Wackwitz, 2005; Rich, 1979). Some activist research, however, documents participants' disdain for "talking over doing" and pitting "awareness raising" against "more productive action" (Pottinger, 2016 p. 219), which mirrors Confucian understandings of silence discussed earlier in the chapter. While problems arise from privileging speech or silence, one does not have to be loud, or even audible, to effectively fulfill a purpose (Pottinger, 2016). The Albert Einstein Institution, which studies and advocates the use of nonviolent approaches to social issues, provides a list of "198 methods of nonviolent action," in which they explicitly mention "silence," along with a variety of methods that might include silence or invisibility, such as "walkouts," "turning one's back," "collective disappearance," and even "stay[ing] at home" (Albert Einstein Institution, 2020).

As communicated elsewhere, though I focus on sexual violence as a particular lens through which to explore silence, activism, and social justice, many of my arguments remain applicable to other causes and contexts. Like with other forms of violence, we must acknowledge that sexual violence often furthers social inequalities because of the many ways in which silence becomes part of the offense: perpetrators silencing victims during an attack—or after via threats (Armstrong, Gleckman-Krut, & Johnson, 2018; Barringer, 1992), survivors' silence as a means of protecting others from their stories (Fivush, 2010), the inadequacy of words to communicate such experiences (Barringer, 1992; Lawless, 2001), the silence of society and erasure (e.g., lack of accounting for sexual violence as part of wartime or politically associated violence) (Armstrong, Gleckman-Krut, & Johnson, 2018), and a lack of response to the systemic issues that lead to sexual violence and the perpetuation of sexual violence as a somewhat taboo topic. Women frequently experience censorship or dismissal based on expression of emotions such as anger, and are met with criticism of them as individuals rather than with criticism of the social structures that led to their traumatic experiences and expressions of anger (Orgad & Gill, 2019).

Ahrens (2006) revealed five reasons sexual violence survivors choose to remain silent about their experiences: "1) lack of options; 2) fears of negative reactions or consequences; 3) ineffectiveness of support; 4) self-blame or embarrassment; and 5) [belief that they] didn't qualify for support" (p. 269). Negative responses to survivors, such as victim blaming, may take place because those responses makes others feel less vulnerable; they can believe that they live in a society where sexual violence doesn't "just happen," but rather happens based on something within someone's control (such as how one dresses) (Murphy et al., 2011). When people to whom survivors disclose their experience urge survivors to remain quiet going forward, "they could be giving voice to fears for their own safety or the safety of their loved ones" (Murphy et al., 2011, p. 706). In a complex way, then, a survivor's voice gives voice to others' fears, which then silences the survivor's voice. Sexual violence thus serves as one systemic example of how society strips women of their power and control, both during and after an act of violence (Ahrens, 2006) (though the same applies to other marginalized groups, such as homosexual men).

Moreover, certain populations, such as Black women, may remain silent, in part, because of issues like racism, fearing that speaking about their experience will reinforce stereotypes such as that of the "Black rapist" (Armstrong, Gleckman-Krut, & Johnson, 2018, p. 109). By aiming to protect others (Barringer, 1992), women use silence as a means to preserve social relationships. While survivors' silence, to some degree and in certain circumstances, yields detrimental psychological effects, due to the factors discussed thus far, disclosure of the experience also often yields detrimental psychological effects (Ahrens, 2006).

Silence, nevertheless, can move beyond mere protection to empowerment. As a matter of fact, Jungkunz (2012) asserts five "insubordinate" silences (p. 135): those that empower by bringing attention to silencing, in which case the silence serves as the "message" itself (p. 147); those that protest the status quo, in which case the silence symbolizes something; those that are untimely by defying expectations for silence or speech (such as refraining from singing during the National Anthem), in which the timing of the silence matters greatly; those that resist by not telling, sharing, or reporting information, in which case the silence usually functions covertly; and those that refuse, in which case silence allows one to refrain from taking action regarding a particular matter (such as not revealing sexual identity)—in other words, "turning away from a given reality or narrative—refusing to be present via one's voice upon and within topographies, structures, constructs, and/or relationships" (p. 144). Silence, in these instances, communicates dominance rather than oppression; after all, "deviations from the norm [typically] call for voice," and with power, one can refuse to explain (Fivush, 2010, p. 88) or choose what to say and what to remain silent about (Bruneau, 1973).

When Anita Hill remained silent, she left her perpetrators in anticipation of what she would say and when she would say it, thereby asserting her own power over them and her narrative, at least to an extent (Glenn, 2002). While the circumstances surrounding Anita Hill's disclosure about harassment committed by Circuit Judge, Clarence Thomas, demonstrates "disciplinary pigeon-holing," in which one does not feel able to speak out without suffering negative repercussions to their career (Glenn, 2002,

p. 264), the kairotic moment at which Hill chose to speak perhaps afforded a more powerful effect than if she had spoken out at the time of her experience (Glenn, 2002).

Still, much like Anita Hill's testimony (and that of other survivors), acts of self-disclosure and protests require open critique of leaders and those who hold power, as well as demand a lot of time (Jung, 2017) and bravery of survivors and activists. We have, for instance, witnessed the danger of protest in the Black Lives Matter movement ("US law enforcement violated Black Lives Matter protesters' human rights, documents acts of police violence and excessive Force," 2020). Via silence and/or invisibility, some activist events allow for safer advocating of causes, whether as "one-off" events (such as the University of California, Davis protest; the Jeffco "Screaming with Silence" protest; or what has become known as the "Standing Man" protest in Turkey) or yearly events (such as "The Saturday People" vigils, LGBTQ's National Day of Silence (DOS), or The Clothesline Project).

More specifically, in 2011, University of California, Davis students engaged in silent protest after campus police pepper-sprayed students protesting tuition increases and other budget modifications (Hatzisavvidou, 2015). Students held the chancellor accountable, calling for her resignation, to which she responded by residing in a University building, supposedly out of fear of students; when she finally emerged (after students had communicated their intent to remain peaceful), students interlocked arms to create a silent "walk of shame" (Hatzisavvidou, 2015, p. 511). Hatzisavvidou (2015), then, reiterates the power of silence:

> The silence of the students at UC Davis does not insinuate patience and consideration; it is demanding and dynamic...This is not to neglect the relation between listening and silence...However, the modality of silence visited here is characterized more by intrusiveness, even ferocity, rather than by attentiveness. (p. 517)

The silence here embodies intention, purpose, and action.

Since the UC Davis protest, students across the country have engaged in silent protests. In 2013 and 2014, the Jeffco, Colorado Board of Education (Colorado's largest school district, with more than 85,000 students) underwent a series of administrative changes that led to a proposed "pay for performance" salary for teachers (Donofrio, 2020,

p. 556). Teachers met the proposed salary structure with a planned, NEA-encouraged "sick out" (Donofrio, 2020, p. 556). Meanwhile, the Board's vice president, "who believed the College Board's new AP. U.S. History (APUSH) framework painted a negative image of America, proposed a new curriculum review committee—circumventing the two existing committees—to review the framework for any objectionable materials" (Donofrio, 2020, p. 557). Students protested both the proposed salary structure for teachers and the proposed curriculum committee, perceiving the Board's efforts as censorship (Donofrio, 2020, p. 557). After the Board repeatedly silenced students at Board of Education meetings—which the Board justified as an appeal to civility—students left the Board members having to decide whether to let students speak or to solidify students' message of being silenced (Donofrio, 2020). Finally given permission to speak, with their hands clasped and with tape or stickers of the American flag over their mouths, students requested a moment of silence (Donofrio, 2020). As a result, the Board faced another dilemma: to refuse to stand in silence would suggest a lack of support for students, but to stand in silence would "relinquish their power to insist that public comment time should include only speech, thus undercutting their use of standards of decorum to silence the students"; having finally been "heard," the students named their efforts "Screaming with Silence" (Donofrio, 2020, pp. 561–562). Similarly, in 2018, student Emma González, who survived the mass shooting at Washington, DC's Marjory Stoneman Douglas High School, stood silent for six minutes and twenty seconds at the consequent "March for Our Lives" protest, the exact timeframe in which the shooting had taken place(Reilly, 2018).

Outside of an educational context, the Standing Man protest initiated by Erdem Gunduz in Turkey in 2013 demonstrates purposeful silence (Seymour, 2013). In response to police brutality against protesters, Gunduz took a silent stand in Taksim Square; and his protest went viral with the hashtag, "duranadam" ("standing man"), as people joined him around the country of Turkey (Seymour, 2013, para. 4). Seymour notes that the protest "was both an affront and a question for the authorities: beat him? Why? He's just standing there. Leave him alone? Then he wins, doesn't he?" (Seymour, 2013, para. 3).

Turkey also serves as the site of the long-running activist event, "The Saturday People." Twenty-five years ago, who became known as "The Saturday People," or "The Saturday Mothers," began meeting for weekly silent vigils, and for the sake of inclusivity, resisted the use of slogans, banners, or other genres that would use words to communicate (Göker, 2011, p. 110). The vigils, in response to the disappearance of men arrested after Turkey's coup in the 1980s, relied on silence in order to protest without deterrence by the government (Göker, 2011). The Saturday Mothers' vigils counter Olson's (1997) claim that while people sometimes perceive silence as more proper in some circumstances, it will likely fail to gain support or bring about change regarding its cause. The protests continued for decades, until 2018, demonstrating Wagner's (2012) notion of silences as "embodied actions" (p. 100).

Another long-running event, created by Maria Pulzetti and occurring since 1996 (Yep & Shimanoff, 2013), Day of Silence (DOS) achieves rhetorical effectiveness via the choice of participants to remain silent for their own purposes rather than being silenced by oppressors (Glasby, 2016). DOS, however, typically ends with a "Break the Silence event" at which participants speak about their experiences throughout the day; "as the Gay, Lesbian, and Straight Education Network (GLSEN) explains, in DOS, 'silence is used as a tactic to provide a space for personal reflections about the consequences of being silent and silenced'" (Glasby, 2016, pp. 3–4).

Despite the notion that the silence and speaking involved in DOS contribute meaningfully to each other (Yep & Shimanoff, 2013), the event rests upon the notion of "breaking the silence" (as Brown, [2012] pointed out with commemorative events). Furthermore, while positive and negative *consequences* exist, the use of the word "consequences" in GLSEN's statement implies that the silence used by DOS participants serves only to point out the negative consequences of silence. For example, the text printed on many DOS cards handed out by participants reads, "What are you going to do end the silence?" (Glasby, 2016, p. 4). Perhaps the question, "What are you going to do to end the *silencing*," would provide a more accurate way of discussing silence in this context, since this question targets oppressive silence in particular.

Glasby (2016) notes conflict within the LGBTQ community regarding silence, as silence raises notions of "both death and safety" (p. 6) (in part because of the association of the LGBTQ identity with HIV/AIDS) (Yep & Shimanoff, 2013). In other words, due to continued discrimination, to remain silent ultimately leads to violence or death for people within the community; simultaneously, remaining silent about sexual identity provides protection from discrimination. Likewise, the "don't ask, don't tell" policy in the military served to protect members of the homosexual community from discrimination and/or hate crimes (Yep & Shimanoff, 2013), though that silence perpetuated stigma by denying military personnel their identity. These facets of silence within the LGBTQ community and DOS demonstrate the complexities of silence, and the ways in which any use of silence can be simultaneously detrimental and advantageous, depending on stakeholders.

In the Clothesline Project, similar to the way disembodied tee shirts embody women's experiences, survivors themselves "are both the scene and witness to the crime" (Armstrong, Gleckman-Krut, & Johnson, 2018, p. 111). Whereas Brown (2012) noted silence during commemorative events as representative of post-tragedy silence ("the calm after the storm") (p. 247), the silence surrounding the CP represents the experiences during and after assault. This, however, does not mean that survivors lack agency or do not communicate in powerful ways. Just like the expectation for women to look and act certain ways as victims (such as "easy"), an expectation exists for them to look and act certain ways as survivors (such as clean and sexually conservative). Without fulfilling this expectation, a case will likely fail to go to trial (Miller, 2019; Murphy et al., 2011). Activist events like the Clothesline Project, though, permit one to represent their experience how they choose and makes the survivor seen (in a sense) while avoiding subjection to "tests" of authenticity.

Finally in this section, I address Gallaudet University's "Deaf President Now" (DPN) protest, which rather than *use* silence protested the privileging of voice within society. In 1988, the University—the world's only university for deaf and hard of hearing people—hired a hearing person as its president (Gallaudet University, 2020). Protests shut down the University, and within a week, the University met students' demands (those for the resignation of the newly hired hearing president; the resignation of the chairperson of the Board of Trustees; the requirement that deaf people constitute 51% of board members; and the requirement that faculty, students, and staff involved in the protest face no negative consequences) (Gallaudet University, 2020).

Levitt (2013) points out the similarities between colonialism and treatment of deaf people within the United States, noting that society considered "native" people and deaf people in need of being "civilize[d]," often via society seeking methods to "make [deaf people] as 'hearing' as possible" (p. 70). Historically, schools prohibited the use of sign language in the education of deaf children, with hearing people believing that they knew best how to deal with the needs of deaf students (Gallaudet, 2020).

Not only did this directly impact deaf students, but it meant a loss of jobs for deaf teachers (Gallaudet University, 2020). Levitt (2013) argues silence as a "technique" and a method for which hearing people can experience solidarity with Deaf people (p. 71). But hearing people who support other social justice issues, such as race and gender equality, often forget to include those with other abilities in their efforts (Levitt, 2013). Levitt (2013) writes:

> Audism as a normalizing discourse privileges hearing bodies, spoken communication, and hearing culture over Deaf bodies, signed communication, and Deaf culture. There are important points of resonance between audism and racism (in its privileging of whiteness), homophobia (in its demonizing and pathologizing Queer bodies), and colonialism (with its state-based exertion of power aimed at the suppression of difference through civilizing projects). (pp. 76–77)

The Gallaudet University DPN protest drew attention to the privileging of oral and auditory engagement as equally problematic as denying them.

Activism commonly spouts phrases such as "speaking out," "finding voice," "breaking silence," and "coming out" as assertions of power and even "political acts," but that language reinforces the language of the dominant (Jungkunz, 2012). Pattie Duncan (2004) writes:

> Hence, we might ask, How effective are 'speaking out,' 'finding a voice,' 'breaking silence,' and 'coming out' as liberatory rhetoric and political acts when such notions rely on the very discursive practices through which social and political domination occurs? (pp. 13–14)

To argue for the valuing of silence within particular rhetorical contexts, we need to stop "breaking" it. On the other hand, we must also stay mindful of speaking for those who choose silence; for us to tell their story, in part, takes away their right to *remain* silent (Wagner, 2012). As some activist events have suggested, sometimes silence *is* the means to solidarity (Wagner, 2012).

In close, in 1969, Susan Sontag observed that the ability to mass produce and disperse printed language accompanied a shift in understanding silence. She argued that the "degeneration of public language within the realms of politics and advertising and entertainment, have produced, especially among the better-educated inhabitants of modern mass society, a devaluation of language…And, as the prestige of language falls, that of silence rises" (Sontag, 1969, p. 21). As the rise of "fake news" and our struggle to grasp information literacy increases, we ever more so might see the value in remaining silent, at least until we have time to conduct research and speak or write with great attention to ethos. Wilke (2017) states, "Memes shouting accusations about what 'silence' means tend to forget that, in the cacophony of relentless media exchange, sometimes there is no message in the madness; it's just noise" (para 6). Indeed, speaking out and remaining silent can prove equally problematic and lead to injustices in their own ways (Oyler, 2017).

All notions of silence, therefore, have in common Fivush's (2010) observation that voice and silence are socially constructed and can only be understood contextually (Hatzisavvidou, 2015). Social constructions create a difference between "being silenced" and "being silent," the former of which implies imposition and the latter of which implies agency. What is more, silences are often intersectional, dependent upon "subject positons" (Clair, 1998, p. 151) and circumstances. The difficulty of determining *why* someone chooses silence only further cautions against ascribing meaning to anyone's choice. Because of the diverse ways we can use silence, there is no "ultimate politics" associated with it (Ferguson, 2011); and the complexity of determining whose interests get served with any act of enclosure or disclosure (Black, 1988) also creates grounds for caution. Contrary to many beliefs, speech and silence can "disrupt one another in intelligible ways" (Kalamaras, 1994).

The next chapter revisits and illustrates many of the notions surrounding silence within the context of a Clothesline Project event.

Discussion Questions

1. How might people use silence as a rhetorical device to shape information literacy and imagine a new democratic paradigm within the U.S.?
2. Identify some personal moments, on a local or global scale, in which you may have used or experienced silence in a positive manner. Does reflecting on those moments inform any area of your life now?

References

Ahrens, C. E. (2006). Being silenced: The impact of negative social reactions on the disclosure of rape. *American Journal of Community Psychology, 38*(3–4), 263–274. https://doi.org/10.1007/s10464-006-9069-9

Albert Einstein Institution. (2020, August 22). *198 methods of nonviolent action*. Albert Einstein Institution. https://www.aeinstein.org/nonviolentaction/198-methods-of-nonviolent-action/.

Alden, L. E., & Taylor, C. T. (2010). Interpersonal processes in social anxiety disorder. In J. G. Beck (Ed.), *Interpersonal processes in the anxiety disorders: Implications for understanding psychopathology and treatment* (pp. 125–152). American Psychological Association.

Anzaldúa, G. (1981/1983). Speaking in tongues: A letter to third world women writers. In C. Moraga & G. Anzaldúa (Eds.), *This bridge called my back: Writings by radical women of color* (pp. 165–174). Kitchen Table: Women of Color Press.

Armstrong, E. A., Gleckman-Krut, M., & Johnson, L. (2018). Silence, power, and inequality: An intersectional approach to sexual violence. *Annual Review of Sociology, 44*, 99–122. https://doi.org/10.1146/annurev-soc-073117-041410

Bakhtin, M. M. (1986). Erom notes made in 1970–71. In C. Emerson & M. Holquist (Eds.), *Speech genres and other late essays* (pp. 132–158). University of Texas Press.

Barringer, C. E. (1992). The survivor's voice: Breaking the incest taboo. *NWSA Journal, 4*(1), 4–22.

Basso, K. H. (1970). To give up on words: Silence in the Western Apache culture. *South-Western Journal of Anthropology, 26*(3), 213–230.

Ben-Ze'ev, E., Ginio, R., & Winter, J. (Eds.). (2010). *Shadows of war: A social history of silence in the twentieth century*. Cambridge University Press. https://doi.org/10.1017/CBO9780511676178.

Black, E. (1988). Secrecy and disclosure as rhetorical forms. *Quarterly Journal of Speech, 74*(2), 133–150. https://doi.org/10.1080/00335638809383833

Bokser, J. A. (2006). Sor Juana's rhetoric of silence. *Rhetoric Review, 25*(1), 5–21. https://doi:https://doi.org/10.1207/s15327981rr2501_1.

Bondy, C. (2015). *Voice, silence, and self: Negotiations of Buraku identity in contemporary Japan*. Harvard University Press. https://doi.org/10.1093/ssjj/jyx005

Bravesmith, A. (2012). Silence lends integrity to speech: Transcending the opposites of speech and silence in the analytic dialogue. *British Journal of Psychotherapy, 28*(1), 21–34. https://doi.org/10.1111/j.1752-0118.2011.01263.x

Brown, S. D. (2012). Two minutes of silence: Social technologies of public commemoration. *Theory & Psychology, 22*(2), 234–252. https://doi.org/10.1177/0959354311429031

Brummet, B. (1980). Towards a theory of silence as political strategy. *The Quarterly Journal of Speech, 66*, 389–303. https://doi.org/10.1080/00335638009383527.

Bruneau, T. J. (1973). Communicative silences: Forms and functions. *Journal of Communication, 23*(1), 17–46. https:// doi: https://doi.org/10.1111/j.1460-2466.1973.tb00929.x.

Cain, S. (2012). Quiet: The power of introverts in a world that can't stop talking. *Crown*. https://doi.org/10.3389/fpsyg.2017.00155

Carrillo Rowe, A., & Malhotra, S. (2013). Still the silence: Feminist reflections at the edges of sound. In S. Malhotra & A. Carrillo Rowe (Eds.), *Silence, feminism, power: Reflections at the edges of sound* (pp. 1–24). Palgrave Macmillan. https://doi.org/10.1057/9781137002372

Clair, R. P. (1998). Organizing silence: A world of possibilities. *State University of New York Press*. https://doi.org/10.5860/choice.36-3743

Coleman, L. M. (2006). Stigma: An enigma demystified. In L. J. Davis (Ed.), *The disability studies reader* (2nd ed., pp. 131–140). Routledge.

Covarrubias, P. (2007). (Un)biased in Western theory: Generative silence in American Indian communication. *Communication Monographs, 74*, 265–271. https://doi:https://doi.org/10.1080/03637750701393071.

Dobson, A. (2014). Listening for democracy: Recognition, representation, reconciliation. *Oxford University Press*. https://doi.org/10.1093/acprof:oso/9780199682447.001.0001

Donofrio, A. R. (2020). If you don't want to be silenced, be silent: Tactical silence & Jeffco Students for change. *Western Journal of Communication, 84*(5), 550–567. https://doi.org/10.1080/10570314.2020.1780303

Duffey, S. (2011). Student silences in the deep South: Hearing unfamiliar dialects. In C. Glenn & K. Ratcliffe (Eds.), *Silence and listening as rhetorical arts* (pp. 293–303). Southern Illinois University Press.

Duncan, P. (2004). Tell this silence: Asian American women writers and the politics of speech. *University of Iowa Press*. https://doi.org/10.2307/j.ctt20q1x8x

Eades, T. (1996). Plato, rhetoric, and silence. *Philosophy & Rhetoric, 29*(3), 244–258.

Ephratt, M. (2011). Linguistic, paralinguistic and extralinguistic speech and silence. *Journal of Pragmatics, 43*(9), 2286–2307. https://doi.org/10.1016/j.pragma.2011.03.006

Farmer, F. (2001). Saying and silence: Listening to composition with Bakhtin. *Utah State University Press*. https://doi.org/10.2307/j.ctt46nxt4

Ferguson, K. (2011). Silence: A politics. In C. Glenn & K. Ratcliffe (Eds.), *Silence and listening as rhetorical arts* (pp. 1–22). Southern Illinois University Press. https://doi.org/10.1080/07350198.2011.604613

Field Belenky, M., McVicker Clinchy, B., Rule Goldberger, N., & Mattuck Tarule, J. (1997). *Women's ways of knowing.* Basic Books.

Fivush, R. (2010). Speaking silence: The social construction of silence in autobiographical and cultural narratives. *Memory, 18*(2), 88–98. https://doi.org/10.1080/09658210903029404

Gallaudet University. (2020, August 16). *History behind DPN.* About Deaf President Now. https://www.gallaudet.edu/about/history-and-traditions/deaf-president-now/the-issues/history-behind-dpn

Glasby, H. (2016). [ ]: National Day of Silence's rhetorical silence as performative rhetorical activism. *Liminalities: A Journal of Performative Studies, 12*(3), 1–13.

Glenn, C. (2002). Silence: A rhetorical art for resisting discipline(s). *JAC, 22*(2), 261–291.

Glenn, C. (2004). *Unspoken: A rhetoric of silence. Southern Illinois University Press.* https://doi.org/10.5860/choice.42-4476

Glenn, C., & Ratcliffe, K. (2011). Introduction: Why silence and listening are important rhetorical arts. In C. Glenn & K. Ratcliffe (Eds.), *Silence and listening as rhetorical arts* (pp. 1–22). Southern Illinois University Press. https://doi.org/10.1080/07350198.2011.604613

Göker, Z. (2011). Presence in silence: Feminist and democratic implications of the Saturday vigils in Turkey. In J. Beinin & F. Vairel (Eds.), *Social movements, mobilization, and contestation in the Middle East and North Africa* (pp.107–124). Stanford University Press. https://doi.org/10.1515/9780804788038.

Greene, A. B. (1940). *The philosophy of silence.* R.R. Smith.

Gries, L. (2015). *Still life with rhetoric: A new materialist approach for visual rhetorics.* Utah State University Press.

Hao, R.N. (2010). Silence as cultural pedagogical performance: Possibilities in silence research. *The Review of Communication, 10*(4), 290–305. https://doi.org/10.1080/15358593.2010.498523

Hao, R.N. (2011). Rethinking critical pedagogy: Implications on silence and silent bodies. *Text and Performance Quarterly, 31*(3), 267–284. https://doi.org/10.1080/10462937.2011.573185

Hatzisavvidou, S. (2015). Disturbing binaries in political thought: Silence as political activism. *Social Movement Studies, 14*(5), 509–522. https://doi.org/10.1080/14742837.2015.1043989

Hesford, W. S. (2004). Rhetorical projections and silences. *JAC Online, 24*(3), 785–797.

hooks, B. (2015). *Talking back: Thinking feminist, thinking black.* Routledge.

Horsman, J. (2009). *Too sacred to learn: Women, violence, and education*. Routledge.

Hull, A.G. (2001). *Soul talk: The new spirituality of African American women*. Inner Traditions/Bear & Co.

Jandt, F. E. (2017). An introduction to intercultural communication: Identities in a global community. *SAGE Publications*. https://doi.org/10.1080/17475759.2011.581035

Jaworski, A. (2005). Introduction: Silence in institutional and intercultural contexts. *Multilingua—Journal of Cross-Cultural and Interlanguage Communication, 24*, 1–6. https://doi.org/10.1515/mult.24.1-2.1

Jung, T. (2017). Le silence du peuple: The rhetoric of silence during the French Revolution. *French History, 31*(4), 440–469. https://doi.org/10.1093/fh/crx062

Jungkunz, V. (2012). The promise of democratic silences. *New Political Science, 34*(2), 127–150. https://doi.org/10.1080/07393148.2012.676393

Kalamaras, G. (1994). *Reclaiming the tacit dimension: Symbolic form in the rhetoric of silence*. State University of New York Press.

Keating, C. (2013). Resistant silences. In S. Malhotra & A. Carrillo Rowe (Eds.), *Silence, feminism, power: Reflections at the edges of sound* (pp. 25–33). Palgrave Macmillan. https://doi.org/10.1057/9781137002372

King, J. (2013). Silence in the second language classrooms of Japanese universities. *Applied Linguistics, 34*(3), 325–343. https://doi.org/10.1093/applin/ams043

King, J., & Atsuko, A. (2017). Talk, silence and anxiety during one-to-one tutorials: A cross-cultural comparative study of Japan and UK undergraduates' tolerance of silence. *Asia Pacific Education Review, 18*, 489–499. https://doi.org/10.1007/s12564-017-9503-8

Kohrs Campbell, K. (1989). *Man cannot speak for her: Key texts of the early feminists* (Vol. 2). Praeger Paperback.

Kovač, P., Tolsma, H. D., & Dragos, D. C. (2020). In search of an effective model: A comparative outlook on administrative silence in Europe. In D.C. Dragos, P. Kovač, & D.C. Dragos (Eds.), *The sound of silence in European administrative law* (pp. 3–29). Palgrave Macmillan. https://doi.org/10.1007/978-3-030-45227-8.

Kurzon, D. (2007). Towards a typology of silence. *Journal of Pragmatics, 39*(10), 1673–1688. https://doi.org/10.1016/j.pragma.2007.07.003

Lawless, E. J. (2001). *Women escaping violence empowerment through narrative*. University of Missouri Press.

Lehtonen, J., & Sajavaara, K. (1985). The silent Finn. In D. Tannen & M. Saville-Troike (Eds.), *Perspectives on silence* (pp. 193–201). Ablex Publishing.

Levitt, R. (2013). Silence speaks volumes: Counter-hegemonic silences, deafness, and alliance work. In S. Malhotra & A. Carrillo Rowe (Eds.), *Silence, feminism, power: Reflections at the edges of sound* (pp. 67–82). Palgrave Macmillan. https://doi.org/10.1057/9781137002372

Li, H. (2005). Rethinking silencing silences. In M. Bowler (Ed.), *Democratic dialogue in education: Troubling speech, disturbing silence* (pp. 69–86). Peter Lang.

Lorde, A. (1984). The transformation of silence into language and action. In *Sister outsider: Essays and speeches* (pp. 40–44). Crossing Press.

Lynch, T. (2001). Temperance, temptation, and silence. *Philosophy, 76*(296), 251–269.

Lyon, A. (2004). Confucian silence and remonstration: A basis for deliberation? In C. S. Lipson & R. Binkley (Eds.), *Rhetoric before and beyond the Greeks* (pp. 131–145). State University of New York Press.

Lyons, S. R. (2000). Rhetorical sovereignty: What do American Indians want from writing? *CCC, 51*, 447–468.

Maslow, A. H. (1993). Health and pathology. In *The farther reaches of human nature* (pp. 3–51). Penguin Compass.

McIntyre, A. (2013). The value of "silence" in the lives of post-incarcerated women. *Journal of Offender Rehabilitation, 52*(1), 1–15. https://doi.org/10.1080/10509674.2012.713452

Miller, C. (2019) *Know my name: A memoir*. Viking.

Moraga, C., & Anzaldúa, G. (Eds.). (1981/1983). *This bridge called my back: Writings by radical women of color*. Kitchen Table: Women of Color Press.

Motsemme, N. (2004). The mute always speak: On women's silences at the Truth and Reconciliation Commission. *Current Sociology, 52*(5), 909–932. https://doi.org/10.1177/0011392104045377

Murphy, S. B., Banyard, V. L., Maynard, S. P., & Dufresne, R. (2011). Advocates speak out on adult sexual assault: A unique crime demands a unique response. *Journal of Aggression, Maltreatment & Trauma, 20*(6), 690–710. https://doi.org/10.1080/10926771.2011.595381

Nagar-Ron, S., & Motzafi-Haller, P. (2011). "My life? There is not much to tell": On voice, silence and agency in interviews with first-generation Mizrahi Jewish women immigrants to Israel. *Qualitative Inquiry, 17*(7), 653–663. https://doi:https://doi.org/10.1177/1077800411414007.

Nwoye, G. O. (1985). Eloquent silence among the Igbo of Nigeria. In D. Tannen & M. Saville-Troike (Eds.), *Perspectives on silence* (pp. 185–191). Ablex Publishing.

Oliveros, O. L., (2012). Silence in the musical scores of human phenomena. *Culture & Psychology, 18*(4), 465–471.https://doi.org/10.1177/1354067X12456717.

Olsen, T. (1978). *Silences*. Delta/Seymour Lawrence.

Olson, L. C. (1997). On the margins of rhetoric: Audre Lorde transforming silence into language and action. *Quarterly Journal of Speech, 83*(1), 49–70. https://doi.org/10.1080/00335639709384171.

Orgad, S. & Gill, R. (2019). Safety valves for mediated female rage in the #MeToo era. *Feminist Media Studies, 19*(4), 596–603. https://doi.org/10.1080/08164649.2016.1148001

Oyler, L. (2017, March 9). How the push to 'Break the Silence' fails the feminist movement. Vice. https://www.vice.com/en_us/article/xwqyxj/rebecca-solnit-break-the-silence-review

Picard, M. (1963). *Man and language*. H. Regnery Co.

Price, M. (2011). *Mad at school: Rhetorics of mental disability and academic life*. University of Michigan Press. https://doi.org/10.3998/mpub.1612837

Poling, N. (1997). Can we talk? In B. M. Hodge & J. Preston-Sabin (Eds.), *Accommodations–or just good teaching?: Strategies for teaching college students with disabilities* (pp. 103–104). Praeger.

Pollock, D. (2013). Keeping quiet: Performing pain. In S. Malhotra & A. Carrillo Rowe (Eds.), *Silence, feminism, power: Reflections at the edges of sound* (pp. 159–175). Palgrave Macmillan.https://doi.org/10.1057/9781137002372

Pottinger, L. (2016). Planting the seeds of a quiet activism. *Area, 49*(2), 215–222. https://doi.org/10.1111/area.12318.

Rakow, L. F., & Wackwitz, L. A. (2005). Feminist communication theory: Selections in context. *SAGE Publications*. https://doi.org/10.1108/09649420510609203

Reda, M. M. (2009). *Between speaking and silence: a study of quiet students*. State University of New York Press.

Reilly, K. (2018, March 24). *Emma Gonzalez kept America in stunned silence to show how quickly 17 people died at Parkland*. Time. http://time.com/5214322/emma-gonzalezmarch-for-our-lives-speech/

Reinharz, S. (1994). Toward an ethnography of "voice" and "silence." In E. Trickett & R. Watts (Eds.), *Human diversity: Perspectives on people in context* (pp. 178–200). Jossey-Bass, Inc.https://doi.org/10.2307/2547646.

Rich, A. C. (1979). *On lies, secrets, and silence*. Norton. https://doi.org/10.1080/10894160903048122

Samovar, L. A., Porter, R. E., McDaniel, E. R., & Roy, C. S. (2017). *Communication between cultures*. Cengage Learning.

Saunders, G. R. (1985). Silence and noise as emotion management styles: An Italian case. In D. Tannen & M. Saville-Troike (Eds.), *Perspectives on Silence* (pp. 165–183). Ablex Publishing.

Seymour, R. (2013, June 18). Turkey's 'standing man' shows how passive resistance can shake a state. *The Guardian*. https://www.theguardian.com/commentisfree/2013/jun/18/turkey-standing-man.

Sirc, G. (2002). *English composition as a happening*. Utah State University Press. https://doi.org/10.2307/j.ctt46nx7x

Solnit, R. (2017, March 8). Silence and powerlessness go hand in hand— Women's voices must be heard. *The Guardian*. https://www.theguardian.com/commentisfree/2017/mar/08/silence-powerlessness-womens-voices-rebecca-solnit.

Sontag, S. (1969). *Styles of radical will*. Farrar.

Spivak, G. C. (1988). Can the subaltern speak? In C. Nelson & L. Grossberg (Eds.), *Marxism and the interpretation of culture* (pp. 271–313). Macmillan.

St. Clair, R. (2003). The social and cultural construction of silence. *Intercultural Communication Studies, 12*(3), 87–91.

Sunda, M. (2015, October 23). *Japan's hidden caste of untouchables*. BBC News. https://www.bbc.com/news/world-asia-34615972.

Tannen, D., & Saville-Troike, M. (Eds.). (1985). *Perspectives on silence*. Ablex Publishing.

US law enforcement violated Black Lives Matter protesters' human rights, documents acts of police violence and excessive Force. (2020, August 4). *Amnesty International*. https://www.amnesty.org/en/latest/news/2020/08/usa-law-enforcement-violated-black-lives-matter-protesters-human-rights/

van Manen, M. (1990). *Researching lived experience: Human science for an action sensitive pedagogy*. State University of New York Press.

Voegelin, S. (2010). *Listening to noise and silence: Towards a philosophy of sound art*. Continuum.

Wagner, R. (2012). Silence as resistance before the subject, or could the subaltern remain silent? *Theory, Culture & Society, 29*(6), 99–124. https://doi.org/10.1177/0263276412438593.

Wilke, L. D. (2017, December 7). *Silence isn't always compliance... Sometimes it's the activism of listening*. HuffPost. https://www.huffpost.com/entry/silence-isnt-always-compl_b_7260302.

Yep, G. A., & Shimanoff, S. B. (2013). The US day of silence: Sexualities, silences, and the will to unsay in the age of empire. In S. Malhotra & A. Carrillo Rowe (Eds.), *Silence, feminism, power: Reflections at the edges of sound* (pp. 139–156). Palgrave Macmillan. https://doi.org/10.1057/9781137002372

Yuan, Y. Q. (2015). Analysis of silence in intercultural communication. In W. Striełkowski & J. Cheng (Eds.), *Advances in social science, education and humanities research* (pp. 155–159). Atlantis Press.

CHAPTER 3

Case Study of the CP Archive

On a rainy April afternoon, a group of volunteers gathered to hang tee shirts in a university student center. Some of the shirts had been created recently and some created years ago; but they all address the continuing narratives of thousands of women across the world. The shirts depict screams and tears and music and wings, turmoil and defiance and healing. One CP participant says she chose the particular design of her shirt because she "wanted to give voice to the many women who are denied that opportunity, for the women who scream with no one to hear them."[1] And though her participation, as she reported, made her feel proud, empowered, bold, and daring, it made her nervous too; after all, she wrote, "It's a constant battle. Survivors, we have to be resilient in the face of some pretty terrible memories and echoing voices in our heads." A closer, systematic examination of such sentiments provides an understanding of the dynamics that yield and perpetuate acts of violence and trauma, and the ways in which those who suffer them also survive them.

To engage in a systematic examination of the way written and visual communication mediate resilience on the part of survivors, I turned to a CP shirt collection at a large public university. This CP collection

---

[1] Communicated through an anonymous online survey.

© The Author(s), under exclusive license to Springer Nature Switzerland AG 2021
J. R. Corey, *Materializing Silence in Feminist Activism*, https://doi.org/10.1007/978-3-030-81066-5_3

consisted of 74 tee shirts that yielded 897 data points,[2] which provide responses to the larger questions driving this book:

- How does written and visual literacy function in relation to understandings of female embodiment and violence against women?
- How can literate artifacts be used as an archive to continue revising social narratives?
- How does multimodal composition serve as a mediator between silence (imposed or un-imposed) and meaningful communication?

The first question explores patterns in linguistic and illustrated content, and how women use the content to position themselves in relation to their experiences of violence. The second question, subsequently, investigates the influence of cultural narratives on CP participants' designs and the way these designs adopt or counter narratives about what it means to be a woman. The second question, furthermore, conceptualizes the tee shirts and the ideologies they implicate as a potential archive, a collection of artifacts that documents the past, expands the collection, and influences understandings of present society (as discussed in Chapter 1). The third question looks at the media women use to communicate their messages through the lens of rhetorics of silence in order to explore limitations and affordances of particular uses of silence.

This chapter first details methods, followed by results of the rhetorical and semiotic analyses of CP tee shirts, arguing that women's activist messages align with patriarchal narratives of oppression and marginalization, even as the activist messages attempt to counter narratives about women's identity as sexual objects or people to be conquered and oppressed.[3] Four major findings support this argument:

---

[2] Formula for configuration of data points: 1 shirt with visual representation only × 5 points of semiotic analysis = 5; 26 shirts with text only × 9 points of rhetorical analysis (characters, actions, and setting × logos, ethos, pathos) = 234; 47 shirts with text and visual representations × 9 points of rhetorical analysis + × 5 points of semiotic analysis = 658 (5 + 234 + 658 = 897).

[3] CP participants receive no instructions for the composing of their shirts other than that they cannot use perpetrators' names if perpetrators were not found guilty by a court of law. From a legal standpoint, disclosure without an official guilty verdict can be considered slander. All other design decisions are determined by CP participants at their own discretion.

- Participants' messages lack details of experiences with gender violence.
- In their messages, participants invoke the use of one's physical body, rather than the use of literate practices and artifacts, for social action.
- Participants make covert assertions of agency.
- Participants' visual messages rely on preconceived socially constructed representations of ideas rather than on original representations of experiences.

I also argue that activists employ alphabetic text messages and visual messages but rely on alphabetic text to make meaning even of the visuals. The fifth finding supports this argument:

- Visuals' content show that participants tend to use alphabetic text and visual components in their work, but that alphabetic text and visuals lack a rhetorical relationship between one another. (By "rhetorical," I mean that text and images do not support one another in messages' attempt to persuade or influence CP audiences and instead appear as separate and disjointed elements.)

I organize this chapter around the first principal research question and the data that responds to it, presenting the rhetorical analysis of text and semiotic analysis of visuals, respectively. Information in this chapter establishes *what* literate (including rhetorical) practices occur in the CP.[4] Then, the "Analysis" section of this chapter explores the theoretical underpinnings for understanding these results within the framework of composing, revising, and archiving social narratives and the role of silence in this process.

---

[4] Rhetorical analysis, in addition to the words used on the shirts, included record of capitalization, underlining, grammar and spelling errors, punctuation, and general position of the text (i.e., AT = across top, BL = bottom left, etcetera). I ceased keeping track of the colors of text. Semiotic analysis, in addition to identification of images, included record of the colors of images, but not the position of images. Because of the scope of this project, however, this chapter discusses only the content of text and images.

Methods[5]

For the rhetorical analysis, I use Foss's (2009) Fantasy-Theme Criticism to identify characters, actions, and settings. Fantasy-Theme "is designed to provide insights into the shared worldview of groups" (Foss, 2009, p. 97). Here, "'fantasy' is the creative and imaginative interpretation of events and a 'fantasy theme' is the means through which the interpretation is accomplished in communication" (Foss, 2009, pp. 97–98). This approach allows for determining the degree to which a shirt makes personal or public appeals as they relate to logos, ethos, and pathos. More specifically, my interest in using data to understand divides between the personal and the public meant that I needed to form a connection between personal disclosure of characters, actions, and settings related to CP participants' experiences and the rhetorical appeals used to engage the public (viewers of the CP). To do so, I determined what logical appeals with characters, actions, and settings would look like, as opposed to the characters, actions, and settings that people might use in ethical and emotional appeals. In other words, logical appeals would require inclusion of certain kinds of characters, actions, or settings, or different relationships among these elements, than emotional appeals. Logos, ethos, and pathos, though unaddressed specifically in the results and analysis, facilitated a finite breakdown of the data, which I could then piece together to identify larger patterns *in*, and significant contributions *to*, understandings of feminist activism. This initial breakdown of data included the following scheme:

Logos—Appeals to logic involve the least amount of self-disclosure on the part of CP participants (the greatest distance between CP participants' emotional experiences and the emotional nature of their messages).

- characters: groups of people or 3rd-person pronouns
- actions: calls to public to act
- setting: no setting or large, undefined setting (e.g., "society")

---

[5] Portions of the methods and results presented in this chapter were previously published in two articles (see "Corey, 2014, 2017). The first article, Beyond 'Digital': What Women's Activism Reveals About Material Multimodal Composition Pedagogy, focuses on one of the five major findings of the study presented in this chapter, specifically as it relates to pedagogy (which inspired Chapter 4 of this manuscript). The second article, 'My sister went to Steubenville, OH and all I got was this lousy shirt': Composing Feminist Activism with the Clothesline Project, details the results of my pilot study of the CP, covering 12 of the 74 shirts discussed in this chapter.

Ethos—Appeals to credibility involve a balance between logical and emotional appeals. Too much logic (non-disclosure) may fail to meet activists' objectives to persuade or influence people's thoughts and behaviors regarding social issues. Too much emotion (disclosure) may alienate viewers or invoke stereotypes of the emotional woman.

- characters: proper nouns or 1st- and 2nd-person pronouns
- actions: actions carried out against or by (collectively) the tee shirt writer/artist or a specific individual (e.g., "Sharon")
- setting: public time during, or place in, which actions were carried out in relation to writer/artist or specific individual named by writer/artist (e.g., "college" or "the woods")

Pathos—Appeals to emotion involve the greatest amount of self-disclosure on the part of CP participants. The greater the amount or degree of CP participants' self-disclosure, the greater the opportunity for CP audience members to have an emotional experience in response to the CP.

- characters: people named in specific relation to the writer/artist (e.g., "my sister") or 1st-person pronouns
- actions: actions carried out against or by the tee shirt writer/artist or person with specific relation to writer/artist
- setting: personal time during, or place in, which actions were carried out in relation to writer/artist or specific individual named by writer/artist (e.g., "home" or "January 17")

Given that the questions motivating my research pertained to how women navigated intersections of the personal and the public—how they 'spoke out' and how they were 'silenced'—I devised a scheme that made clear distinctions between general and specific information. In my study, specific information alluded to personal details of women's experiences with gender violence. Given my initial ideas of the rhetorical nature of the CP, I aligned personal disclosure with emotional appeals; activist events with and for the general public seemed to prioritize making emotional appeals (as opposed to those with policy-makers, who might rely more on logical information, such as statistics, to influence actions). Emotional appeals, by nature, involve disclosure of tee shirt designers' experiences of violence (as survivors themselves or as individuals who knew survivors/victims). Emotional appeals can also address ethos, since they make the case for firsthand knowledge.

The further tee shirt messages appear removed from tee shirt creators' personal experiences, the less they involve emotional and ethical appeals and the more they appeal to logical understandings of the issue (as with statistics). The most general information puts the most distance between the tee shirt creator, their experience, and their audience. This general information includes: non-specific groups of people and third-person pronouns; calls to the public; and exclusion of a setting related to experiences with gender violence, or inclusion of a large and undefined settings such as "society." On the other hand, placing the audience in closer relation to the tee shirt creator and her experiences (making emotional appeals) includes: people named in specific relation to the tee shirt creator, or first-person references to the tee shirt creator; mention of actions carried out directly against or by tee shirt creators; and references to specific settings in which these acts occurred. The closer audience members get to tee shirt creators via creators' compositions, the greater opportunity for audience members to experience empathy.

Ethical appeals put audience members in closer proximity to tee shirt creators than logical appeals but may or may not evoke an emotional response. To illustrate, my curriculum vitae speaks to my credibility as a scholar but probably does not illicit deep emotional responses in those who review it. Therefore, ethical appeals give credence to what tee shirt creators communicate and put audience members in relation to tee shirt creators, with specifically named individuals and second-person pronouns; actions carried out against or by the tee shirt creators in a collective unit or by a specific individual; and public time or place in which actions were carried out in relation to these people. But, again, ethical appeals do not bring them as close as emotional appeals do, or distance them as much as logical appeals do. Taken together, these elements create the "theme." As seen in my study of the CP, though most shirts that use "I" appeal to ethos, not all of them appeal to pathos. One shirt communicates a personal relationship with a boy/man named Zachary, but exclusion of the nature of the relationship and other details keeps viewers from making a more intense connection with the tee shirt creator. Characters' relationship to the actions and settings incorporated into the shirt determine the shirt's ethical or emotional appeals. A child-size shirt that reads "Mommy please don't make me go to daddys [sic] house. Please I love you" creates its emotional appeal with the disclosure of the nature of the relationship between the shirt creator and the other characters (mommy and daddy), the actions (make me go), and the setting (daddy's house). This kind of analysis allows for the discussion of how these themes and patterns in language relate to the idea of psychosocial compositions—how the rhetorical positions these messages, as created by tee shirt writers/artists, subscribe to or resist cultural narratives about violence against women.

My attempt to differentiate between personal and public messages, therefore, required use of a rhetorical method conducive to creating my own coding scheme. Moreover, while I could have conducted a visual rhetorical analysis, the use of signs and symbols on most shirts (such as an arrow or sign for "female") lends itself to semiotic analysis. For example, visuals such as awareness ribbons prove difficult to label as a character, action, or setting.

The rhetorical analysis speaks to psychosocial compositions in that it looks at personal and public appeals of messages as they relate to cultural narratives. Semiotic analysis addresses psychosocial compositions differently, as explained by Berger (2011):

> A science that studies the life of signs within society is conceivable; it would be a part of social psychology and consequently of general psychology; I shall call it semiology (from Greek semeion "sign"). Semiology would show what constitutes signs, what laws govern them. (p. 7)

Visuals acquire meaning as elements related in a system, especially a social system. I looked for patterns in the visuals' content rather than at features (such as color and placement); as such, traditional notions of semiotics served my purpose of finding the frequency of use of text and image, and the relationships between text and visuals. Thus, extensive development of a scheme was unnecessary.

I, therefore, use Silverman's (2011) notion of semiotic analysis, which involves examining signifiers and signified concepts, the autonomous nature of images, the arbitrary/unmotivated nature of images, and the relationships between images and concepts. Such an analysis allows me to determine how images acquire their meaning in the context of other images, words, and the CP as a whole. In this project, then, the semiotic analysis looks at how images and their parts converge and diverge to construct evidence of particular rhetorical approaches within social narratives. In other words, examination of the relationship between signifier and signified shows patterns in participants' conceptualizations of images' symbolic meaning. These patterns implicate cultural narratives such as those related to gendered communication (e.g., the frequent use of hearts). Cultural narratives are also implicated in the idea of images gaining their meaning from their placement in a system, rather than from an inherent connection between image and meaning. According to Silverman (2011), semiotic analysis includes responding to the following criteria:

1. "Signs bring together an image or word (the 'signifier) and a concept (the 'signified')."
2. "Signs are not autonomous entities—they derive their meaning only from the place within a sign system. What constitutes a linguistic sign is only its difference from other sights (so the colour red is only something which is not green, blue, orange, etc..)"
3. "The linguistic sign is *arbitrary* or unmotivated. This, Saussure says, means that the sign 'has no natural connection with the signified'."
4. "Signs can be put together through two main paths. First, there are possibilities of combining signs…Saussure calls these patterns of combinations *syntagmatic relations*. Second, there are contrastive properties…Here the choice of one term necessarily excludes the other. Saussure calls these mutually exclusive relations *paradigmatic oppositions*." (p. 330)

The semiotic analysis permitted me to categorize the frequency of images and explore what those frequencies suggest about gendered discourse as it relates to activism and understandings of multimodal composing. To demonstrate an abbreviated semiotic analysis, hands painted in red and blue paint on one CP shirt derive their meaning from the context of an activist event bringing awareness to the issue of gender violence. Without this context, and without the accompanying words, the drawing of hands on a tee shirt would provide for other interpretations. Given the messiness of the image, for instance, we could envision the tee shirt as a child's art project. Hands could also signify affection and communion (holding the hand of a significant other, holding hands during prayers and vigils), the act of welcoming (shaking a hand upon meeting someone), and labor (working with one's hands). Arms could signify these same elements:

affection and communion (embracing someone in a hug), the act of welcoming (welcoming someone with open arms), and labor (performing a job or exercising). Without the context of the CP, these many possibilities could easily make the sign arbitrary to viewers. In addition, the meaning of the message rests on its placement on clothing. The same image and words placed on a blanket or banner, or as a sidewalk drawing, would fail to uphold the integrity of the message. The image, then, relies on its relationship to the words on the shirt; the context of the CP; and the context of a culture in which wearing clothing is the norm and in which tee shirts have particular social value.

I move now to an analysis of the results yielded from use of these methods.

RESULTS

Activists' Textual Messages Lack Details of Gender Violence (See Fig. 3.1)

Of the 74 tee shirts in the collection, 59 (80%) remove the activist from the setting in which they encountered violence. These shirts either make no mention of setting, or mention large, undefined settings (e.g., "night," "day," "jail," "external") (Fig. 3.1). Shirt 54 introduces the audience to a 3-year-old girl (though her relation to the activist remains undisclosed) and to an action ("it," which in this context suggests assault). But lack of further details prevents viewers from connecting with the girl as an individual. Similarly, shirt 65 avoids providing a time and place for a powerfully worded "daddy's doll" among seemingly randomly placed

Fig. 3.1 Shirts excluding designers' personal details

nouns and adjectives. Shirt 67 (not pictured) takes the reader to a place where "a light came in from outside," but becomes rather abstract with the notion of "two worlds" and "invisible boundaries."

Some shirts (66%) offer details of experiences, such as relationships, but do not offer *enough* detail for viewers to make full sense of the experience (Fig. 3.1). We can see this on shirts that include a person's name other than the CP participant's name but not the relationship of that person to the CP participant, and on shirts that include acontextualized actions (e.g., "I was 5 and he did it for 3 years"). Viewers would have *enough* detail only when actions, characters, and settings supplement one another in the construction and understanding of a scene, thought, or sentiment, which does not occur in this study. Shirts that did not offer enough detail made logical appeals (e.g., via statistics), but also included some element of ethos and/or pathos. Elements of ethos and pathos, as conceptualized in this research, are more personal than elements of logos (see preceding Methods section). This does not mean, however, that these shirts are, overall, personal in nature or that they disclose vivid details of personal experiences. With shirt 3, the participant seems to label herself a survivor and describes herself as "bent but not broken," but then quickly turns attention away from herself to instruct unspecified others to "speak out." She focuses attention back on herself, however, by telling the audience about her friend, one of her acquaintances, and a stranger. But she does not disclose the relation of these people to her. Are these people who have assaulted her, or people whom she knows or whom she has heard of and who have been assaulted? Finally, the participant turns attention to a general group of survivors, which she addresses with a second-person pronoun ("you"/ "your"). Though the use of "you" and "your" may demonstrate a willingness to be direct and assert power in the form of making a demand, the overall lack of cohesion among elements seems to undermine this power.

Similarly, shirt 26 (not pictured) refers to a relationship between the activist and a boy/man named Zachary. But audience members have no idea what relationship the character Zachary shares with the CP participant or why the participant feels proud of Zachary. Is he a survivor of sexual violence? Is he a supportive intimate partner, a family member, or a friend to the tee shirt activist? Though the creator refers to herself and her personal relationship, she stops short of letting viewers fully understand the nature of that relationship, which hinders the overall clarity and rhetorical effectiveness of the message.

This first major finding, that participants' messages lack details of personal experiences with gender violence, aligns with larger cultural narratives about what society deems appropriate for women to disclose (Ahrens, 2006; Clover & Stalker, 2008; Droogsma, 2009; Ehrlich, 2014; Julier, 1994). Women who have suffered gender violence have also frequently suffered the "second assault" (Williams & Holmes, 1981, p. xi; Lewis-O'Connor et al., 2017, p. 19), known too as victim blaming and re-victimization—the act of blaming women for their experiences of gender violence (e.g., 'leading men on' by wearing revealing clothing, emasculating men, etc.) (Droogsma, 2009; Skinner, 2009). Even in 1981, Williams and Holmes acknowledged:

> The controlling, restrictive fear of rape is part of being a female. It is part of socialization to the feminine role. It is one of life's cruel ironies, however, that the experience of rape which a woman has been taught to fear and to resist to the point of death brings not a public show of support but a public display of skepticism and even blame. (p. 3)

Williams and Holmes (1981) equally note the influence of subject positions on perceptions of rape; society associates sex and gender, race, and ethnicity with rape "by frequency of victimization, by frequency of being labeled the 'alleged rapist,' by social reaction, [and] by impact and consequences" (p. xii). Such subject positions, then, may further influence presence and degree of disclosure.

Specific to sexual violence on college campuses, both *The Hunting Ground* (2015) documentary and books like *Missoula: Rape and the Justice System in a College Town* (Krakauer, 2015) have discussed the issue of victim blaming. *The Hunting Ground* sheds light on administrators' jobs to "protect the institution from harm, not the student from harm" (12:22), which means administrators often discourage students from going to the police so that the matter does not become one of public record (12:54); furthermore, while fraternities and student athletes have often been reported as offenders, universities have too much to gain from fraternities and athletes to intervene (1:05:15–1:06:19). In a multitude of ways, then, society has encouraged women to avoid revealing their experiences at all, let alone in detail.

When CP participants, however, exclude details, such as setting, they decontextualize the characters and actions they *do* disclose; this separates viewers from the space in which characters and actions gained their

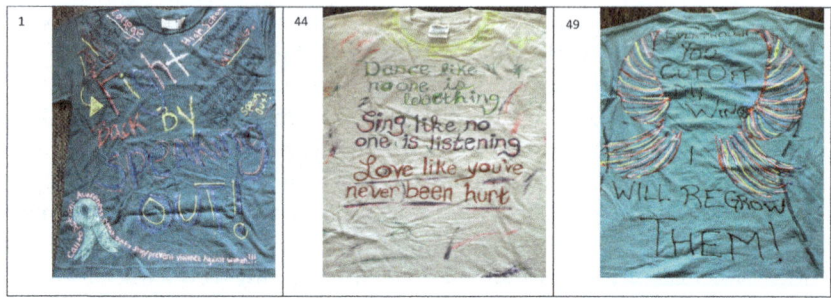

Fig. 3.2 Shirts with references to use of the body as active participation

meaning. Inclusion of details creates connection between an audience and the story or event and reduces viewers' disorientation, therefore likely increasing the impact of the activists' messages. In essence, greater understanding allows for greater connection. But while activists attempt to defy expectations placed on them by larger social narratives, activists in this study, to some extent, adhere to those expectations. Shirts that take this approach provide "appropriate" barriers between people, as exposure to graphic personal accounts may alienate non-survivors by making them feel uneasy (Clover & Stalker, 2008). In addition, the non-individualized nature of statistics presented on some shirts can put serious social issues into perspective in ways that personal stories may fall short. Statistics establish that a problem exists on a large scale, but their collective nature also provides an element of comfort, taking focus off of the individual and, therefore, allowing the individual to communicate in socially acceptable ways.

ACTIVISTS' TEXTUAL MESSAGES MAKE REFERENCES TO USING THE PHYSICAL BODY AS ACTIVE PARTICIPATION (SEE FIG. 3.2)

About one-third (34%) of all shirts refer to the body,[6] with 82% of these references suggesting the body as a means of asserting empowerment, whether directly or indirectly. Direct references include statements such

---

[6] 15 (60%) refer to the use of the body in relation to the audience 7 (28%) refer to the participant herself 2 (8%) refer to survivors 1 (4%) refer to men specifically.

as "fight back by speaking out," "dance and sing," and "stand up." With direct references, then, activists make explicit what characters are doing or ought to do with their bodies. Indirect references, on the other hand, include statements of action such as "express," "we will not be silenced," and "even though you cut off my wings, I will regrow them." Though indirect references do not specify how one would use their body, "expressing" and "breaking silence" would require action of some kind (whether speaking, writing, marching, or engaging in other ways). In addition, the metaphorical nature of some actions, such as having wings cut off and re-growing them, makes these actions indirect.

Much like the shirts that eliminate details related to personal experience, these shirts leave much of the sense-making up to viewers. Shirt 1 instructs people to "fight back by speaking out." But how does "speaking out" stop or prevent violence against women? Likewise, how does "dancing like no one is watching" and "singing like no one is listening" address the issue of sexual violence? And when "speaking out against sexual violence," what should people say? Viewers unfamiliar with the political issues surrounding sexual violence, or those unfamiliar with activist efforts in general, may need more concrete guidance in regards to what they can do in response to the issue. Ideas that audience members should "speak out" or assert liberation (shirt 44) require overt explanations of what these actions entail, signify, and mean in relation to the issue of sexual violence.

That participants invoke references to the body in their tee shirt messages aligns with cultural narratives that place focus on the female body (King, 2004; Siebel Newsom, 2011). In many of these messages, CP participants refer to using the body to defy expectations (e.g., standing up and speaking out). These uses of the body suggest three ideas on the part of activists: (1) that they see themselves or audience members as able to *do something* about gender violence; (2) that they think about 'action' in terms of physical movement (speaking and standing) rather than in terms of literate practices (such as writing to Congress or city officials) or practices such as attending bystander-awareness training[7]; (3) that audience members will know *how* to enact "speaking out" and "standing up," that they will know how to engage in meaningful responses to the problem of

---

[7] While activities like writing, reading, and attending trainings requires use of the body/movement, the focus in these activities is not on the movement itself, as it is with speaking and standing in this context.

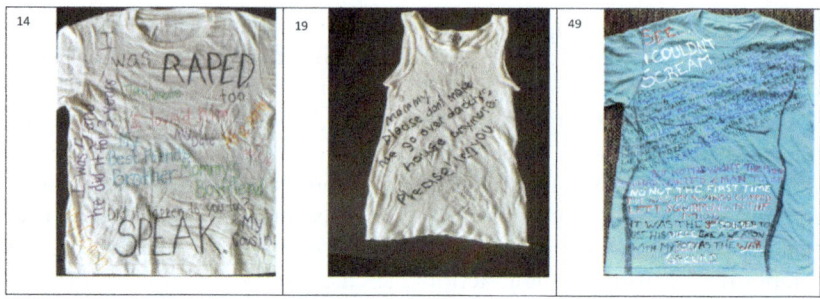

Fig. 3.3 Shirts that include covert assertions of agency with characters (pronouns)

gender violence. What does "speaking out" or "standing up" entail? What does it do or what should it do, and how can viewers (with varying abilities) engage in those activities? With an activist agenda, such questions remain important; simply drawing attention to injustice remains crucial to activists' purposes, but if creating awareness fails to empower or motivate people to act meaningfully, the status quo will likely remain (for individuals on a journey to recovery and for society as a whole). Additionally, as activists attempt to counter cultural narratives, they seem to perpetuate the idea that use of one's body supersedes more intellectual or collaborative pursuits, such as using literacy for social change or volunteering one's time with relevant non-profit organizations.

ACTIVISTS' TEXTUAL MESSAGES INCLUDE COVERT ASSERTIONS OF AGENCY (SEE FIGS. 3.3 AND 3.4)

Covert assertions of agency[8] occur in multiple ways: the use of "you" pronouns, the use of "I" pronouns, a focus on perpetrators' actions, and a focus on survivors' healing rather than on survivors' states of vulnerability. Twenty-eight shirts (38%) include individuals or groups in their messages, which fall into the following categories: survivors (10 shirts); friends, family members, or specific people known to tee shirt activists (8 shirts); perpetrators (7 shirts); members of the public (4 shirts); and others such as authors and sororities (4 shirts). Eighteen of these shirts

---

[8] I define "agency" as an "ability or capacity to act or exert power" ("Agency").

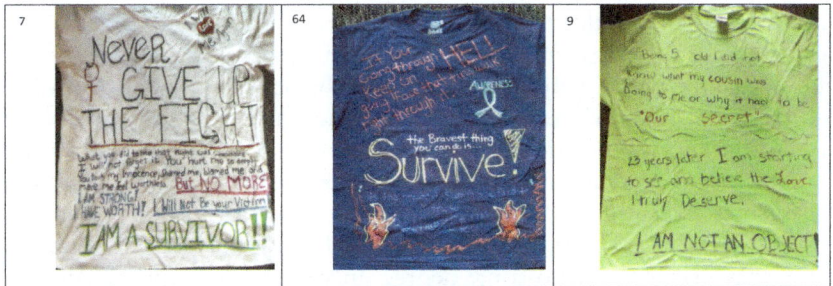

Fig. 3.4 Shirts that include covert assertions of agency with actions

(64%) refer to these characters as "you" (Fig. 3.4). For example, shirt 16 (not pictured) addresses the general public, warning that "You have to know what you stand for, not just what you stand against." Though the viewer reads this within the context of the CP, the generic nature of the message makes it applicable to anyone. Shirt 31 (not pictured), as determined by the context of the CP, addresses survivors. But eliminating "assault" or "rape" and just saying "Not Your Fault" allows the viewer to personalize the message. These commands, and the way they are made personal by addressing "you" rather than a larger and more general audience, demonstrate activists' covert assertions of agency. "You," as a personal pronoun, puts audience members in closer proximity to the CP participant. CP participants, thus, engage in activism by using the "you" pronoun and framing their messages as an empathetic dispensing of indirect advice (e.g., shirt 14), putting themselves in authoritative positions without a domineering stance that might alienate viewers.

Furthermore, 23 shirts (31%) make first-person mention ("I" or "me") of CP activists. Some of these personal references include details of women's experiences with violence, as seen in Figs. 3.3 and 3.4. Shirt 14 discloses that the participant was raped, along with the timeframe of her abuse (though subsequent information becomes confusing for readers, as the activist lists a number of characters but not much else). Shirt 19 makes a rhetorical move to communicate with a child-like voice, with the activist using common youthful appeals to beg her mother to not make her go to "daddys" [sic] house; this participant uses a child-size shirt to enhance the rhetorical strategy of connecting with an audience from the point of view of a child, therefore making an emotional appeal. In addition, shirt 49, perhaps the most vivid shirt in the collection, invites the viewer, as much as possible, to experience the activist's assault from her point of view as the violence took place. The activist discloses the name of her attacker, the position of her body, her view of the setting during the attack, and graphic images of the attacker "ramm[ing]" her. Though these shirts assert agency via activists' explicit implication of themselves as survivors of sex crimes, they too either lack details or present details in a way that makes them, to some degree, inaccessible to viewers. Also, in the case of the child's shirt, the agency involved in identifying one's self as a survivor becomes undermined by the activist taking the perspective of a vulnerable child.

Finally, 33 shirts (45%) involve assertions of agency by way of implicating actions related to perpetrators. These actions, more specifically, function by building ethos (by citing participants' personal experience with the issue) or showing activists in a process of healing (Fig. 3.4). Shirt 7 speaks directly to an offender, stating, "What you did to me that night was inexcusable" while also proclaiming, "I will love me again...I have worth." Shirt 64 shows this implication of perpetrators' actions and a process of healing by calling for women to "survive" the acts committed by "those bastards," to "go through [the] hell" that offenders have caused. Shirt 9 refers to the activist "starting to see and believe the Love [they] deserve." Shirts 27 and 33 (not pictured) assert activists' control over their lives and emotional well-being, "rising" and once again embodying emotional and psychological strength. To some extent, all actions mentioned on tee shirts refer back to perpetrators; tee shirts, after all, exist within the context of an activist event intended to name and defy gender violence. But shirts in Fig. 3.4 take a more direct approach to implicating actions related to perpetrators.

Nonetheless, these shirts show assertions of agency separate from the time or other details of attacks or experiences with gender violence. To depict moments in which the violence took place, one could argue, would require assertions of agency in the most explicit way and, therefore, with the most graphic imagery and language. Rather than focus on the moments of the attack, activists focus on moments of healing; moments of healing may allow activists to avoid imaginatively re-embodying their violent experience, to communicate with less aggressive images and words and, perhaps, to discourage attitudes of re-victimization within the context of the CP. By focusing on the healing rather than on the violence, these participants' accounts demonstrate a sense of agency. A focus on healing also provides a decentering of the violence and places the 'self' as emerging from the experience empowered; in this way, participants can reconfigure their bodies as not just having been acted upon but as capable of healing and carrying out positive action.

In many ways, then, women take a protective stance in regards to their experiences and messages. For the most part, they avoid revealing details about their violent experiences, reveal in such a way that limits viewers' understanding of experiences, and/or assert messages of covert agency and healing. We most clearly see this protection (of themselves or others) in the fact that, as a collection, 54 of 74 shirts, or 70% of the archive, consist of shirts that make 'bumper sticker' messages, messages we would see either on bumper or campaign stickers (Table 3.1). While some of these shirts (6) contain references to personal details, most of them do not.

The dynamic in which participants assert agency but do so subtly speaks to influences discussed in relation to the first finding: hesitation to disclose personal experiences (or to disclose too explicitly), perhaps because of definitions of *what* society deems appropriate for women to disclose, criteria for *how* women should communicate, and the consequences that come from communicating negative personal experiences. Survivors of violence face re-victimization and silencing from perpetrators, family, and society (Ahrens, 2006; Rose, 1999). In addition, cultural narratives have communicated to women the inappropriateness of certain types of expression, and expression of certain types of emotions or thoughts (Clarke, 2018; Droogsma, 2009; Ehrlich et al., 2014; Ruggles Gere, 1997), especially in regards to sexual violence as a public versus private matter (Payne, 2000). If CP activists assert agency directly or forcefully, rather than subtly, they risk alienating viewers (Clover & Stalker, 2008) and perhaps making viewers defensive against CP messages.

Covert assertions of agency may also prove more rhetorically effective because of their ability to command action without audience members perceiving such demands as coming from a figure of authority; the more CP activists can connect with viewers, the greater ability to influence them. Using the pronoun "you" may grab readers' attention, as it appears personal to viewers (even though, upon closer read, it may have nothing to do with them). While logical appeals make the case that others are part of the issue of sexual violence, the ethical appeal makes the case that "you" and the activist share an experience, an attitude, or a goal. This

Table 3.1 "Bumper Sticker" messages in the CP (written as displayed on shirt)

1 out of 2 women WILL BE IN A VIOLENT relationship	I DESERVE BETTER	Hands ARE NOT for hurting	I will Not let One Asshole Influence who I Become	VA Cares about Military Sexual Trauma …ASK	
SPEAK OUT FIGHT BRAVE	Every 2 min some one is Sexually Assaulted 1/5 of college aged women will be assaulted	…BUT Where theres a monster theres a MIRACLE	Break the SILENCE LOVE should not HURT	TAKE BACK THE NIGHT	
You may trod me in the very dirt, But still like dust, I'll rise!	NO MEANS NO	Dance like no one is watching Sing like no one is listening Love like you've never been hurt	This little light of Mine IM goNNA Let it shiNe	Got Consent?	
REAL MEN ASK PERMISSION	NOT ALL SCARS ARE EXTERNAL	WORDS ARE POWERFUL SPEAK OUT Against SEXUAL Assault	SURVIVOR 75% of battered women attempt suicide Stay Strong	Stop the Violence!	
Be Strong Stand against VIOLENCE [w/ sorority letters]	NOT YOUR FAULT	(…) Silence No More	I will love	[Front] Just because your Past taps you on the Shoulder doesn't mean you have to turn Around [Back] I am a warrior	

approach, therefore, lends credibility to CP participants. Activists, then, assert agency via their rhetorical approach to gaining viewers' attention by subtly aligning their experiences with those of viewers.

Covert assertions of agency draw attention to the use of the body as agentive and to the process of healing that survivors endure (rather than the violence itself). Such assertions meet gendered demands for subtlety or passivity by avoiding 'aggressive' statements. Still, CP participants assert agency with their focus on taking control and moving forward, rather than mentally and emotionally staying in the vulnerable, frightening position they occupied during the acts of violence committed against them. As mentioned earlier, participants reconfigure their bodies as agents and not the objects perpetrators saw them as during an attack, therefore also pushing against mainstream culture's continued notion of women and women's bodies as objects.

In addition, the use of actions that directly refer *to*, or create strong associations *with*, perpetrators' actions hint at activists' credibility. The ability to refer to these personal experiences, whether activists themselves or people close to them suffered the actions, makes the argument that tee shirt participants *know what they're talking about*. Being affected, directly or indirectly, by gender violence gives CP participants authority or merit with which to broach the subject. Tee shirts suggest that participants have personal knowledge or experience and a philanthropic agenda; this information gives viewers reason to trust and take seriously what CP tee shirts communicate (although, this communication seemingly must occur in certain forms to have this effect).

ACTIVISTS' VISUAL MESSAGES RELY ON PRECONCEIVED SOCIALLY CONSTRUCTED REPRESENTATIONS OF CONCEPTS (SEE FIGS. 3.5 AND 3.6)

Of 74 tee shirts, 47, or 64% of the collection, include visual components in their messages. Just as with linguistic messages, participants exclude detailed representations of experience and instead rely on 'bumper sticker' notions of activist communication. Table 3.2 provides a categorization of the types of visual representations found in the CP.

Table 3.2 shows, then, that CP activists tend to gravitate toward common, socially constructed representations of concepts such as happiness, love, awareness, peace, religion/faith, and liberation or healing.

108　J. R. COREY

Fig. 3.5 Shirts depicting personal experiences

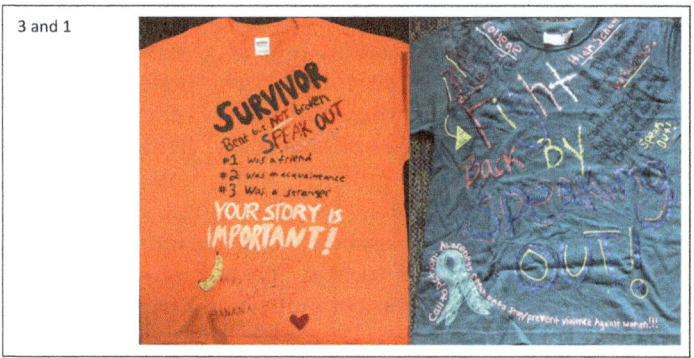

Fig. 3.6 Shirts depicting socially constructed representations

Only 2 shirts (24 and 69) depict scenes from activists' experiences with violence (Fig. 3.5); both of these representations fall into the category of Bodies/Body Parts. These two shirts rely on participants' imagination to envision moments or scenes from their attack, to determine which moments to illustrate on their shirts, and to determine *how* to portray those moments. These shirts may show evidence of preconceived notions about elements such as the symbolism of color, but nothing routinely suggests their meaning based on prior social understandings of their elements. In other words, the images in Fig. 3.5 would likely receive varying interpretations, as opposed to an image of a heart, which people

Table 3.2 Visual representations on CP tee shirts

Visual categories	Examples	Frequency
Depictions of bodies/body parts	Stick figures or drawings of people, handprints, happy and sad faces, mouth/lips, "female" symbol (circle with ' + ')	19
Depictions of awareness to social causes	Teal ribbons, purple ribbons, blue ribbons, TBTN logo, peace sign	16
Depictions of emotion	Hearts and tears	15
Depictions of religion/spirituality	Angel wings, candle, cross, demons	5
Depictions of natural elements	Flowers, stars, ladybug	4
Depictions of location	"downtown" buildings, home, an outline of a state, directional arrow	3
Depictions of social guidelines	"anti" or "no" symbol (circle w/ diagonal line through it)	2
Depictions of food	Banana	1

would likely describe as representing love. In contrast, Fig. 3.6 shows shirts that rely on socially constructed representations.

The finding that activists' messages rely on socially constructed representations of concepts suggests that even in communicating against normative narratives regarding what women should say and how they should say it, activists adopt patriarchal narratives into their messages. Again, activists tend to rely on preconceived notions in their representations (happy faces, sad faces, hearts, and awareness ribbons), representations already deemed appropriate by the general public. As a case in point, people do not inherently or instinctively associate hearts with the issue of sexual violence, and many of the shirts omit a direct linguistic (alphabetic) reference to the hearts. Therefore, no evidence directly explains why activists made the choice to include them; hearts could, however, represent emotional healing or a sense of victory. Lives become shattered by sexual violence; experiencing happiness, security, and a sense of wholeness—a reconfiguring of identity—requires engagement in cognitive and affective processes which the hearts may represent. The hearts, similarly, may represent a sense of victory, a statement that, though survivors have reason to distrust others or to isolate themselves, they choose to interact with others in ways that make themselves vulnerable, and to believe that positive experiences will come from this effort. Hearts may suggest conflicting emotions toward intimate partners or friends who committed acts of violence against them; acts of violence do not necessarily sever emotional ties to some perpetrators. The use of hearts, in addition, suggests something about the ways in which culture socializes women to communicate. One might question the extent to which the hearts truly represent activists' experiences and the extent to which activists used them because they were an appropriate option among other 'feminine' symbols and 'feminine' messages.

As for the awareness ribbons, they provide another example of communication that considers what a public audience might deem appropriate. People commonly use awareness ribbons in activist communications; a single color represents dozens of medical conditions and social issues. In other words, individual activists and global, national, and local organizations rely on the same symbol for their own causes, thereby making it an acceptable option for survivors of sexual violence. Because viewers recognize the symbolism of ribbons, ribbons serve as a reliable and quick 'go to' for people looking to broach a subject. In the case of the CP, activists can rely on the context of the CP, and the way that shirts work together, to bring attention *to*, and construct an understanding *of*, sexual violence or other forms of gender violence. Creating scenes from experiences, linguistically or visually, puts great demands on the CP participants; in such cases, activists must revisit their experiences and try to find a way to put those experiences into words and images. This can prove difficult, given that people often refer to traumas as 'indescribable' or 'unspeakable.' Participants might figure that viewers who have not experienced gender violence will be unable to understand the experience regardless of the detail used. Personal disclosure also puts weight on the viewer, as such disclosure may disturb the viewer, given the nature of the trauma and/or the fact that the viewer feels helpless in confronting such an incident. With these factors in mind, awareness ribbons address issues in impersonal, appropriate ways for public consumption.

These first four findings focus on a description of content. That participants' messages lack details of experiences with gender violence, that participants make covert assertions of agency, and that participants' visual messages rely on preconceived socially constructed representations of concepts all suggest the presence of dominant narratives that influence individual composers' designs.⁹ In addition, participants' invocations of the body suggest ways of thinking about activism and action as separate from literate practices. Repeatedly, given the opportunity to say anything, and in any way, CP participants 'play it safe.' They avoid profanity. For the most part, they avoid graphic textual and pictorial representations of their violent experiences. And they rely on images such as androgynous figures, hearts, awareness ribbons, and flowers and ladybugs. This evidence suggests that women may have internalized culturally normative narratives about what it means to 'speak out,' either as survivors of violence, activists, or women in general. This evidence is made stronger by the fact that shirt-making sessions are held in private, often with one or a few people attending a single session—and with the shirts being collected over a number of years. In other words, the possibility for groupthink decreases under these circumstances.¹⁰ Therefore, we must look to a larger influence than what participants may have on one another in particular moments of creating.

The fifth finding, which I discuss next and which deals with patterns in overall usage of text and images, pertains to the collection as a whole and exists across the four points discussed thus far (lack of details, invocation of the use of the body rather than literate practices, covert assertions of agency, and reliance on socially constructed representations).

ACTIVISTS' TEXTUAL AND VISUAL MESSAGES DO NOT FUNCTION RHETORICALLY IN RELATION TO ONE ANOTHER (SEE FIG. 3.7)

Data suggest that activists see importance in both linguistic (alphabetic text) and visual representations. Seventy-three of 74 tee shirts (99%) present a written message, whereas 48 of 74 tee shirts (65%) use some sort of visual (even if just a heart to dot an "i"). But despite pushes toward multimodal and more visual-laden composing in education (The DeVoss

---

[9] Dominant narratives, or patriarchal narratives, are those that perpetuate the oppression of women and other marginalized groups. The "Analysis" section of this chapter, as well as Chapter 4, present a more thorough discussion of such narratives.

[10] Arguments exist for CP participants' influence on one another in regards to participation (i.e. validating one another and showing the issue of gender violence as more than anomaly). But evidence does not suggest that CP participants influence one another's design decisions.

et al., 2005; Kress, 2003; New London Group, 1996; Selfe & Takayoshi, 2007), only 1 participant communicated without the use of words. This starkly contrasts Kress's (2003) notion that words have been subsumed by visual communications. This one participant, moreover, relied on the awareness ribbon and confetti-looking dots, visuals that already offer some standardization of form and meaning.

Of 48 shirts with visual representations, only 8 of them (16% of shirts with visuals) have visuals that render the words no longer sensible, or at least less powerful, if the visual is removed from the shirt. In these cases, the meaning of the activist's message relies on visual composition. Shirt 2 (not pictured) presents a rebus; the statement, "One in two women will be in a violent relationship," uses symbols to represent "women" and "relationship." Shirt 19 (in Fig. 3.3) has the words, "MOMMY Please don't make me go over daddys [sic] anymore. Please! I ♥you"; this message appears on a child's shirt, used visually to create a more powerful impact for an audience. Though symbiotic to an extent, with these shirts, activists place emphasis on the visual element to convey meaning.

On the other hand, 23 shirts (48% of shirts with visuals) have visuals that would not make sense without the words on the shirts. Though these shirts contain visuals, they rely on alphabetic text to convey their meaning. Removing the text from shirt 3, for instance, would leave us with a shirt with drawings of a heart and a banana. Shirt 22 (not pictured) presents the Take Back the Night (TBTN) logo, along with the phrase "Take Back the Night." Without the words, viewers would see only a picture of a half moon and some stars contained in a circle. While people familiar with the issue of sexual violence or TBTN might recognize the symbol, the general population most likely would not; to reach a vast audience, then, the shirt relies on the text. Shirt 60 (not pictured) has a purple ribbon with the words, "Stand up [&] speak out against sexual violence." Similar to the teal ribbon, the purple ribbon can symbolize numerous causes. Only through the words on the shirt can we connect the purple ribbon to the issue of violence. Though symbiotic to an extent, with these shirts, activists place emphasis on the textual (alphabetic) element to convey meaning.

Overall, then, with only 1 of the 74 shirts eliminating the use of words altogether, and 23 shirts creating a relationship between text and image such that the image depends on the text to make sense (versus 8 shirts that have a relationship between text and image such that if the image is removed, the text no longer makes sense), activists seem to rely on linguistic text more than on visuals to communicate their ideas. While 65% of tee shirts incorporate a visual element, 48% of the 65% have visuals that depend on alphabetic text to make sense, whereas only 16% of the 65% use visuals necessary to maintaining the meaning of alphabetic text.

Finally, 16 shirts (33% of shirts that have visuals) have neither words nor visuals that make sense without the context of the larger CP. Messages on these shirts include general statements such as "Speak Out Fight Brave" (shirt 15); "I will take back my strength" (shirt 33); and "Not all scars are external" (shirt 72, not pictured) (Fig. 3.7). These shirts also suggest the influence of cultural narratives on such designs (discussed in the next section of this chapter).

Activists' reliance on text to communicate, even when including images, challenges society's current emphasis on visual and digital communication. Perhaps participants recognize the immediacy that can come with images; images can be quickly recognized in passing and draw a viewer's attention to alphabetic text, or communicate messages in and of themselves. Tee shirts do suggest that participants look to images to communicate (whether because they find images easier to work with, a better rhetorical strategy for gaining viewers' attention, or a means to align with an increased focus on visual communication within university and global settings). But nearly all shirts used alphabetic text, and more than half of them used both alphabetic text and images. Data

Fig. 3.7 Shirts relying on the CP context for meaning

suggest, therefore, that participants did not have a substantial understanding of how they could use the two modes together to communicate more effectively.

To reiterate, these findings create an opportunity to reconsider Kress's (2003) assertion that visual communication has supplanted linguistic communication. Besides, while technology may allow people to engage with visuals more often, it may fail to motivate people to 'create' visual texts or consider available opportunities and means for communication more widely. To illustrate, Pinterest invites users to choose among photographs, GIFs, and videos to 'pin' on their 'boards.' Facebook and Twitter allow one to quickly choose a 'sticker' or emoji that conveys one's emotions, as well as share photographs, GIFs, and videos. Snapchat allows people to temporarily exchange messages that contain stickers; emojis; bitmojis; and photographs, GIFs, and videos. Instagram allows people to create by editing and posting photographs and videos, while TikTok allows for sharing personal videos (but only those between 15 seconds and one minute in length). Though not an exhaustive list of either social media platforms or the potential uses of each one mentioned (which continue to evolve), I aim simply to differentiate between the kinds of creating in which people engage in popular digital spaces and the kinds in which people engage at some activist events like the CP. I especially recognize that the pervasiveness of these online social spaces may limit people's notions of composing more broadly or their appreciation for the kinds of creating that can occur outside of digital spaces (discussed further in Chapter 4).

The CP invites people to use materials (shirts, paint, markers, and in some cases, fabric and other supplies) to think of and carry out creating a representation, as opposed to choosing from a menu of preconstructed representations, sharing a readily available image or video, or composing within the confines of social media stipulations. Put another way, while many people *use* visuals, a smaller subset of people may actually *create* visuals. CP participants in this study did not provide evidence of a substantial understanding of how they could create with materials, or that they had a desire to take fullest advantage of the opportunity if they did understand the various ways they could use materials. Calling this finding into question implicates activist communication and pedagogical practices related to these issues. Finally, participants' reliance on text and preconceived visual representations raises questions related to work on women's use of fabric arts (and other forms of art) as a means of transgressive communication rather than for traditional and domestic purposes. In this study, data show that the use of fabric and art remains conservative.

Looking at all five findings as a whole through the framework of psychosocial compositions, including the notion of archives, reveals intersections between historical and contemporary cultural ideologies, as well as ways in which activists might respond to unjust narratives, actions, and policies. Moreover, the archival lens reveals findings as present across time and, therefore, as linked to larger, prevalent social narratives.

All five of the findings speak to the shirts' reliance on the context of the CP and to activists' work in the context of psychosocial compositions. This work establishes a pattern in composing practices of individual women who worked in various settings (private and hall- or group-sponsored shirt-making sessions or isolated settings) and across years of an event. These patterns establish the existence of a dominant influence on composing practices, establish commonalities in personal experience, and suggest impacts on the outcome of activist events like the CP. As suggested in Chapter 1, the intersections of these elements *are* psychosocial compositions at the same time that they are *products of* psychosocial compositions.

Within this study of the CP, evidence of psychosocial compositions regarding dominant culture comes in the fact that we can remove these shirts from the CP collection and take them to practically any activist event or archive, and the tee shirts could, arguably, adopt that cause. Due to the generic 'bumper sticker' nature of the messages, we only know that the shirts address sexual assault or gender violence because they take their place in the CP among other shirts addressing the same issue, and because promotional and other informational materials explain the purpose of the CP. In these instances, CP participants seem to use activism to connect themselves to an experience or a cause, but use composition to remove themselves from an experience. In other words, by choosing to participate in, and contribute to, the CP, activists connect themselves to the cause and/or an experience with it. But in their acts of composing, they remove themselves from any personal experience; perhaps composing *is* the process or medium that allows them to do so, to temporarily remove themselves from the narrative.

While activists adapt cultural narratives to their work, thereby re-inscribing and producing psychosocial compositions, they also attempt to revise psychosocial compositions or cultural narratives about what it means to live as a woman (Fig. 3.8). Shirt 70 asserts that men who ask

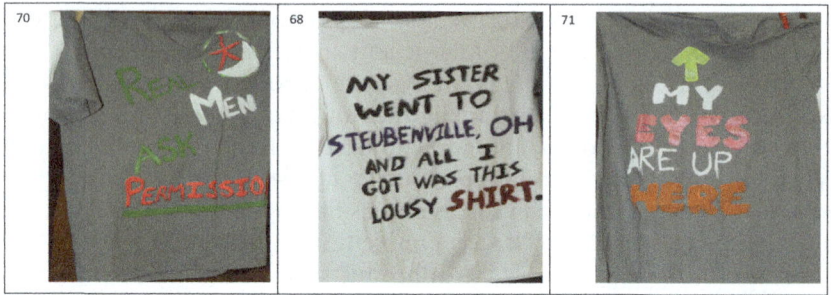

Fig. 3.8 Content of shirts providing commentary on cultural narratives

permission and, therefore, refuse to force themselves on women (in this context, physically) have character as genuine males. Men who fail to ask permission of women suffer a flaw that undermines their status as a particular sex and gender. Rhetorically, the shirt appeals to the ethos of what it means to be a man. Therefore, it may appeal to one's ego and sense of self; generally speaking, one avoids feeling inadequate in a particular role, and the alternative to being a 'real' man is being a 'fake' one. Activists push, then, to define or redefine what it means to be a man in current culture.

The activist who created shirt 69 (see Fig. 3.5) uses painted hands to represent a woman fighting off her attacker. Interestingly, she poses a question without punctuation, which indicates a statement or request for action, often with an expected or obvious answer. The fact that the activist needs to ask the question, to literally *paint a clear picture*, implies a flaw or lack of intelligence on behalf of the perpetrator. In this case, it seems as though the activist makes a demand for society to understand both voiced and silent embodied resistance. Many women's voices are silenced during an attack (via the use of items like duct tape or via the threat of weapons or harm to loved ones). The activist makes the argument here that speaking "no" is a sufficient but not a necessary condition for expressing one's decision.

The activist behind shirt 71 also provides commentary about current culture. On a very basic level, identity gets constructed, in part, through a connection between name and face. By referring to the face ("My eyes are up here"), the activist suggests that she wants viewers to communicate with the parts of her that make her an individual person who can reciprocate communication.[11] Furthermore, the author of shirt 68 appears to comment on how the Steubenville rape case reduced Steubenville's reputation to one particular event and made the school/city a cultural icon of the event.[12] The *takeaway* (figuratively and materially) is the realization of violence and its emptiness ("all I got was this lousy shirt"). Shirt 4 (not pictured) simply states that survivors will not be silent about their experiences; in particular, they will forbid others to silence them. This shirt, then, suggests how the writer understands the ways in which survivors become silenced, intentionally or unintentionally, in current culture.

The way in which these activists position themselves or their work additionally speaks to awareness of social narratives about the woman's body as a site for sexual male aggression (see Gavey, 2005). Miller and Bowdon (1999) argue:

> The civic tradition in rhetoric and moral philosophy was programmatically political in its effort to teach citizens how to draw on received values to address public problems. While the politics of the civic tradition were often sexist, elitist, and ethnocentric, a critical reappraisal of the civic virtues of 'the good man speaking well' can help us assess the opportunities for historical transformation in prevailing ideologies precisely because the civic tradition was so concerned with the craft of translating 'shared' values into political action. (p. 593)

What CP participants choose to disclose and how they choose to disclose it sheds light on the relationship between literacy, rhetoric, and activism. The tee shirts demonstrate that the activist imagines a particular audience of the CP. While CP activists may imagine themselves, perpetrators, fellow survivors, or the general public as their audience, the nature of the CP means that the actual audience will extend beyond the imagined audience; this makes the audience difficult to define. But survivors of violence, most likely, know the dominant cultural narratives pertaining to rape culture (Harding, 2015) and, therefore, double victimization. One such narrative

---

[11] This analysis and others are based on an understanding of the tee shirts as representing embodiment, being understood as if embodied at the moment of viewing.

[12] This shirt refers to the 2012 rape of a high school girl from Steubenville, Ohio. Captured by peers via electronic devices and posted on the internet, the rape raised awareness of the violent acts committed by offenders, but also of the unjust acts of those committed by bystanders.

appeared in a *TIME* magazine opinion piece titled, "It's Time to End 'Rape Culture' Hysteria," in which the female author claimed:

> Recently, rape-culture theory has migrated from the lonely corners of the feminist blogosphere into the mainstream.... Rape-culture theory is doing little to help victims, but its power to poison the minds of young women and lead to hostile environments for innocent males is immense. (Kitchens, 2014, para. 2 & 1)

And more recently, women have encountered the political narrative that it is a "very scary time for young men in America" as women come forward with their accounts of sexual violence (Diamond, 2018). Again, CP composers likely remain aware of the fact that people who share rape culture attitudes to varying degrees will view their tee shirts. CP tee shirts, therefore, contribute knowledge to how those in oppressed subject positions—those who occupy subject positions that may conflict with those of the audience—use literacy publicly and subversively to create social change, whether that change occurs on an individual level or a collective scale. In other words, this study shows literate artifacts as they produce, reproduce, and become products of various and competing social narratives. As discussed earlier, I refer to this process as literate artifacts being contextualized in psychosocial compositions.

Bakhtin supports this notion of psychosocial compositions, arguing that the "world" and the individual share a symbiotic relationship (Warshauer Freedman & Ball, 2004, p. 5). Warshauer Freedman and Ball (2004) further note:

> As we form our own ideas, we come into contact with the discourses of others and those discourses enter our consciousness much as authoritative discourse does. The discourse of others also influences the ways we think and contributes to forming what ultimately is internally persuasive for us. (p. 8)

CP activists' shirt designs certainly suggest that the dominant narratives about women influence women's communication. Scott (1990) claims that individuals learn to act out roles subscribed to them by dominant culture, and that the acted role becomes enmeshed with individuals' view of themselves. Both the individual and the message are "cultured" (Harris, 2007, p. 261). CP activists' approach to their messages speaks to Scott's (1990) examination of how "resistance is disguised, muted, and veiled for safety's sake" (p. 137). Such resistance must conceal the message and/or the messenger, and yet, as discussed earlier, must be neither too covert nor too overt (Scott, 1990). Messages and messengers must attract attention but not overwhelm or offend in such a way that attention gets diverted and opportunities for activism diminished. To the extent that CP activists document and display their commentary yet avoid appearing threatening to the status quo in a patriarchal society, they achieve success. Furthermore, CP activists achieve success by countering Scott's (1990) suggestion that remaining, in a sense, undetected means that the work of oppressed groups will fail to be archived; in the case of the CP activists, they achieve the dynamic of making and displaying commentary while avoiding pushback in the very act of creating archival materials.

Not only does the CP meet Danielson's (2010) criteria for forming an archive (see Table 3.3), but the CP also engages activists, their literate practices, and psychosocial compositions in the dynamics discussed by other archival researchers. These notions frame archival research as "a lived process," rather than an isolated examination of isolated documents (Schultz, 2008, p. ix). The tee shirts document past and present individual and cultural narratives, erasure, rhetorical silence, public commentary, personal healing, and activist theory.

CP activists' awareness of their subject positions as survivors, in relation to re-victimization and other social narratives about sexuality and sexual and gender violence, make them a "counterpublic"; this counterpublic attempts to modify social beliefs and structures that perpetuate participants' struggles and the rhetorical ways they approach these struggles with a public audience (Coogan, 2010, p. 161). Conceptualizing the CP as initiating an archive aligns with these considerations and objectives. As a collection of individual compositions, the CP documents the past and present while composing the present and (one hopes) the future. As potential archivists, then, CP activists participate in the act of record-making as "imposing control and order on transactions, events, people, and societies through the legal, symbolic, structural, and operational power of recorded communication" (Harris, 2007, p. 242). The CP archive aids its creators' attempt to assert control over their experiences, their narratives, their identities, and over cultural attitudes about gender violence. The archive, then, connects its creators to a history of activism.

Table 3.3 Parallels between the CP and Danielson's (2010) conceptualization of archives

Term/process involved in archives	Definition/criteria	How the CP meets the definition/criteria
Appraisal	The process of "determining which documents have permanent historical or evidentiary value" (p. 48)	I argue that CP artists and writers do this when determining the design of their shirts. In addition, CP though rare, administrators or planners sometimes call the inclusion of particular tee shirts into question
Solicitation, collection development, and documentation strategy	The process of "proactively seeking appropriate collections" (p. 48)	This occurs when planning committee members advertise the Clothesline Project and shirt-making sessions leading up to the event and determine the most promising sites to acquire additions to the collection of shirts. For example, they reach out to particular campus organizations (Inter-Hall Council, the Health Center, Psychological Services, Sororities) and strategically schedule shirt-making sessions based on student behavior and campus events
Loans and deposits	Loaned or donated artifacts attained from individuals/institutions	CP writers and artists donate their work for the sake of a humanitarian effort. They give full authority over the work to an individual CP event
Accretion, accrual, and increment	The process of adding, or objects added, to a collection	As an annual event that features shirts made for prior events and the current year's event, the CP archive continuously accrues new artifacts

(continued)

The CP, however, aligns with the notion that the "the archive is first the law of what can be said…And *when* it can be said, *how*, and *by whom*" (Harris, 2007, p. 245). The CP activists' disclosure, or lack thereof, has been established as rhetorical (in that activists attempt to persuade or influence people's taking action against sexual violence, and that messages suggest consideration of audience and the context of the CP event itself). But the patterns in the approaches spanning a number of years suggest that, though informed, decisions about design may involve an act of silencing by patriarchal narratives.

Initially, I viewed the CP as a bridge between the public and the private, serving as a means to circumvent calls to 'speak' that disregard the difficulty introverts, trauma survivors, and those dealing with mental

Table 3.3 (continued)

Term/process involved in archives	Definition/criteria	How the CP meets the definition/criteria
Research value	The contribution the artifact can make to scholarship	Though CP organizers may not think of "research" per se, the CP shirts, and the purposes of the project, contribute to research value within the notion of research as "creative work undertaken on a systematic basis in order to increase the stock of knowledge, including knowledge of man, culture and society, and the use of this stock of knowledge to devise new applications" (Organisation for Economic Co-Operation and Development 2002). Shirt-making sessions and the CP event are planned, and tee shirts are acquired, in a systematic manner for the purpose of increasing knowledge of the individual, humanity, culture and society and contributing to new applications of such knowledge (such as policy development or civic engagement)
Artifactual value	The monetary worth of the artifact	CP organizers assess the monetary value of artifacts to be acquired only to the extent that tee shirts and materials must be purchased. The CP itself, and the value of the writing/art on each tee shirt, is not assessed in terms of monetary value

health issues may face in trying to meet such demands. Malchiodi (2008) described the CP as an opportunity for "telling without talking," telling without the loss of anonymity or pressure to censor for the sake of protecting personal or professional identity. But the shirts in this study suggest that participants adopt a more complex understanding and experience of the CP. As it turns out, women seemed to approach their task with particular ideas of who constituted their audience and how they should address those audiences (perpetrators, fellow survivors, the general public). Audience members, like CP participants, have worldviews embedded in narratives of sexual 'deviance' as a crime committed by an individual rather than as a result of systemic social problems (Armstrong et al., 2018); sexual liberation; virgin/vamp dichotomies; government initiatives and policies addressing (or failing to address) the issue of sexual violence; colloquial language for sexual acts; and gendered communication, including various uses of silence.

THE CP AND RHETORICS OF SILENCE

The literature on silence suggests many ways people interpret and misinterpret women's silence. My study reveals the complexity of women's communication in that it exposes a cultural space in which women assert their voice in ways that resist dominant expectations for women to remain silent and yet, in part, remain silent. These expectations may involve eliminating communication or calls to communicate within confines determined by setting, topic, degree of disclosure, or mode. The CP and other movements (e.g., Take Back the Night, Slut Walk, One Billion Rising) contribute in a material way to resisting the act of being silenced and remain crucial to reconfiguring the cultural narrative of silenced women. Data analysis reveals that while the very existence of the CP engages these dynamics, women's acts of speaking out involve complex negotiations. In their nuances, the women's tee shirt compositions are not simply straightforward re-writings of the narrative of silence. They reveal the same kind of holding back that results from more general silencing, which might serve as evidence of the difficulty of speaking against one's culture, the challenge in composing work that resists cultural narratives but remains accessible to an audience, the limits of written language, and (to some extent) the presence of tacit genre expectations for tee shirts.

This evidence suggests that cultural narratives silence women even as women attempt to "speak out" and encourage others to do so (Ahrens, 2006; Clover & Stalker, 2008; Fivush, 2010). Cook (2019) argues:

> Without risk, there is no reward. The person who risks nothing does nothing. When we risk going too far, we discover how far we can go. In today's era of motivational speak, risk has been singularly rebranded as a badge of honour. In turn, risk is considered a cornerstone of art, innovation, creativity, and ultimately, change. Perhaps ironically, then, it is the #MeToo, Idle No More, and Black Lives Matter movements, among others, that have shone light on the dark underbelly of taking chances: the demand for individuals to step forward and share their voice paints targets on the already vulnerable and marginalized for fear- and anger-filled hate and aggression, repeatedly and relentlessly beating down the voices of change. (pp. 408–409)

We can view the categories identified across all tee shirts as shared expectations about what the women can, cannot, or should say. Though the generic 'bumper sticker' messages allow activists to appeal to a broad audience, perhaps even allowing audience members to relate CP messages to a variety of their personal experiences, the generic 'bumper sticker' messages also seem to shy away from appealing to pathos, and perhaps limit their effect in that regard. In these ways, participants might comply with the regulations and stipulations society attempts to place on them as women and as survivors of gender violence. Whatever the reason, tee shirts do not reveal what society has deemed inappropriate—or dangerous—for survivors to say. The relationship between silence as subversion, silence as a convention, and silence as a result of coercion, therefore, remains complex.

Aminzade and McAdam (2001) examine the silencing of emotions, despite their importance (especially anger and hope) in collective action, which Gregory et al. (2002) also take up in their work. Gregory et al. (2002) argue for the CP as a site that "does not privilege the dominant form of political communication, rational speech," which increases the emotional effect of the event (pp. 445–46). First, however, results from this study raise questions about where in the process of collective action emotion exists as a primary motive and how that relates to outcomes for activist events. Without having interviewed CP shirt creators and viewers, I cannot comment on the affective experiences of either of these groups. Clearly, experiences with gender violence are emotionally charged; though in the case of this study, participants do not make emotional appeals. Similar to the "trope of the angry feminist" (Tomlinson, 2010, p. 1), any emotion expressed by women may serve to undermine women's arguments. Dominant discourse characterizes women as typically overly emotional in a way that inhibits their ability to think and act rationally (e.g., Clarke, 2018). Furthermore, from the perception of viewers, emotion may individualize any arguments women make, rather than show women's experiences as the result of problematic social structures. Historically, cultural norms silenced women's verbal expressions of emotion and taught women to avoid displays of emotion, such as facial expressions or gestures, that would indicate dissent from authority (Tomlinson, 2010). Gaining information about if, where, how, and why emotions get silenced would further enlighten the work conducted in this study. Writing specifically about anger, Tomlinson (2010) asserts:

We also need to consider the costs of not following a path simply because we have been told not to travel on it. Textual vehemence or anger may appear in arguments of social critique asserting that current or historical conditions and politics are not desirable or equitable, but damaging, demeaning, despicable, disgraceful, divisive... compelling reasons [may exist] to use textual vehemence or anger as a *strong component of persuasion*. Textual vehemence can convey a sense of moral responsibility—and of moral revulsion—demonstrating importance of the stakes of the debate. It can operate as a battle cry or rallying cry, drawing together into action those who already agree or who have been swayed by the argument. It can appeal to those who have not been reached by other methods. It can also operate as a site of expressive power: the power of expressing anger—not just to influence others, but also to influence oneself—not spewing forth of emotion, but constructed reflection of anger designed not so much expressively as rhetorically—to communicate rather than to combust. (pp. 83–84)

Noting the silencing of emotion and the consequences of such silencing for others and one's self, Tomlinson's arguments echo work such as that in Lashgari's (1995) *Violence, Silence, and Anger: Women's Writing as Transgression*, and informs future directions for activist work. Second, much political communication throughout the years spanning the writing of this book lacked "rational speech" referred to by Gregory (2002). So how do, or how can, the emotional experiences behind the CP take a meaningful place in politics?

The CP seems to value silence (the silence of the room during composing, the opportunity for telling without talking) yet align with political agendas of breaking silence (the direct references to silence on tee shirts, the ways in which individuals and society might silence participants). Perhaps CP participants embody Fivush's (2010) notion that the need to speak represents loss of power and silence represents assertion of power. More specifically, perhaps they recognize the fact that they have personal and potentially influential knowledge, and that their power comes, in part, from the fact that they withhold the truly personal nature of their knowledge. CP participants' potential motives may align with Jungkunz's (2012) notions of "democratic silences": silence used for empowerment (in which the silence itself serves as the point), protest (in which silence draws attention to another issue), resist*ance* (simply choosing not to speak about a particular topic), or resist*ing* (purposely remaining ambiguous about what we say) (p. 136). Jungkunz's (2012) notion of democratic silences bridges Brown's (2012) idea of the inefficiency of silence to disrupt norms and Fivush's (2010) perceptions of silence *as a norm*—in that it is democratic in a democratic society—*yet a tool for civil dissent*. We see the CP representing these ideas as it fits within norms for carrying out activism (avoiding violence), yet interrupting cultural narratives and physical spaces.

CP participants must balance the status quo with subversion so that neither sabotages the other. That participants chose not to disclose personal details might suggest an awareness of the fact that changing, too much, the 'status quo' of viewers' lives may end up counterproductive. If CP participants disturb CP viewers with graphic accounts of violence, CP viewers may actually try to put those accounts out of their minds. In addition, invocations to the body and reliance on socially constructed visual representations introduce an element of familiarity to CP viewers. The common display of clichés on tee shirts (such as "Stand up and speak out" or "Dance like no one's watching") make CP participants' calls for change less ominous. The use of common representations of the body (such as stick figures, handprints, and happy and sad faces) also appear non-threatening amidst calls to change reality. Likewise, the covert rather than overt assertions of agency that CP participants employ may make women appear as though they are abiding by expectations for women to behave in a passive manner. In other words, CP participants align their messages with certain cultural narratives while attempting to undermine others, whether consciously or subconsciously.

Furthermore (as stated in Chapter 2), Ferguson (2011) argues that because of the diverse ways we can use silence, we cannot assert an "ultimate politics" with which to associate it (p. 12). Therefore, we should avoid asserting ideas that silence is only oppressive (a conclusion that people seem to jump to without consideration of alternative interpretations and examples). McIntyre (2013) writes about post-incarcerated women and the complexities of disclosing their experiences rather than remaining silent about them, documenting that, upon incarceration, women often remain silent about their crimes as a way for them to believe in a difference that sets them apart from fellow inmates. In other words, psychologically, the women need to believe that they do not share characteristics or experiences with "criminals"; they need to believe that they and their experiences remain fundamentally different. Not communicating with other inmates, at least about their crimes, increases this sense of difference. Post-incarceration, their motives for silence change, or the focus weighs more heavily on others; they remain silent as a means to protect loved ones from having to face the harsh realities of their crimes and their experiences in prison (McIntyre, 2013) (though I recognize that not all incarcerated people actually committed crimes).

Likewise, CP messages might suggest a combination of CP participants' believing in themselves as somehow different while protecting others. More specifically, CP participants' lack of disclosure of personal details, as well as their focus on healing, might suggest similar notions to those which McIntyre (2013) proposes. Perhaps like the incarcerated women, the lack of detail regarding their experiences, in addition to the focus on healing, allows survivors of gender violence to believe that they are (or are not) fundamentally different from who they were before an experience with gender violence. Both the lack of personal detail in messages and the focus on healing also suggests the possible protection of viewers.

Survivors of violence (and perhaps other crimes) likely have different motives for "silence" at different times: fear of perpetrators or social consequences of disclosure, protection of loved ones, or a need for reflection or meditation. Fivush (2010) draws attention to silences, violence, and social action when she notes that, in interviews with survivors of childhood sexual assault, interviewees often asked about the interviewer's certainty of wanting to hear their accounts. The interviewees mindfully navigated helping the researcher, engaging in activism via telling their stories, and censoring—as they knew the power their narratives might hold and the affect they may have on a listener or reader. Women in Fivush's (2010) study demonstrate Droogsma's (2009) sentiment that, "Although powerful patriarchal discourses attempt to prescribe women's experiences, women are never fully controlled by these discourses but rather exercise constrained agency" (p. 484).

Therefore, whether to encourage disclosure or critique enclosure must consider whose interests we serve in any time and place and with any act of disclosure (Black, 1988) or "enclosure" (Glenn & Ratcliffe, 2011, p. 3). In the case of sexual violence, those close to survivors may be unequipped to hear survivors' accounts, leading survivors to feel silenced or to use silence to protect themselves and those they care about; support systems, moreover, can end up using the voice of the survivor to give voice to their own fears surrounding the issue (Murphy et al., 2011). Trauma survivors ask those close to them to face the reality that someone they care about has suffered; and they ask us to face the possibility of our own traumatic experiences. Negative responses to disclosure provide another reason for women to choose silence (Ahrens, 2006), and complicate ideas about freedom and speech, or expression of any kind.

Some women engage in healing via the opportunity to retreat inside themselves and begin to create meaning of their experiences (Motsemme, 2004). In fact, silence sometimes aids in "escape," physical or mental (Hesford, 2004, pp. 9–10). As long as oppression and subversive action exist, so will the need to escape violent or harmful circumstances. Furthermore, as other scholars have argued, pain can interfere with one's ability to produce language (Rose, 1999); in this way, we must look to "dreams, gestures, tears" and art as ways in which "the mute always speak" (Motsemme, 2004, p. 910). Events such as the CP lend themselves to these examinations.

The interaction between trauma and linguistic expression remains difficult to interpret; silence can indicate navigation between old and new identity construction after trauma (Sorsoli, 2010), which further raises ideas about objectives for activism. For protest to exist, people must conceptualize injustice not as fate but as a socially constructed circumstance, and believe in the ability of protest to lead to social progress (Rucht et al., 1999, p. 7). While the public can easily ignore protests or events like the CP, and the social impact of protests remains impossible to measure (Rucht et al., 1999, p. 9), such efforts may bear significant meaning for participants themselves (Rucht & Neidhardt, 1999).

Some scholars assert that an individual can have a voice only when those establishing dominant discourse actually listen to women and account for what they say in political arenas (Droogsma, 2009, p. 494). As noted in Chapter 1, Droogsma (2009) asks, "Do the persons who silenced woman abuse survivors, and therefore remain complicit in their oppression, listen to The Clothesline Project?" (p. 494). Therefore, do we define activism based on some criteria that actually measure social change? It does not seem that way. But the difficulty of measuring *activist outcomes* leaves us with the idea of *activist goals and practices*; and activist goals and practices can provide a means to healing for those in positions of suffering, even in what appears as an act of silencing women. As a result, it remains unclear whether such instances of activism for healing, including using writing for healing, should change what activism means and does. Amidst silence, then, what constitutes 'social action' becomes more complicated. Wood (2019) notes that women have had to behave and communicate with "composure...in order to be taken seriously by cis-gendered, white, straight, middle-class men," though "the rules of 'affective (in)justice" constantly shift (p. 613), thereby further obscuring the 'effectiveness' of activism.

Of course, we must not ignore that silence can and does cause suffering for those who are silenced, and deprives those who are not silenced of alternative, enriching narratives (Rich, 2003). But problems arise from society's overwhelmingly common idea that people always or primarily experience silence as detrimental (Cain, 2012). We must pay attention to what we perceive in CP participants' designs, and the context that influences such communications. Jones' (2009) notion of psychogeography (p. 3) speaks to the CP because—along with events like Take Back the Night, One Billion Rising, Slut Walk, and Walk A Mile In Her Shoes— the CP aims to change ideas via changing physical space, whether quiet and calm or loud and chaotic. As discussed in Chapters 1 and 2, Take Back the Night has women complete a candle-lit march as a representation of working toward a society in which women feel safe to go out alone at night. One Billion Rising involves flash mob dances performed on Valentine's Day, across the country and internationally, as a way of addressing violence against women and rethinking Valentine's Day as a commercialized holiday that fails to address love and relationships in a worthwhile manner. Slut Walks take the form of public marches that protest victim blaming (i.e., to avoid being raped, you need to first avoid dressing like a slut). During Walk A Mile In Her Shoes, men parade in high heels to make a statement about understanding the unique experiences of women. All of these events disrupt one's typical experience of a given place and time. My work, then, addresses Jungkunz's (2012) criticism of the discourse surrounding silence and speaking. Jungkunz (2012) argues that to advocate for alternative and equal forms of resistance (other than speaking), we must eliminate the use of phrases like "breaking the silence" (p. 145). We might think of the examples of homosexual individuals talking about "coming out of the closet"; such descriptions of their experiences enact the very discourse that suggests that they should have been "in the closet" or "closeted" in the first place (Jungkunz, 2012, p. 145). We must, therefore, find alternate ways of speaking about our values. Descriptions of the CP as an opportunity for "telling without talking" (Malchiodi, 2008) offer a way to discuss communicating effectively or freely without enacting an oversimplified dominant discourse of silence. Similarly, Wagner (2012) points out that the marginalized people choosing to remain silent open themselves up to others speaking for them; therefore, we must question whether it is not sometimes better to join a marginalized person or group of people in their silence (p. 116). LGBTQ's National Day of Silence serves as one event that calls for joining marginalized people in their silence and which allows for more inclusive conceptualizations of composing, protesting, and advocating. Harris (2007) posits:

> Can the mainstream ever accurately represent the marginal? How can we invite in what is always beyond our limits of understanding? How can we avoid the danger of speaking *for* these voices? How can we avoid reinforcing marginalization by naming 'the marginalized'? (p. 262)

Wagner (2012) seems to suggest that, to some extent, we can. Investigations of events like the CP help to invite participation in ways that seem, as yet, beyond our limits of understanding.

Moreover, my subject position as a survivor leads me to argue that the mainstream can accurately represent the marginalized, but in limited ways. For instance, the secondary sources cited in this book often accurately represent the experiences of survivors of violence, but only to the extent of documented patterns in research about how assault survivors cope or respond rhetorically to their experiences and to a public audience. The truly personal, tragic, chaotic experiences of traumatic events themselves, and the continuous (re)construction of identity that takes place thereafter, can be represented by no one other than an individual survivor, and perhaps not even by them. Earlier in this work (Chapter 1), I made similar comments in regards to my ability to advocate for, but not make the same appeals as, members of communities like the LGBTQIA community or even for male survivors of sexual violence.

Therefore, this work suggests opportunities for future inquiries. For example, further research may involve interviewing CP participants about why they chose the messages they did, especially as messages pertain to emotion. The chaos and pain accompanying feelings of vulnerability that come from violence may keep some CP participants from wanting to re-access those feelings for the sake of their participation. Some CP participants may need to feel and express feelings of control (Bex Lempert, 2003). The incompleteness in many of the messages in my study leads viewers to fill gaps and may exist because of the difficulty of using language to describe experiences that remain difficult to put into words.

Alternatively, the context of the CP may empower some participants and motivate them to share their feelings of strength or acts of courage. Again, Aminzade and McAdam (2001) note much "silence about emotions" (p. 23), and suggest further inquiry into emotional intelligence as it relates to social movements, as well as "dominant emotion rules of the wider society" (p. 25). Given arguments about the gendered nature of emotional intelligence (Aminzade & McAdam, 2001, p. 34), women's activist events may serve as particularly rich sites for such examination.

Future work may also inquire about the influence of the physical space of tee shirts. Goodnow (2005) points out that the tee shirts leave little room for development of stories about experiences, and that participants' communication would likely differ if delivered verbally (an issue I address in the next section). Future investigations could undertake CP participants' understandings of tee shirt literacy. Finally, future endeavors could attempt to account for cultural differences such as race and ethnicity. Smith (2005) reports that:

> Some communities enforce victim/survivors' silence more than others due to the presence of other societal oppressions.... For example, communities of color often 'advocate that women keep silent about the sexual and domestic violence in order to maintain a united front against racism. (p. 417)

These opportunities for future work, however, must not inaccurately influence the interpretation and value of findings in this study. The next section provides a response to alternative interpretations of the data and the issues with those interpretations. Therefore, the "Legend of Cautions" that follows addresses Fine, Weis, Weseen, and Wong's (2000) call to examine the ways in which "outsiders" might misinterpret or misuse findings (p. 123).

Conclusion to the Chapter

In a situation that we might think of as relatively "free" or "liberating," the CP participants revealed very little about their personal experiences. They create short, declarative statements addressing the general public rather than more detailed narratives about personal journeys and relationships. Overall, they forgo gut-wrenching accounts of their own suffering and healing, or that of someone close to them. Even if participants choose this approach, in part, based on the convention of tee shirts having less rather than more text, they could still choose to include more explicit or graphic words or images. Participants' more impersonal approach, however, remains as significant as approaches that include more detail. As with much writing, the difficulty comes not in knowing what one wants to say but in struggling to say it, struggling with how to say it, and struggling with the consequences of sharing thoughts and feelings—with others and, in the case of some survivors, with themselves. The opportunity to "tell without talking" anonymously does not seem to lead to expressions of catharsis on CP tee shirts. This suggests that larger social narratives inform the narratives of women's experiences of violence and, therefore, call for continuing efforts to serve survivors, activists, and the broader public. Changing these larger cultural narratives might then change women's experiences.

Findings from this study align with findings from other studies pertaining to women's activist art. In particular, Clover and Stalker (2008) conducted interviews and focus groups regarding activism with fabric arts in Canada and New Zealand; they reported one of the themes from their work as "external and internal censorship" (p. 9). The lack of details presented in my study additionally suggests the role of censorship in messages; even when activists assert agency, they do so covertly, as if with a sense of caution. I, again, look at this phenomenon in relation to what I call psychosocial compositions, the ways in which messages on CP tee shirts converge with, or diverge from, larger circulating narratives governing social practices and beliefs. Likewise, Droogsma (2009) points to the influence of social narratives on tee shirt design decisions; her work revealed "double victimization" as a theme in a sample of CP shirts (p. 484). Ardener (2005) writes about these dynamics more generally:

> The voices of nondominant group members often become 'muted' not only due to the repression of speech but also by the regulation of what they say, when they speak, how much they say, and in what mode they say it. In other words, muting occurs not due to the 'voicelessness' of women and others from marginalized groups but rather transpires when dominant discourses that exclude women's realities become embedded in many different social spaces. (p. 485)

The covert assertions of agency and lack of disclosure of details suggests the work of such forces in the context of some CP participation.

Relatedly, Clover and Stalker (2008) assert art as a "private protest movement against your circumstances...[art] allows you to keep your tongue still through difficult moments...so it can be quite protective too" (p. 7). The art involved in the CP additionally provides engagement with Gregory et al.'s (2002) four "faces of power": "explicit, observable uses of power to control the behavior of others"; "social norms that keep issues off public agendas"; "people's self-understanding and perceptions of their own interests, which may be influenced or manipulated"; and "the creation of subjects" (people's identities) (pp. 435–436). According to Gregory et al. (2002), the CP pushes against these faces of power by providing a public space for political communication, providing a nontraditional mode of communication, informing others about an issue that exacerbates calls for silence, and serving a role in social change (p. 433). The nontraditional mode of communication (multimodal communication) involved in the CP allows for women to "silently" and anonymously address the silencing of oppressive experiences.

Still, while Hipple (2000) claims that concealing the identity of CP participants "emboldens" their speech (p. 174), similar to what Malchiodi (2008) claims, this study, in some ways, counters these arguments. While artistic forms and silence offer opportunities for empowerment, evidence in this study suggests that this empowerment remains difficult to navigate. Participants tend to make *covert* assertions of agency, as demonstrated with the elimination of personal details, reliance on the physical body rather than on more globalized efforts such writing letters to the government, and the use of pronouns. My work, to this end, aligns with Julier's (2000) findings that women "tend to tell what happened in abbreviated elliptical forms" (p. 378). The fact that the results in this chapter align with the work of Julier, conducted *15 years* prior to my study, further implicates larger social narratives in the activist participation of women and the ways they use communication to support themselves, each other, and their causes. Unfortunately, data suggest that these larger social narratives, to some degree, place limitations on messages and continue to create patriarchal structures.

These psychosocial compositions, as influences on activists' literate practices and the literate artifacts activists produce, construct the CP as a potential archive that shows unchanging and changing aspects of difficult work. A number of sources throughout this chapter establish the phenomena of "silencing" or "censoring" women's communication, in general and as it pertains to gender violence and sex crimes. Additionally, as mentioned above, an analysis of the large data set presented in this chapter (897 data points) yields results that align with Julier's (2000) research on the CP, as well as Clover and Stalker's (2008) research on women's use of fabric arts for activism. That the research taken up in this study yields findings similar to work conducted 15 years prior, as well as to work carried out internationally, attests to the fact that the same narratives continue to suggest what it means to communicate as a woman. The CP examined in this study in and of itself implicates the same and continuous cultural narratives, given that the 74 tee shirts were accumulated over a number of years and with artists (for the most part) isolated from one another. In other words, data from the single CP event examined here reveal consistent patterns in women's communication, despite the fact that shirts were not created in the same time or in the same places. In essence, the archive, though consisting of artifacts from across time and by a number of contributors, establishes the same historical narratives; the CP traces the same psychosocial compositions of what it means to communicate as a woman, and to do so regarding an issue commonly categorized among "women's issues." But explorations of visual rhetoric draw attention to the CP as a rich site for further questioning the dynamics of a live audience at an event that includes previously constructed materials by anonymous creators (Hocks & Balsamo, 2003), the "active" relationships formed among narrative images (Kress & van Leeuwen, 2006) on CP tee shirts, and the materials used in feminist activism and what those materials suggest about changing dominant culture (Wysocki, 2005/2014) and activists changing themselves.

Tal (1996) points out that political discourse that "shapes the rhetoric of the dominant culture and influences future political action" determines, in part, the meaning ascribed to various forms of trauma (p. 7). As part of this meaning-making process, composing "revise[s]" individuals (Rose, 1999) and seemingly omnipresent cultural narratives (Fiandt, 2006). In the instance of the CP, artists may now "re-vision" personal blame as a social issue (Julier, 1994, p. 253). Payne (2000) states that survivors of abuse "have lost confidence in a stable, knowable reality. Signifiers and signified constantly shift. Thus, reality and one's sense of identity are deconstructive texts" (p. 151). But Baur (1994) notes that in attempts to fit extenuating circumstances or experiences into a sense of normal life, "language is our main tool for creating and then negotiating what we think of as 'reality'" (p. 60). Similarly, women involved in the CP "seem to see that language can be amended to reshape experience" (Julier, 2000, p. 373), to rewrite—deconstruct and reconstruct—themselves. Thiongo (2002) argues:

> Our pens should be used to increase the anxieties of all oppressive regimes. At the very least the pen should be used to 'murder their sleep' by constantly reminding them of their crimes against the people, and by letting them know that they are seen. (p. 221)

The art of the CP, like other art, makes no attempt to solely solve major social issues related to oppression, but rather to serve as a political act by providing honest accounts of the intersection of such issues with real people (Escobar, 2002). Choosing and engaging with images [and words] instills a sense of autonomy, even over past events (Peacock, 1991). Writing *can* change power structures (Hyland in Bremner, 2006). CP participation, then, may contribute to an understanding of individuals' subject positions as survivors in the larger society, and their relation to fellow survivors, victims, offenders, and cultural attitudes. CP participants' work, their rhetorical understandings and strategies, remains crucial because if society "appropriate[s] the trauma and can codify it in its own terms, the status quo will remain unchanged...[and] the penalty for repression is repetition" (Tal, 1996, p. 7). In other words, through words and art, survivors take command of what was done *to* them and make an attempt at taking command of audience members' internalization of victim's/survivors' experiences.

LEGEND OF CAUTIONS: WAYS TO MISREAD, MISAPPROPRIATE, AND MISUSE PRESENTED ANALYSES[13]

One of the primary explanations for the lack of disclosure on tee shirts comes in the idea of the tee shirt as limited in space and traditionally not conducive to graphic, personal accounts. First, this argument conflates detail with length. Participants could create graphic, personal messages even within the limited space of tee shirts, such as the child-size tee shirt with the plea, "Mommy, please don't make me go to Daddy's house

---

[13] Fine, Weis, Weseen, and Wong (2000) recommend publishing a Legend of Cautions "that warns readers how *not* to read our work" (p. 202).

anymore" or the shirt that says "I was so drunk my friends were checking my pulse before you carried me into your bed." As a matter of fact, at times, concision can have greater rhetorical effects than lengthier communications. Second, tee shirts often serve as a way of disclosing personal identity in public spaces. Tee shirts can inform people of one's music preferences, political party alliances, religious beliefs, sports team participation or fandom, university or organization affiliations, travel excursions, or coalition with social causes. Third, the existence of websites, such as roadkilltshirts.com, tshirthell.com, and foulmouthshirts.com, indicate that the graphic nature of some tee shirts is not only socially acceptable but desirable.

The argument that CP participants adapt messages to normative uses of tee shirt space further becomes undermined by the fact that CP participants violate these norms in other ways. Whereas the counterargument claims that women do not disclose because of the limited space that tee shirts provide, women, in fact, often provide lengthy communications about experiences, though these lengthy accounts may be fragmented or impersonal. The reliance on text further suggests that CP participants do not abstain from disclosure because of tee shirt literacy conventions, as tee shirts generally rely on limited use of text and extended use of graphics. That participants ignore tee shirt literacy conventions in the ways discussed above further demonstrates the influence of cultural narratives on design decisions.

Another way people might reduce the importance of my findings is to overly simplify any notion of oppression or agency demonstrated in this study of the CP. As discussed throughout the chapter, evidence shows that women abstain from personal disclosure and emotional appeals and, instead, rely on "bumper sticker" messages related to gender violence. But CP participants also assert agency. The women assert agency in their very act of choosing to participate in the CP to begin with, to comment descriptively or generically. They further assert agency in covert ways, by using particular pronouns and by presenting themselves as healed or healing. Silence and voice both serve as forms of expression and function in relation to oppression, subversion, and liberation, depending on a variety of circumstances and contexts, such as audience, access to resources, emotional and psychological development, and individual and collective relationships.

At a conference in New York City, I presented the results of my pilot study of the CP. During the question and answer period, a male audience member expressed his displeasure with the statistic that motivated the creation of the CP in the first place—that during the time that 58,000 men were killed in the Vietnam War, approximately 51,000 women had been murdered due to gender violence (Hipple, 2000, p. 168). The audience member disliked the fact that the statistic failed to recognize the Vietnamese and other soldiers who perished in the war. While his point has validity, his focus on the statistic merely distracted from the issue at hand: women and gender violence. In fact, discussions about victim blaming and rape culture demonstrate attempts to distract from, or even deny, the fact that gender violence remains part of the dominant narrative in American culture (and many other cultures). Likewise, to attribute women's design decisions to the material of the tee shirt alone dismisses more profound social influences on such decisions.

Moreover, to locate CP participants and their messages solely in narratives of silencing and oppression only furthers the injustice suffered by participants. And to focus only on the agency CP participants have and assert in their messages distracts us from social and political structures of power that, directly or indirectly, lead to gender violence as a cultural problem to begin with. In a legend of cautions, then, we must remain aware of the necessity of categorizing; we make sense of an overwhelming and complex set of data by categorizing. At the same time, we must stay attentive to how others will use such categorizations to create oppositions where dynamics are much more complex than simple alliances and oppositions.

Understanding the plural identities of the participants discussed in this study relates to the issue of avoiding simplification. We must not reduce women (or other participants) to their experiences with trauma (or any other experiences); doing so assumes an overly simplified shared identity. Trauma survivors *do* share an identity to the extent that they frame their experiences in terms of, or as related to, identity. They also share a cultural identity to the extent that they share a discourse. The fact that dissociative identity disorder often results from trauma (Mayo Clinic, n.d.) supports these assertions about identity, as do many publications that have addressed relationships between trauma and identity (re)construction (Alexander et al., 2004; Eyerman, 2001; Rosenthal, 2015; Seeburger, 2012).

Phillips and Daniluk (2004) note how survivors of childhood sexual abuse progressed through therapy in such a way that they developed an understanding of their trauma as one part of a multi-faceted identity, and that an "ability to put the abuse into a broader social and political perspective enabled them to start sharing and connecting with others" (p. 179). As many survivors recognize positive outcomes from their trauma and their identities as survivors, Layton (1995) points out that people can sometimes glorify fragmentation for its opportunities to explore and reinvent one's self. In a doctoral seminar, I once announced my status as a survivor (because it related to the discussion); upon doing so, a fellow student asserted that, despite my experience, I remained "privileged." To some extent, I make no argument. But my story is not hers or anyone else's to tell. And "privilege" is complex. I have tried to remain mindful of my position as survivor and writer in relation to CP participants' messages. In other words, I have tried to explore the complex ways in which multiple facets of gender violence and multiple facets of identity intersect. As we talk about social phenomena, we must recognize individuality. These notions arise in my final thoughts on disclosure as it relates to identity and education in the next chapter.

DISCUSSION QUESTIONS

1. This research revealed that women abstained from strong emotional appeals, at least in the activist event under examination. But given the political trend of increasingly relying on emotional appeals, should activists meet politicians "where they are at" or maintain a rhetorical stance toward logical reasoning? Which might be more effective in the pursuit of revising cultural narratives? Or do we aim to achieve balance? To what extent can or should pathos be voiced or silenced in advocating for political agendas?
2. What are some affordances and limitations of various modes of communication in regards to the above questions?

REFERENCES

Ahrens, C. E. (2006). Being silenced: The impact of negative social reactions on the disclosure of rape. *American Journal of Community Psychology. 38*, 263–274. https://doi.org/10.1007/s10464-006-9069-9

Alexander, J. C., Eyerman, R., Giesen, B., Smelser, N. J., & Sztompka, P. (2004). *Cultural trauma and collective identity*. University of California Press.

Aminzade, R., & McAdam, D. (2001). Emotions and contentious politics. In R. Aminzade, J. A. Goldstone, D. McAdam, E. J. Perry, W. H. Sewell, S. Tarrow, & C. Tilley (Eds.), *Silence and voice in the study of contentious politics* (pp. 14–50). Cambridge University Press.

Ardener, S. (2005). Ardener's '"muted groups"': The genesis of an idea and its praxis. *Women and Language, 28*, 50–73.

Armstrong, E. A., Gleckman-Krut, M., & Johnson, L. (2018). Silence, power, and inequality: An intersectional approach to sexual violence. *Annual Review of Sociology, 44*, 99–122. https://doi.org/10.1146/annurev-soc-073117-041410

Baur, S. (1994). *Confiding: A psychotherapist and her patients search for stories to live by.* HarperCollins.

Berger, A. A. (2011). Semiotic analysis. In *Media analysis techniques* (4th ed., pp. 3–44). Sage.

Bex Lempert, L. (2003). The clothesline project as student production: Creativity, voice, and action. *Teaching Sociology, 31*(4), 478–484. https://doi.org/10.2307/3211371

Black, E. (1988). Secrecy and disclosure as rhetorical forms. *Quarterly Journal of Speech, 74*(2), 133–150. https://doi.org/10.1080/00335638809383833

Bremner, S. (2006). Politeness, power, and activity systems: Written requests and multiple audiences in an institutional setting. *Written Communication, 23*(4), 397–423. https://doi.org/10.1177/0741088306293707

Cain, S. (2012). Quiet: The power of introverts in a world that can't stop talking. Crown. https://doi.org/10.3389/fpsyg.2017.00155

Clarke, L. (2018, September 9). *In her anger, in defeat, Serena Williams starts an overdue conversation: Tennis's double standard remains in effect, in ways the 23-time Grand Slam champion is still showing us.* The Washington Post. https://www.washingtonpost.com/

Clover, D. E., & Stalker, J. (2008). Feisty fabrics: Women's education, learning and activism through fabric arts in Canada and Aotearoa New Zealand. *Studies in the Education of Adults, 40*(1), 80–95. https://doi.org/10.1080/02660830.2008.11661557

Coogan, D.J. (2010). Sophists for social change. In J. M. Ackerman & D. J. Coogan (Eds.), *The public work of rhetoric: Citizen-scholars and civic engagement* (pp. 157–174). University of South Carolina Press. https://doi.org/10.2307/j.ctv6wghr9

Cook, K. (2019). EmboDIYing disruption: Queer, feminist and inclusive digital archaeologies. *European Journal of Archaeology, 22*(3), 398–414. https://doi.org/10.1017/eaa.2019.23

Corey, J. (2014). 'My sister went to Steubenville, OH and all I got was this lousy shirt': Composing feminist activism with the Clothesline Project. *Gender Forum* (special issue: *Early Career Researchers II*), 50.

Corey, J. (2017). Beyond 'digital': What women's activism reveals about material multimodal composition pedagogy. *Journal of Multimodal Rhetorics, 1*(1).

Danielson, E. S. (2010). *The ethical archivist*. Society of American Archivists.

DeVoss, D. N., Cushman, E., & Grabill, J. T. (2005). Infrastructure and composing: The when of new-media writing. *College Composition and Communication, 57*(1), 14–44.

Diamond, J. (2018, Oct. 2). *Trump says it's 'a very scary time for young men in America.'* CNN. https://www.cnn.com/2018/10/02/politics/trump-scary-time-for-young-men-metoo/index.html

Droogsma, R. A. (2009). "I am the woman next door": The Clothesline Project as woman abuse survivors' societal critique. *Communication, Culture & Critique, 2*, 480–502. https://doi.org/10.1111/j.1753-9137.2009.01049.x

Ehrlich, S., Meyerhoff, M., & Holmes, J. (Eds.). (2014). *The handbook of language, gender, and sexuality* (2nd ed.). John Wiley & Sons. https://doi.org/10.1002/9781118584248

Escobar, E. (2002). Art of liberation: A vision of freedom. In J. Hirschman (Ed.), *Art on the line: Essays by artists about the point where their art and activism intersect* (pp. 246–254). Curbstone Press.

Eyerman, R. (2001). *Cultural trauma: Slavery and the formation of African American identity*. Cambridge University Press.

Ferguson, K. (2011). Silence: A politics. In C. Glenn & K. Ratcliffe (Eds.), *Silence and listening as rhetorical arts* (pp. 1–22). Southern Illinois University Press. https://doi.org/10.1080/07350198.2011.604613

Fiandt, J. (2006). Autobiographical activism in the Americas: Narratives of personal and cultural healing by Aurora Levins Morales and Linda Hogan. *Women's Studies, 35*(6), 567–584. https://doi.org/10.1080/00497870600809772

Fine, M., Weis, L., Weseen, S., & Wong, L. (2000). For whom?: Qualitative research, representation, and social responsibility. In N. K. Denzin & Y. S. Lincoln (Eds.), *Handbook of qualitative research* (pp. 107–131). Sage.

Fivush, R. (2010). Speaking silence: The social construction of silence in autobiographical and cultural narratives. *Memory, 18*(2), 88–98. https://doi.org/10.1080/09658210903029404

Foss, S. K. (2009). *Rhetorical criticism: Exploration and practice*. Waveland Press.

Gavey, N. (2005). *Just sex?: The cultural scaffolding of rape*. Routledge.

Glenn, C., & Ratcliffe, K. (2011). Introduction: Why silence and listening are important rhetorical arts. In C. Glenn & K. Ratcliffe (Eds.), *Silence and listening as rhetorical arts* (pp. 1–22). Southern Illinois University Press. https://doi.org/10.1080/07350198.2011.604613

Goodnow, T. (2005). Empowerment through shifting agents: The rhetoric of the Clothesline Project. In K. Smith, S. Moriarty, G. Barbatsis, & K.

Kenney (Eds.), *Handbook of visual communication: Theory, methods, and media* (pp. 179–192). L. Erlbaum.

Gregory, J., Lewton, A., Schmidt, S., Smith, D., & Mattern, M. (2002). Body politics with feeling: The power of the Clothesline Project. *New Political Science, 24*(3), 433–448. https://doi.org/10.1080/0739314022000005455

Harding, K. (2015). *Asking for it: The alarming rise of rape culture—And what we can do about it*. DaCapo Press.

Harris, V. (2007). *Archives and justice: A South African perspective*. The Society of American Archivists.

Hesford, W. S. (2004). Rhetorical projections and silences. *JAC. Online, 24*(3), 785–797.

Hipple, P. C. (2000). Clothing their resistance in hegemonic dress: The Clothesline Project's response to violence against women. *Clothing and Textiles Research Journal, 18*(3), 163–177. https://doi.org/10.1177/0887302X0 001800305

Hocks, M. E., & Balsamo, A. (2003). Women making multimedia: Possibilities for feminist activism. In B. E. Kolko (Ed.), *Virtual publics: Policy and community in an electronic age* (pp. 192–214). Columbia University Press.

Jones, R. (2009). The aesthetics of protest: Using image to change discourse. *Enculturation: A Journal of Rhetoric, Writing, and Culture, 6*(2).

Julier, L. (1994). Private texts and social activism: Reading the Clothesline Project. *English Education, 26*(4), 249–259.

Julier, L. (2000). Voices from the line: The Clothesline Project as healing text. In C. M. Anderson & M. M. MacCurdy (Eds.), *Writing and healing: Toward an informed practice* (pp. 357–384). National Council of Teachers of English.

Jungkunz, V. (2012). The promise of democratic silences. *New Political Science, 34*(2), 127–150. https://doi.org/10.1080/07393148.2012.676393

King, A. (2004). The prisoner of gender: Foucault and the disciplining of the female body. *Journal of International Women's Studies, 5*(2), 29–39.

Kitchens, C. (2014, March 20). It's time to end 'Rape Culture' hysteria. TIME. http://time.com/30545/its-time-to-end-rape-culture-hysteria/

Krakauer, J. R. (2015). *Missoula: Rape and the justice system in a college town*. Doubleday. https://doi.org/10.1080/19496591.2017.1284673

Kress, G. R. (2003). *Literacy in the new media age*. Routledge. https://doi.org/10.4324/9780203299234

Kress, G. R., & van Leeuwen, T. V. (2006). *Reading images: The grammar of visual design* (2nd ed.). Routledge.

Lashgari, D. (1995). *Violence, silence, and anger: Women's writing as transgression*. University Press of Virginia.

Layton, L. (1995). Trauma, gender identity and sexuality: Discourses of fragmentation. *American Imago, 52*(1), 107–125. https://doi.org/10.1353/aim.1995.0010

Lewis-O'Connor, A., Wolbert Burgess, A., & Harvey Marchetti, C. A. (2017). Victim services and SANE/SART programs. In R. Hazlewood & A. Wolbert Burgess (Eds.) *Practical aspects of rape investigations* (5th ed., pp. 19–34). Taylor & Francis.

Malchiodi, Cathy. (2008, September 26).*Telling without talking: Breaking the silence of domestic violence*. Psychology Today. https://www.psychologytoday.com/us/blog/arts-and-health/200809/telling-without-talking-and-domestic-violence

Mayo Clinic. (n.d.). *Dissociative disorders*. https://www.mayoclinic.org/diseases-conditions/dissociative-disorders/symptoms-causes/syc-20355215

McIntyre, A. (2013). The value of "silence" in the lives of post-incarcerated women. *Journal of Offender Rehabilitation, 52*(1), 1–15. https://doi.org/10.1080/10509674.2012.713452

Miller, T. P., & Bowdon, M. (1999). Archivists with an attitude: A rhetorical stance on the archives of civic action. *College English, 61*(5), 591–598. https://doi.org/10.2307/378977

Motsemme, N. (2004). The mute always speak: On women's silences at the Truth and Reconciliation Commission. *Current Sociology, 52*(5), 909–932. https://doi.org/10.1177/0011392104045377

Murphy, S. B., Banyard, V. L., Maynard, S. P., & Dufresne, R. (2011). Advocates speak out on adult sexual assault: A unique crime demands a unique response. *Journal of Aggression, Maltreatment & Trauma, 20*(6), 690–710. https://doi.org/10.1080/10926771.2011.595381

New London Group. (1996). A pedagogy of multiliteracies: Designing social futures. *Harvard Educational Review, 66*(1), 60–93. https://doi.org/10.17763/haer.66.1.17370n67v22j160u

Payne, M. (2000). A strange unaccountable something: Historicizing sexual abuse essays. In C. M. Anderson & M. M. MacCurdy (Eds.), *Writing and healing: Toward an informed practice* (pp. 115–157). National Council of Teachers of English.

Peacock, M. E. (1991). A personal construct approach to art therapy in the treatment of post sexual abuse trauma. *American Journal of Art Therapy, 29*, 100–109.

Phillips, A., & Daniluk, J. C. (2004). Beyond "Survivor": How childhood sexual abuse informs the identity of adult women at the end of the therapeutic process. *Journal of Counseling & Development, 82*(2), 177–184. https://doi.org/10.1002/j.1556-6678.2004.tb00299.x

Rose, S. (1999). Naming and claiming: The integration of traumatic experience and the reconstruction of self in survivors' stories of sexual abuse. In K. L. Rogers, S. Leydesdorff, & G. Dawson (Eds.), *Trauma and life stories: International perspectives* (pp. 160–179). Routledge.

Rosenthal, M. (2015). *Your life after trauma: Powerful practices to reclaim your identity*. W.W. Norton & Company.
Rucht, D., Koopmans, R., & Neidhardt, F. (1999). Introduction: Protest as a subject of empirical research. In D. Rucht, R. Koopmans, & F. Neidhardt (Eds.), *Acts of dissent: New developments in the study of protest* (pp. 7–30). Rowman & Littlefield Publishers Inc.
Ruggles Gere, A. (1997). Introduction. In *Intimate practices: Literacy and cultural work in U.S. women's clubs, 1880–1920* (pp. 1–16). University of Illinois Press.
Rich, A. C. (2003). Compulsory heterosexuality and lesbian existence (1980). *Journal of Women's History, 15*(3), 11–48. https://doi.org/10.1353/jowh.2003.0079
Schultz, L. M. (2008). Foreward. In G. Kirsch & L. Rohan (Eds.), *Beyond the archives: Research as a lived process* (pp. vii–x). Southern Illinois University Press.
Scott, J. (1990). *Domination and the arts of resistance*. Yale University Press.
Seeburger, F. (2012). *The open wound: Trauma, identity, and community*. CreateSpace Independent Publishing Platform.
Selfe, C. L., & Takayoshi, P. (2007). Thinking about multimodality. In C. Selfe (Ed.), *Multimodal composition: Resources for teachers*. Hampton Press.
Siebel Newsom, J. (Director). (2011) *Miss representation* [Film]. The Representation Project.
Silverman, D. (2011). *Interpreting qualitative data* (4th ed.). Sage.
Skinner, J. (2009). Recovery from trauma: A Look into the process of healing from sexual assault. *Journal of Loss and Trauma, 14*(3), 170–180. https://doi.org/10.1080/15325020902724537
Smith, A. (2005). Looking to the future: Domestic violence, women of color, the state, and social change. In N. J. Sokoloff (Ed.), *Domestic violence at the margins: Readings on race, class, gender, and culture* (pp. 416–434). Rutgers, NJ: Rutgers University.
Sorsoli, L. (2010). "I remember", "I thought", "I know I didn't say": Silence and memory in trauma narratives. *Memory, 18*(2), 129–141. https://doi.org/10.1080/09658210903168046
Tal, K. (1996). *Worlds of hurt: Reading the literatures of trauma*. Cambridge University Press.
Thiongo, N. W. (2002). Freedom of the artists: People's artists versus people's rulers. In J. Hirschman (Ed.), *Art on the line: Essays by artists about the point where their art and activism intersect* (pp. 203–221). Curbstone Books.
Tomlinson, B. (2010). *Feminism and affect at the scene of argument: Beyond the trope of the angry feminist*. Temple University Press.

Wagner, R. (2012). Silence as resistance before the subject, or could the subalternremain silent? *Theory, Culture & Society, 29*(6), 99–124. https://doi.org/10.1177/0263276412438593

Warshauer Freedman, S. & Ball, A. F. (2004). Ideological becoming: Bakhtinian concepts to guide the study of language, literacy, and learning. In A. F. Ball & S. Warshauer Freedman (Eds.), *Bakhtinian perspectives on language, literacy, and learning* (pp. 3–33). Cambridge University Press. https://doi.org/10.1017/CBO9780511755002

Williams, J. E. & Holmes, K. A. (1981). *The second assault: Rape and public attitudes*. Greenwood Press.

Wood, H. (2019). Fuck the patriarchy: Towards an intersectional politics of irreverent rage. *Feminist Media Studies, 19*(4), 609–615. https://doi.org/10.1080/14680777.2019.1609232

Wysocki, A. (2014). awaywithwords: On the possibilities in unavailable designs. In C. Lutkewitte (Ed.), *Multimodal composition: A critical sourcebook* (pp. 302–308). Boston: Bedford/St Martin's.

CHAPTER 4

"Making" Progress in the Classroom and Beyond

Literacy, Ideology, and Multimodality in Rhetoric and Composition Studies

In 1982, Shirley Brice Heath (2001) introduced the idea of literacy events, which occur when "a piece of writing is integral to the nature of participants' interactions and their interpretive processes" (p. 445). Heath's (2001) examination of uses of literacy in the Trackton community revealed that its members read and wrote when occasions demanded such acts, but that understanding of written products relied on oral, group-oriented communications. While residents engaged in the same processes used to make sense of print (reliance on the text itself, prior experience related to the text, and creative thinking), increased knowledge of oral communication, especially in regards to asking questions, would have helped residents further navigate their daily lives. Heath (2001) makes the point that oral and "literate traditions," rather than existing along a spectrum, exist in interconnected relationships with one another (p. 466). While my own research supports the interconnectedness of literate traditions, including voice and silence, I argue that voice and silence also exist along a spectrum. In particular, my idea of psychosocial compositions argues that personal composing practices intertwine with cultural definitions of womanhood, which set limits on what and how women communicate (or 'should' communicate). Cultural traditions in censoring or masking women's communication (Lashgari, 1995;

Tomlinson, 2010) influence individuals' literate practices, as women's literate practices influence various understandings of the aforementioned cultural traditions. Each act of communication, then, interconnects with current and historical context, but each interconnected act of communication also discloses to varying degrees along a continuum, ranging from complete silence to complete disclosure.

Similarly, Street (1984) postulates the ideological model of literacy in opposition to the autonomous model. The autonomous model argued for literacy as the root of intellectual and personal development but treated literacy as a variable that people could study in isolation from the social contexts in which such development took place; on the other hand, the ideological model suggests reading and writing practices as embedded in ideological, cultural purposes and processes, and opens the idea of literacy to multiple modes (Street, 1984). Therefore, we can think of any act of reading and writing as embedded in cultural processes, yet place it along a spectrum in terms of the degrees to which its mode influences its rhetorical effectiveness. The use of tee shirts in the CP, for instance, lends itself to such an examination. First, the androgyny suggested by tee shirts helps defy gender stereotypes and their associated disempowerment (Hipple, 2000); we might think of the way society has placed men's and women's clothing along a spectrum, on which tee shirts fall toward the middle and support some CP activists' purpose of defying gender stereotypes. To decorate skirts, for example, might only perpetuate stereotypes associated with victim blaming (women who wear revealing clothing invite acts of sexual violence), and therefore influence CP activists' communication in a different way.

We might also think of CP founders' decision to use tee shirts as a way of "sponsoring" communication that attempts to defy stereotypes surrounding gender violence. Deborah Brandt (2001) introduced the idea of literacy sponsors, defined as "any agents, local or distant, concrete or abstract, who enable, support, teach, model, as well as recruit, regulate, suppress, or withhold literacy—and gain advantage by it in some way" (p. 556). This definition draws attention to dominant groups' and activists' stake in explicitly or implicitly creating and using social structures that break or defy communication boundaries for marginalized populations. To investigate sponsors of literacy, Brandt (2001) interviewed more than 100 people across the United States and traced influences on attitudes toward reading and writing and the resulting social "stratification" (p. 557). In so doing, Brandt (2001) demonstrates the importance of being able to place our findings along a spectrum; the idea of the spectrum helps us explore how cultural narratives and literacy interconnect to place people in particular subject positions with varying degrees of power (and perhaps keep them there). Brandt's work, then, hints at a psychosocial understanding of literacy.

Building upon Brandt's work, James Paul Gee argued in 2001 that "a new field of study, integrating 'psych' and 'socio' approaches to language from a variety of disciplines, is emerging, a field which we might call *literacy studies*" (p. 525). He encourages examination of the "saying (writing)-doing-being-valuing-believing combinations," more simply known as "Discourses" (Gee, 2001, p. 526). Gee (2001), therefore, differentiates the meaning of discourse with a lowercase "d" from Discourse with a capital "D," conceptualizing discourse as a solely linguistic construction and Discourse as all forms of communication acted out in relation to various identities and social contexts (p. 526). While my research does not use the term "discourse," my notion of psychosocial compositions builds on Gee's (2001) idea of Discourses, as psychosocial compositions encompass "saying (writing)-doing-being-valuing-believing combinations" associated with an individual's dynamic (rather than static) identity, and the influence of various social contexts on identities (p. 526).

To further encourage investigation of intersections between literacy, individual ways of being, and social context, Higgins et al. (2006) introduced the term "community literacy" as a way of thinking about literacy as "the public act of writing and taking social action" (p. 9). Long (2008) later questioned: "What does it take for ordinary people to go public?" (p. 15). My research explores the follow-up question of *how* people use literacy to go public, taking particular interest in the communication of people occupying multiple oppressed subject positions (women and survivors). To engage in such work, Long (2008) suggests a rhetorical framework that includes identifying: the guiding metaphor (description of the space), context (location and factors that give literacies their meaning), tenor of the discourse (register, affective quality of the discourse), literacy (practices that comprise how people organize and carry out going public), and rhetorical invention (the process by which people respond to the exigencies that call the local public into being) (p. 16). She further hopes that examination of local publics will lead to "useful generalizations" (Long, 2008, p. 18) with implications for understandings of literacy in a variety of disciplines. Correspondingly, my study includes a discussion of the CP's metaphor of "airing dirty laundry" (Julier, 1994, p. 255); the context of shirt-making sessions and the larger cultural context; use of emotional appeals; literacy involved in going public; and the possible influence of silencing on invention.

While scholars in the field of rhetoric and composition examined the use of literacy for civic engagement and social change before Long (2008), and have examined such use since Long's focus on community literacy (e.g. Addison, 2010; Cushman, 1996; George, 2002; Lieblich, 2013), these investigations remain part of a line of work on the psychological and sociological functions of writing. For example, Rosenwald and Ochberg (1992) assert that cultural narratives create an identity and shape how people understand identity. In essence, Rosenwald and Ochberg (1992) recognize a symbiotic relationship between one's narrative, one's audience, and one's life. As we find ourselves in constant tension with authoritative discourse and the discourse of all others we encounter, we must deal with persuasion and ideology as "not within us, but between us" (Warshauer & Ball, 2004, p. 29). Similarly, Kock and Villadsen (2012) use the term "rhetorical citizenship" to discuss the way in which discourse serves not as a precedent to action but as part of action itself (p. 1). Together, these scholars bring attention to "macro and micro [social] practices" (Kock & Villadsen, 2012, p. 6) and their implications.

In contemporary culture, multimodality remains pertinent to macro and micro literate practices. Bezemer and Kress (2008) define a mode as "a socially and culturally shaped resource for making meaning" and assert that "meanings are…always made with more than one mode" (p. 171). Multimodality, then, involves the use of a variety of modes, such as image, alphabetic text, color, and layout (Kress, 2010). The New London Group (1996), one of the most influential groups of scholars in the movement to focus on multimodality, suggests any semiotic activity as involving design (available designs, designing, and the redesigned). In their view, discourse both reproduces and changes social conventions, and design decisions and products are always historically interwoven with other texts (Cope & Kalantzis, 2009). Likewise, CP participants' design decisions suggest that the seemingly ubiquitous discourse of digital composition influences understandings and uses of composing practices in other modes.

Furthermore, Gunther Kress (2003) asserts that a shift in visual culture requires a move from literacy theories of linguistics to those of semiotics. He argues that semiotic change occurs when the change in mode echoes "the values, structures and meanings of the social and cultural world of the meaning-maker and of the socio-cultural group in which they are" (Kress, 2003, p. 40). Again, the semiotic analysis in my study suggests that the change in people's preferred mode of communication may be from material multimodal composing to digital multimodal composing. In other words, generally speaking, engaging with the arts at one time involved more interaction with tangible rather than digital materials (e.g. scrapbooking, card making, architectural designing, sewing/knitting/crocheting, and drawing) than what may be common today. Of course, as noted in Chapter 1, all representations have limitations in their ability to reflect experiences (Kress, 2003). But, as also noted in Chapter 1, while Kress (2003) argues that images have supplanted the use of text in communication, my study shows participants relying on text. Therefore, cultural trends related to mode, in some cases, may pertain more to divides between digital and material composing, rather than to divides between textual and visual composing.

Regardless of these differences, multimodal composing involves design mediated by context, purpose, and materials. Kress (2010) writes of the technicalities of design:

> At the beginning of design stands a task; the parameters of the task and the assessment of the task come from some other source. Design starts with the designer's imagining of the task; a knowledge of the resources available to make the tool that will be used to perform the task; an understanding of the characteristics of the object to be worked on or with—carrot, potato or apple; and understanding of the wider social conditions and a knowledge of the worker/agent and her or his capacities—the fact, for instance, that the hands of a five-year-old differ from those of an adult.
>
> Design projects and organizes the arrangement of an entire ensemble: of the worker; the object to be worked on or with; of a tool for action with or on the object[,] integrated in specific ways into the capacities and affordances of the human body[,] a body with a history or experience of other, prior physical/social processes[—] an ensemble which is subject more or less, and in different ways, to social needs and regulation of the process...The design...has social effects[and] meanings; and produces affect. (p. 137)

Hocks and Balsamo (2003) further write about social design via new media, particularly as it relates to women and feminist activism. They claim that women can envision and carry out activism in "technological artifacts" (p. 192). Their project, "Women of the World Talk Back," involved filming responses to a video archive of international representatives' commentary on global women's politics. With their delivery grounded in technology, they aimed to develop a "virtual public" and use technology to draw attention to feminist issues and to feminist perspectives on technology (2003, p. 195). Hocks and Balsamo (2003) argue:

> We can ask such questions as: Where are the places within a given formation that the technology is given meaning or shape? At what point is the technology designed to serve certain ends and not others? Who benefits from specific technological designs? At what moments do decisions get made to pursue one technological research program and not another? (p. 201)

We can ask the same questions of any available (or unavailable) modes of communication and their relation to the situations linked to hegemony and politics.

Wysocki's (2005) "awaywithwords: On the Possibilities of Unavailable Designs" builds on Hocks and Balsamo's (2003) questions by asserting that a dichotomous conceptualization of "word" and "image" perpetuates other oppositional relationships, such as those between men and women (p. 306). Changing or experimenting with textual or visual composition conventions, consequently, can lead to changes in social practices and ideologies, which Kress (2003) suggests, and findings in my study of the CP might also suggest.

Changes in composition conventions and ideologies might, in turn, lead to shifts in the content of images. Kress and van Leeuwen (2006), in their book, *Reading Images: The Grammar of Visual Design*, theorize images as either narrative or conceptual, with the former "presenting unfolding actions and events, processes of change, [or] transitory spatial arrangements" and the latter "representing participants in terms of their more generalized essence, in terms of class, or structure or meaning" (p. 79). Important to the distinction between image types is Kress and van Leewen's (2006) idea of "vectors," or invisible lines that connect people to one another, so that narrative images may not engage in storytelling but form interactions among participants in the images. Conceptual images, then, lack vectors and aim to appear static and acontextualized (Kress & van Leeuwen, 2006). Again, though the study of the CP taken up in my work does not adopt the language of "vectors," psychosocial compositions relate to the idea. Moreover, my exploration of rhetorics of silence situated in cultural narratives suggests the presence of vectors in both linguistic text and images.

Like the invisible lines Kress and van Leeuwen (2006) conceptualize, Jeffrey Grabill (2010) grapples with the under-established (or unseen) connections between composing and its implications in the public sector. As first presented in Chapter 1, Grabill (2010) argues for rhetoric as "work" that involves collaboration and communication via writing, images, and information technology, therefore supporting digital composition and materiality (p. 193). Jefferies (2001) refers to the combination of linguistics and images discussed by Grabill as "scriptovisual" (p. 191) and addresses definitional issues of "feminist visual culture." More specifically, she aligns feminism with politics by tracing patterns in various art forms, which reveal a focus on domestic trends, "the phenomenon of empty garments," and an intersection between personal and political interests (p. 201). Jefferies (2001) states,

> Such work... might just conform to a feminist model of rendering the personal within the political; a site where traditional, gendered biographies and identities are loosened by fragments of cloth and fragile bits of sewing. (p. 201)

To reiterate, Jefferies (2001) records how language and art take their status as subversive only in relation to the dominant; in other words, activists must use the language of the dominant discourse even as they critique it. After all, social critique by those in oppressed positions almost always involves elements of disguise (Jefferies, 2001, p. 182).

The issue becomes not whether art depicts the truth but how it came to exist, what it conveys, and who gets implicated in it (Coogan, 2010). Again, visual rhetoric draws attention to the dynamic of having a live audience at an event that includes previously constructed materials by anonymous creators (Hocks & Balsamo, 2003), the "active" relationships formed among narrative images (Kress & van Leeuwen, 2006) on CP tee shirts, and the CP as a rich site for questioning materials used in feminist activism and what those materials suggest about dominant culture (Wysocki, 2005). The activist research discussed thus far, in many ways, has been conducted by literacy scholars exploring the role of reading and writing in personal and social change; my work provides a more focused extension of this scholarship. My work also emphasizes the stem word "multi" in multimodality; as Huang (2015) points out, all communication is and always has been multimodal and ideological. Shipka (2011) illustrates this notion of multimodality:

> To take as an example a text that in its final form is largely text-based (word processed) and printed on sheets of 8 ½ × 11″ copy paper. Just because the text does not have an online, audio, or visual component (save, of course, for the visual aspects associated with spacing, margins, font choice and size, and so on), it does not mean that doodling, sketching out one's ideas, listening to music, reading the text aloud, discussing one's ideas with others, blogging one's ideas, or exchanging drafts of the text online was not part of the producer's overall composing process. To label a text multimodal or monomodal based on its final appearance alone discounts, or worse yet, renders invisible the contribution made by a much wider variety of resources, supports, and tools. (p. 52)

Such a broad conceptualization of multimodality allows us to examine a text and its implications more fully. Just as Western cultures historically privileged communication in the form of alphabetic writing (especially the manuscript) (Kress, 2005), thereby limiting the types of communication valued and oppressing the voice of people without the skills to engage in such composing (at least to the extent that it would adhere to expectations for Standard English), privileging digital media over alphabetic text or compositions that involve non-digital materials may limit the means by which people can or will communicate. Shipka (2011) raises this concern regarding the texts students produce in our courses, as I will discuss later in this chapter. Terms like "technology" (Shipka, 2011, p. 52), "multimodal," "intertextual," "multimedia," or even "composition" may not only become associated with "digitized, screen-mediated texts" (Shipka, 2011, pp. 7–8) but become conceptualized as being *better* than alphabetic texts or texts that involve non-digital materials. Gollihue (2019) extends the argument by suggesting that focusing entirely on digital composition excludes makers in the realms of everyday life, such as farmers, who use seeds, mechanical and digital technology, waste, and scientific knowledge to yield produce (to create).

Scholars like Kress (2010) have arguably contributed to such notions of linguistic texts and texts made with non-digital materials as inferior to those made with digital materials; he argues that multimodal composition is "inevitably innovative [rather than] competent implementation of conventionally given practices" (p. 33). But to achieve rhetorical effectiveness, all forms of communication must, at least to some extent, competently implement conventions. And as digital composition and the ability to appropriate digital texts has become more popular—and depending on what we define "innovative"—people could consider a plethora of digital compositions mundane, unoriginal, and non-innovative. Even narratives produced by way of new media remain situated within the same "historical and cultural context as other genres" (Andersson et al., 2019, p. 7); and *"writing* like *making* happens in context, through land, material, and cultural practice" (emphasis mine) (Gollihue, 2019, p. 31). Finally, DIYers working with non-digital materials also seek originality in their creations (Wolf & McQuitty, 2011). In the end, all modes have affordances, limitations, and consequences.

More specifically, all modes "have differing modal resources" (Bezemer & Kress, 2008, p. 171). Bezemer and Kress (2008) state:

> Writing, for instance, has syntactic, grammatical, and lexical resources[and] graphic resources such as font type, size, and resources for 'framing,' such as punctuation. Writing might make use of other resources, for instance, the resource of color. Speech and writing share aspects of grammar, syntax, and lexis. Beyond these, speech has intensity (loudness), pitch and pitch variation (intonation), tonal/vocal quality, length, silence. Image has resources such as position of elements in a framed space, size, color, shape, icons of various kinds—lines, circles—as well as resources such as spatial relation, and in the case of moving images, the temporal succession of images, movement. (p. 171)

As new tools get introduced into society, however, it becomes easier to recognize the limitations of the tools that came before them; and which tools people use may have less to do with the affordances of the tools and more to do with how people who have a stake in their use present and conceptualize them (Shipka, 2011). To illustrate, computers have advantages regarding efficiency, assistance with spelling and grammar, and capability to modify and share work with others easily (Shipka, 2011). But they have disadvantages in regards to space (not being able to see all pages/images of a text at one time), lack of portability (bulkiness or weight of carrying/transporting them, reliance on electrical or battery power), and consequences such as dry eyes, screen fatigue (Shipka, 2011), or carpal tunnel. Similarly, paper and pen/pencil have advantages regarding financial accessibility, space (being able to see a full text or multiple pages at one time), and portability (lightweight, no reliance on other resources for them to function). Paper and pen/pencil, though, have disadvantages regarding efficiency, aid with spelling and grammar, capability to modify and share work easily, and consequences such as carpal tunnel. Continued use of particular tools (digital or non-digital), then, affect not only how we interact with the world, but how our bodies perform—which muscles we use and, therefore, which ones become stronger and which ones atrophy (Shipka, 2011). As Breaux (2017) points out, technology in and of itself does not change society; the people who use it change society. We should, therefore, focus our attention and work on "literacies, not just devices and software" (Breaux, 2017, p. 34).

Beyond practical affordances and limitations, and embodied consequences, exist consequences from narratives embedded in the use of tools and products of composing. People create texts to "perform specific social actions or tasks" (Serafini, 2010, p. 89). An increase in available tools means that "political ideologies are infused into the culture more widely," in everything from "software," "administrative processes," and "office furniture design" (Machin & van Leeuwen, 2016, p. 243). The meanings we ascribe to any text depend first on what we understand about the world, which determines which texts we notice and how we understand what we notice (Serafini, 2010). Putting visual images into words is an act of "transduction," and "every act of transduction is an act of interpretation, no matter how literal the emphasis" (Serafini, 2010, p. 95).

We see ideologies infused into culture more widely, along with the subsequent uses of technology to serve certain ends, in the creation and sharing of digital content that documents sexual assaults. On the one hand, such content has served as evidence in survivors' legal cases; while helpful, convictions and punishments remain rare in the legal system, and so online platforms allow women an alternative space in which to find validation, community, and perhaps a sense of "informal justice" (Powell, 2015, p. 573). Use of online platforms, then, "challenge[s] meanings of justice within criminology and the global West more broadly" (Powell, 2015, p. 573). Fileborn's (2017) study of women's online disclosure of experiences with street harassment found that women viewed their disclosure as an "overtly...political" effort to draw attention to harassment and situate their experiences within a broader narrative of gender discrimination (p. 1492). Online spaces may certainly serve marginalized groups excluded from, or dismissed and under-valued in, typical forms of communication (Fileborn, 2017), including disabled/differently abled individuals (Loizou, 2019).

On the other hand, people have used digital content that documents assault, and related content on online platforms, to re-victimize survivors/victims (Powell, 2015). Likewise, perpetrators have used online spaces to *find* victims (Fileborn, 2017). So while technologies and their resulting digital compositions have proven "liberatory" for women and other marginalized populations—and the internet and social media spaces have allowed women to find validation after their assaults by breaking "social and legal norms" such as naming perpetrators (Salter, 2013, p. 237)—technologies can prove equally harmful (Fileborn, 2017; Powell, 2015). Furthermore, evidence continues to suggest that younger and more highly educated people with access to technology engage more with online activism, and so the internet may remain somewhat exclusive (Loizou, 2019). Finally, while Keller, Mendes, and Ringrose (2016) argue that teen Twitter users in their study were "Not simply re-tweeting rape culture posts [but rather] creatively documenting and speaking urgently about the experiences and resistances happening live at school" (p. 32), my research raises questions about how creativity online fosters creativity in non-digital spaces and about how that might relate to hashtag activism and street activism. As with any text or tool, however, we cannot dichotomize online spaces into those that are just and those that are unjust; we must ask questions about which spaces serve which people and how, why, and in what context (Fileborn, 2017). We must also raise questions about which spaces serve people creatively, in what ways, to what extent, and with what consequences.

As with limitations to online spaces, "one-directional" media, such as television, newspaper, and radio, can make it difficult for subaltern voices to gain influence (Salter, 2013, p. 22). One-directional media presents narratives to forward or perpetuate particular ideologies without accounting for counter evidence or counter narratives. While people certainly respond to these narratives in other spaces, the ideal readers or viewers of one-directional media may not enter those alternative spaces. Communication in the public sphere, in fact, approaches viewers as mere consumers of material, increasingly adopting conventions of advertising and entertainment (Machin & van Leeuwen, 2016). I turn now to the ways in which materiality intersects with attempts to forward particular ideologies and political agendas.

Materiality: An Overview of Making

The "maker movement" remains grounded in the sharing of knowledge and resources that allows for advancement (Cook, 2019, p. 401). Historically, beginning in the late eighteenth and early nineteenth centuries, arts and crafts pushed against industrialization and mass production (Willett, 2016), instead advocating for individualism; repurposing; and accessibility to materials, artifacts, and the process of making (Breaux, 2017). In much of the twentieth century, DIY projects pertained mostly to home improvement, though the 1960s and 1970s saw a resurgence in making for activist purposes (Willett, 2016). In contemporary times, the maker movement aligns with movements like Occupy Wall Street and Buy Nothing Day (Breaux, 2017). Hatch's (2014) *The Maker Movement Manifesto: Rules for Innovation in the New World of Crafters, Hackers, and Tinkerers* lists "make," "share" (creations and knowledge), "give" (creations), "learn," "tool up" (use tools appropriate for the project), "play," "participate" (in the maker movement more broadly), "support" ("emotional, intellectual, financial, political, and institutional), and "change" as values and goals of the maker movement (pp. 1–2).

Rooted in learning, play, and advancement, Hackerspaces emerged in the 1960s with graduate students at MIT; hackers then relied on universities for access to technology and became credited with establishing Silicon Valley start-ups that led to the development of the personal computer and other technologies (Willett, 2016). "Fab Labs" also came out of MIT, started in 2002 by Neil Gershenfeld at the Center for Bits and Atoms in MIT's Media Lab; this space encouraged people to create what they needed "to solve their own problems...rather than purchasing and outsourcing" (Marsh et al., 2017, p. 20). Before FabLab, however, C-Base, the first official hackerspace, was launched in Berlin, Germany in 1995; still reserved for "programmers," hackers would "'hack' technology in order to try to make it do something that it wasn't meant to do," though the term now applies to hacking physical objects and even creating "life hacks" (Marsh et al., 2017, p. 18).

Technological development and the "access to tools" movement eventually put technology in the hands of the masses, allowing for a variety of ways to engage in the act of making; concerns, though, about a lack of evidence for the idea that accessibility shifted power in meaningful ways—and questions of continued exclusion—still exist (Willett, 2016, p.315). Accessibility, nevertheless, had a lot to do with the development of makerspaces. In 2005, Dale Dougherty founded *Make* magazine; and a year later, the first Maker Faire occurred, providing a space for people to share their creations (Marsh et al., 2017). Various definitions of hackerspaces and makerspaces exist, with hackerspaces traditionally associated with digital technology and makerspaces associated with material resources; in reality, however, these two types of spaces often blur these distinctions (Marsh et al., 2017).

Still, both hackerspaces and makerspaces remain largely associated with white men in technology fields (Gollihue, 2019; Willett, 2016). Kim et al. (2018) conducted interviews with 80 participants (instructors, students, and administrators) across 30 K-12 makerspaces nationwide. They found a lack of women in leadership roles involving makerspaces and a tendency to perceive boys as having greater technical skills (Kim et al., 2018). Perceptions of boys as more technologically savvy may prevent girls and women from entering such spaces and, as a result, perpetuate the stereotype and lead to an actual difference in skills between men and women.

Moreover, Kim et al. (2018) found that makerspaces tended to be characterized by either those that focused on arts and crafts or those that focused on digital technology (similar to common distinctions between makerspaces and hackerspaces), with those focused on digital technology also more focused on competition (Kim et al., 2018). Separation of arts and crafts from digital technology only further risks students having a dichotomous understanding of making and, therefore, seeing one type of creating as more valuable than another. Hira and Hynes (2018) write:

> [Makerspaces] provide, request for, and dictate the means used[;] the means determine the activities that may be possible in the space[;] and the activities contribute to people's experiences[,] which include their learning experiences. At the same time, the people and their interests, goals, and experiences dictate the activities that take place in a Makerspace[;] the activities determine which means are needed[;] and the means influence what people do in the space. Depending on the purpose behind the space, each Makerspace could be variably focused toward either the people, the means, the activities of the space, or combination of them. (pp. 4–5)

Arguably, all spaces need to focus on the people, the means, *and* the activities, given the constant interaction among them in the process of making and the roles each has in the implications of what gets made and how people use that creation. Malea Powell makes such an argument by reconceptualizing makerspaces as "makingspace," which shifts the focus from the maker and their tools to the process of making and "the embodied ways that humans, nonhumans, and technologies (both electronic and non-electronic) are constantly configuring and reconfiguring one another" (Gollihue, 2019, p. 22). Failure to account for these complexities will perpetuate exclusion and exclusivity in such spaces.

A focus on people, means, and activities remains necessary to achieving craftivism as well. People have credited Betsy Greer with originating the term "craftivism" in the early 2000s, with the goal of inspiring people to engage in less "abrasive" forms of protest (Ey, 2019, p. 957). But Greer (2011) claims she got the word from the Church of Craft, which began using the word around the same time that Greer began circulating the term online. Regardless, craftivism opposes the devaluing of traditionally "feminine" or "domestic" endeavors and argues that women and their work belong in public spaces (Ey, 2019, p. 961). Historically, however, people excluded types of art created by women from consideration as fine art and, therefore, dismissed such work as not much more than a symbol of submission (Parker, 1984).

Still, women have long used crafts as a form of subversive resistance, such as those who knitted or embroidered Morse codes into items like rugs, or those who used the role of a knitting woman as a disguise in spy work (Zarrelli, 2017). In addition, the suffragettes created handmade banners to protest gender inequality (McGovern, 2019). Actually, if we take into account "crafting, sewing, growing, cooking, and fixing—if you consider not only 'garage science' but also 'kitchen science'—then you quickly see that people have been making continuously for centuries" (Cipolla, 2019, p. 266) and for a variety of purposes.

Despite its history and roots in anti-industrialization and other forms of resistance, home goods lines and television shows and networks have commodified crafting (e.g. Martha Stewart and DIY Network) and used crafting to associate companies with social causes, despite the fact that the companies lack any meaningful connection to those causes (Bratich & Brush, 2011). In other words, a perceived revival of making has come from a focus on the activities of upper-middle-class white people (Cipolla, 2019) and its consequent economic benefits. But lack of awareness or acknowledgment of the ways in which women and those of lower socioeconomic statuses have *been* making, combined with privileging new media or tools to which not all people have access, only furthers stereotypes of "domestic" making and undervalues resourcefulness.

Furthermore, people have failed to value or take seriously acts such as "radical knitting"; one reader of an article about "rebel knitting" on *The Guardian* questioned, "Are we to knit our banana covers to show contempt for the ruling powers? Forgive me, but what's next? Rebellious doilies" (Robertson, 2011, p. 188). Additionally, some women not identifying as feminists may perceive both feminism and craftivism as a defilement of traditional feminine values and practices; more specifically, they may find the political use of practices "passed down matrilineally" problematic (Mandell, 2019, p. 5). Others find support of craftivism problematic due to the history of crafts as oppressive to women, thereby preventing them from engaging in other activities for enjoyment or progress (Robertson, 2011). That said, many women now *choose* to craft (Robertson, 2011), and even women with what might be considered more conservative views have used crafting to send political messages, as I discuss in the next section (Mandell, 2019).

Materiality in Activism

Though activism in digital spaces increases awareness of social causes, online activism may lack sustainable structure; in other words, people join causes and disperse easily, which means actual work may not get done (Naím, 2014). As Graham wrote about Donald Trump's presidency in 2019, "We can't hashtag our way out of this roiling mess of an administration" (para. 17). Financial accessibility and "representation" may additionally limit participation in, and effectiveness of, online activism (Fileborn, 2017). In contrast, face-to-face events, such as those revolving around crafting, may yield greater financial accessibility; and face-to-face interactions may allow for the easier allocation of particular roles and greater accountability for completing tasks related to a cause or activity.

Craft politics certainly address a variety of causes and take a variety of forms. Some craftivist works aim for reform (bringing about change and funding causes), some serve as cultural interventions (interrupting spaces encountered in everyday life through art such as graffiti), some accompany "street-based" efforts (such as knit-ins), and some accompany "confrontational street tactics" (such as aggressive protests) (Bratich & Brush, 2011, p. 249). Regardless of the purpose, making can serve as a "means of enacting embodied knowledge" and learning through one's emotions (Hackney et al., 2016, p. 58).

Countless groups and organizations have turned to materials as the mode through which to communicate their messages, both in the United States and abroad. In the United States, just as the AIDS quilt used crafting as a means to getting people to reconsider AIDS in a domestic space (Elsley, 1992), the Pink Tank Project, in protest of the Iraq War, used pink knitted blankets to cover military tanks, thereby disrupting typical schemas of warfare and creating an opportunity for dialog about war (Ey, 2019). Arte Sana, a non-profit organization formed in 2001 and serving Latina women, addresses sexual and gender violence through the arts, including "mixed media, digital art, painting, drawing, photography, and installation art" (Baker & Bevacqua, 2018, p. 365). In addition, The Long Walk Home, a non-profit organization formed in 2003, addresses gender and racial violence through art therapy, including visual and performing arts (Baker & Bevacqua, 2018). And in 2009, activists re-appropriated the Clothesline Project into the Disability Clothesline Project, addressing violence against disabled people (Disability Clothesline, n.d.).

Many additional activist projects utilizing crafting arose across the country following The Pussyhat Project, which began in response to Donald Trump's winning of the 2016 presidential election (Mandell, 2019). Post inauguration, the Welcome Blanket project produced blankets with yarn that collectively measured the length of Trump's proposed border wall between the United States and Mexico (2,000 miles) (Mandell, 2019); refugees in the United States received the blankets, and blanket creators shared welcoming messages and personal stories about immigration with refugees (Zweiman, 2019). The Immigrant Yarn Project solicited yarn artwork from immigrants and immigrant descendants to display on public columns and totems, showing cultural enrichment from the presence of immigrants in the United States (Immigrant Yarn Project). People created "Resistor hats" in support of the March for Science, which draws attention to climate change; "Black Lives Matter hats" in support of the Black Lives Matter movement, which protests violence against Black people; "Enough hats" in support of protests against gun violence; and "Blue Wave hats" in support of a hoped-for democratic majority in the 2018 midterm elections for Congress (Mandell, 2019, pp. 4–5). In addition, the Kudzu Project placed "knit versions of the kudzu plant…over Confederate statues" (Mandell, 2019, pp. 4–5) in an effort to raise awareness of "false narratives about the Civil War and white supremacy" (Markus, 2019, p. 21). "Hearts of Cville" solicited knitted/crocheted hearts to memorialize those killed during the "Unite the Right Rally" in Charlottesville, Virginia (Mandell, 2019, pp. 4–5). And activists knitted and sewed "evil eye gloves" in support of the March of Our Lives protest, which responded to the school shooting in Parkland, Florida (Mandell, 2019, pp. 4–5); the "eye" on the gloves signified that people see the violence and look to Congress to make changes to protect them (Willingham, 2018).

Also in response to concerns about Trump's presidency and the political agenda that would follow, a week before the 2016 election, St. John Fisher College in Rochester, New York held an alternate version of the Clothesline Project, named "Consent Trumps Everything" (Dehoff & Swiencicki, 2019). Meant to "elicit dialogue about how Trump is implicated in issues of sexual assault, objectification, and sexism," this version of the CP broke with the customary guideline of not naming perpetrators without a conviction and served the direct purpose of influencing voters (Dehoff & Swiencicki, 2019, p. 206). Specifically, the project labeled Trump's speech as sexism, not the "locker room talk" he dismissed it as (Dehoff & Swiencicki, 2019, p. 207). With a similar agenda—to respond to Trump's justification of an inappropriate conversation between him and Billy Bush (captured on an *Access Hollywood* tape)—Shannon Downey, a leader in craftivism, embroidered, "boys will be ~~boys~~ held accountable for their fucking actions" (McGovern, 2019, p. 35), a picture of which went viral online. After Trump's inauguration, during the 2017 Women's March, Downey revealed an embroidery that stated, "I'm so angry I stitched this just so I could stab something 3,000 times" (McGovern, 2019, p. 35).

Though not in response to Trump's presidency directly, The Handmaid Coalition, named after Margaret Atwood's novel, *The Handmaid's Tale*, creates replicas of attire in Atwood's novel, specifically red capes and white bonnets, for people to wear at protests and demonstrations (McGovern, 2019). Their message implicates the role of governments in the oppression of women and "marginalized groups" (McGovern, 2019, p. 41). They aim to "keep fiction from becoming reality" (McGovern, 2019, p. 41).

Also using red clothing and now in the United States, the REDress project began in Canada in 2011; the project hangs red dresses in public places to represent missing or murdered native women (Ault, 2019). In

Brussels, Belgium, The Center Communautaire used clothing worn by women when they were assaulted to create an exhibit; items included pajamas, tracksuits, and a child's "My Little Pony" shirt (Exhibition Put Up Clothes From Women to Prove They Were NOT "Asking For It," 2020). The exhibit illustrates that what women wear has no bearing on whether they are assaulted, therefore asserting that society should stop associating clothing choices with such violence (Exhibition Put Up Clothes From Women to Prove They Were NOT "Asking For It," 2020).

In the United States and Mexico, The Monument Quilt addressed sexual violence with a particular focus on consent (McGovern, 2019). Similar to the CP, survivors/victims attended workshops where they created quilt blocks (via writing, drawing, or stitching) pertaining to their experiences with sexual assault and intimate partner violence (McGovern, 2019). Organizers displayed the final quilt in Washington D.C.'s National Mall (McGovern, 2019).

Though unrelated to women and gender violence, in the United Kingdom, craftivists sewed handkerchiefs for distribution to the retailer Marks & Spencer (M&S), a means of advocating for the establishment of a living wage by the company (Corbett, 2019). More specifically, the handkerchiefs were purchased from M&S and made by M&S customers "matched" to a particular board member based on commonalities (such as pairing a new mom with a board member with young children) (Corbett, 2019). Corbett (2019), the leader of the project, writes:

> I mailed the hankies out to the craftivists, and I included 'crafterthought' questions for them to reflect on while they stitched. These included 'What challenges do you think your designated hanky-receiver would face trying to implement the living wage?' and 'How would you feel if you were a staff member working full time for this company but couldn't afford to pay for basic necessities to live comfortably?' These queries were to help the craftivists engage in the issue more deeply, critically and compassionately and inspire them to make empathetic gifts, which, in turn, would make their gifts more impactful. (para. 8)

These efforts, combined with small "stitch-in"s outside M&S stores, resulted in M&S agreeing to pay more than the Living Wage rates; craftivists, however, continued their efforts to get M&S to agree to accreditation that would prevent them from reneging on the implementation of their new remuneration policy (Corbett, 2019).

Bridging collective action centered on crafting and individual benefits of making, researchers have examined self-reported psychological advantages of crafting. For instance, Malema and Naidoo (2017) investigated the relationship between making crafts for a rural community art project and feeling empowered; through field notes and a semi-structured questionnaire given to 18 women, they discovered that participants found that crafting served as a positive distraction from stress; allowed them to interact in relationships (such as those with children) more positively; provided at least one aspect of their lives over which they had control; and yielded feelings of hope, optimism, and pride. Moreover, the crafters felt they gained respect from community members and, because they crafted collectively, that they had a support system (Malema & Naidoo, 2017). Finally, crafting provided a space in which women could discuss personal issues, and an accessible (local and inexpensive) way for women to feel as though they remained contributing members of society (Malema & Naidoo, 2017). Similarly, an online survey of 3,545 knitters (with most respondents identifying as white, female, and under the age of 40) showed a correlation between knitting frequency and feelings of happiness and calmness (Riley et al., 2013). According to the study, knitting with others also correlated with reports of improved communication and feelings of happiness, confidence, and belonging (Riley et al., 2013).

Crafting can also provide a means of taking time for one's self while remaining productive and feeling accomplished (Short, 2018). Some might argue that the need for productivity creates anxiety and should, therefore, be excluded from stress management techniques or personal time. For many, however, abandoning the notion of productivity may prove difficult, or even impractical, and in this way, crafting can 'meet people where they're at.'

Crafting further yields positive benefits to mental health, in part, by creating an opportunity to learn something new and "fail safely," and by allowing us to enter a "flow" state (Huotilainen et al., 2018, p. 1). Flow is characterized by the intensity with which one gets involved in an activity and experiences a sense of purpose (Huotilainen et al., 2018, p. 1). The many chalk drawings created in response to the COVID-19 pandemic, for example, suggest that engaging in art away from digital technology fulfills a sense of purpose and offers a means of catharsis. One needs only to do a quick Google search to find images of chalk drawings dedicated to offering hope to neighbors or giving thanks to the medical community. As one popular media article noted, "Sidewalk chalk is having a real moment during the pandemic" (Gallucci, 2020).

Regarding craftivism in particular, McGovern's (2019) study of yarn bombers found that craftivists were motivated by experiencing personal satisfaction and catharsis, positively affecting the lives of others and creating a sense of community, and communicating and protesting injustices. Participants also appreciated the ways in which yarn bombing defied expectations for how people should use crafting and for how women should behave, though they acknowledged the low likelihood of suffering legal consequences for their actions (McGovern, 2019). Participants, apparently like authority figures, did not see their work as "destructive" (McGovern, 2019, p. 116).

While some may wonder why I account for personal benefits of crafting or making with non-digital materials in a section about activism, doing so interrogates the notions of activism presented in Chapter 1. In addition, it pushes against "traditional academic" notions of activism as "grandiose" and "unquestionably meaning-ful," showing that not all activists carry out activism collectively or within the context of large events, but rather within one's personal spaces and "everyday life" (Pottinger, 2016, p. 216). Hackney et al. (2016) document making in the "micro-emancipatory sense of fostering autonomy" (p. 39). Self-awareness and awareness of the social narratives influencing one's life may, in turn, lead to more collective and intentionally political activist efforts in the future (Hackney et al., 2016).

Converging notions of personal well-being, activism, and rhetorics of silence occurs via the use of materiality to engage in "quiet activism" (Pottinger, 2016, p. 215). Quiet activism involves "small, everyday, embodied acts, often of making and creating, that can be either implicitly or explicitly political in nature" (Pottinger, 2016, p. 215). Pottinger (2016) explored such activism in the United Kingdom in the form of seed saving (harvesting seeds of produce) in order to "conserve biodiversity and challenge the corporate control of food"; participants in seed saving formed a national network that holds local events for seed swapping (p. 215). Though, as established in Chapter 2, people frequently experience silence as awkward and uncomfortable, the silence that accompanies the act of making [including planting and growing] is "meditative" (Page & Thorsteinsson, 2018, p. 8). Quiet or "silent" activism may also enhance ethos. In Corbett's (2019) work to persuade Marks & Spencer to pay a living wage, she addressed ethos by intentionally recruiting quiet people to serve the goal to "encourage" and "not bully" board members (para. 7). Hackney et al. (2016), then, note that "quiet" and "powerful" are not necessarily opposites.

Whether quiet or loud, The Center for Artistic Activism (2018) has called into question the efficacy of artistic activism. They note determining the impact of artistic activism and understanding *how* it accomplishes its goals as necessary to validating such efforts. The Center writes in its 2018 report:

> None of this is to say that we can, or should, create a science of artistic activism. The questions of 'how it works' and 'how do we know' immediately brings up the thornier question of: what do we even mean by 'working' in the context of the marriage of arts and activism?…Understanding the forces at play may not allow us to predict exactly what will happen, but it helps us make sure that something happens, and then, once we've determined what has happened, refocus our efforts. (p. 3)

To help address some of the above questions and concerns, The Center conducted an eight-year study with 57 artistic activists (most of who are from the United States, with some from Canada, Germany, Spain, and Ireland). These activists reported that their work 'works' by presenting ideas "Æffectively" (catering to audience), creating conversations, revealing reality, generating affect and empathy, making openings ("circumventing usual defences" [sic]), causing disruption (creating shock or surprise), encouraging participation, aiding and amplifying existing movements, imagining new worlds, and doing something (impacting the artists themselves) (The Center for Artistic Activism, 2018, pp. 26–36).

Finally, in questioning the integrity and efficacy of craftivism, we must remember (as acknowledged earlier) that not all craftivist endeavors have been carried out by women identifying as "liberal" or "democrat" or advocating for what some consider liberal values. For example, the Sisters of the Good Shepherd created baby blankets in an effort "to save babies from abortion," believing that distributing baby blankets to pregnant women considering abortion "lets them know that someone cares about them" (Mandell, 2019, p. 6). In addition, in Ottowa, Canada, women knitted, crocheted, or sewed 6,978 baby booties and placed them in front of Canada's parliament buildings as a way to protest abortion (Mandell, 2019). Understanding how these messages gain traction through materiality fosters awareness of, and (perhaps) empathy for, counter narratives, as well as knowledge about how to increase our own rhetorical effectiveness.

Materiality in Pedagogy

Because the media targets viewers as consumers (Machin & van Leeuwen, 2016), and the Trump administration increasingly threatened freedom of the press (Pratte, 2019), critical media literacy has become vital to understanding the state of the world. Such literacy provides a foundation for thoughtful and ethical consideration of texts and their consequences. According to Huang (2015), critical media literacy, "is not only concerned with identifying how the media delineate people of different race, class, gender, and sexuality, and the consequences of such depiction, but more importantly emphasizes the production of counter narratives...". (p. 22)

But as previously established, literacy pertains to spoken and written linguistic text, new media, *and* embodied experiences that involve the senses (sight, sound, touch) (Pahl & Escott, 2015); and individual literate artifacts influence "collective existence" (Gries, 2015, p. xviii). Writing teachers can utilize past engagements with multimodality in effective ways, which avoids relying on the newest technology (Palmeri, 2012). That said, we should also avoid considering anything without the label "new media" as "old," as crafting "transforms old into new" (Bratich & Brush, 2011, p. 245).

In our classrooms, then, we should pay attention to students gravitating toward what they perceive as new and exciting—and therefore desired by an audience—rather than thinking critically about how their work meets the demands of rhetorical situations and contributes to important conversations. Every call for communication comes with an array of modes and materials from which to choose, requiring the composer to consider themselves and their message in relation to a particular audience (Kress, 2005). To fail to consider one's creation in relation to how it may impact an audience or community would be unethical (Baumstark, 2019).

Instructors and students must also give considerable thought to how others may use work in unintended ways (Breaux, 2017) and how desires for, and strategies to increase, inclusion can lead to exclusion. As even material texts can circulate broadly as the result of photographs snapped with cell phones and uploaded online, we must consider how people may understand, or even alter, texts. Eagerness can lead to unethical approaches to, or consequences of, a communicative act (Cipolla, 2019). Furthermore, as discussed earlier, valuing and privileging certain literacies or modes over others yields exclusion of people with particular subject positions and critical ideas. Students must understand that one can appreciate and value a tool, material, or technology while at the same time interrogate its potential drawbacks and think critically about how and why people use it, and what the consequences of that use are (Cipolla, 2019). Likewise, because assertions about people's "literacy" have supported oppression (Macedo, 2006), we must stress the multiplicity of the word and the fact that *literacies* change as social and cultural values, practices, infrastructures, and power dynamics change (Kellner & Share, 2009). Allowing students to "make" aids their understanding of "what counts as learning" (Garber et al., 2019) and, therefore, what counts as "literacy." Kellner and Share (2009) argue that teaching only the practical skills of making forces students "to merely reproduce hegemonic representations or express their voice without the awareness of ideological implications or any type of social critique" (p. 7). In order for students to benefit fully from acts of making, pedagogies must help them explore the cognitive intricacies of the process of making and disseminating artifacts.

The act of making (as with any physical activity) can actually enhance cognitive function (Huotilainen et al., 2018), which aids students' learning and understanding of knowledge transfer. As a matter of fact, "embodied cognition" refers to "experiences of the individual in interaction with the material and social environment" (Huotilainen et al., 2018, p. 4). The majority of the 3,545 knitters in Riley et al.'s (2013) study reported higher cognitive functioning, with 61% reporting that knitting aided concentration, 58% reporting that it benefitted memory, 47% reporting that they "usually" or "definitely" found knitting to help them "think through problems," and 39% reporting that it helped them "organize their thoughts" (p. 54). More specifically, participants reported improved cognitive skills in relation to "mathematics, planning and organizing, and visual/spatial awareness" (Riley et al., 2013, p. 55). Aligning with the work correlating materiality and activism, knitters also noted that learning a new skill came with feelings of confidence, adventurousness, self-sufficiency, and contentment (with the last two of these associated with producing goods for one's self or someone else) (Riley et al., 2013).

Learning a new skill and experimenting with materials via crafting also sets a healthy expectation for failure as part of the process; craft, therefore, can help students reconfigure notions of failure as a necessary component of success (Page & Thorsteinsson, 2018). Undoubtedly, many students today carry an increasing psychological and emotional burden. Much of their young lives seems determined by how well they thrive under pressure and compete against others. They must tend to high grade point averages and standardized test scores, show engagement in a variety of extracurricular activities, work part- or full-time jobs to earn places in higher education and the workforce, all while facing a plethora of environmental and social problems (global warming; mass shootings; racism; sexism; homophobia; xenophobia; and in 2020–2021, a pandemic). Amid teachers, coaches, bosses, school admissions personnel, and social media users, it seems that students may rarely find space in which they feel free of stringent evaluation, if not outright judgment. Additionally, the ways in which education systems assess student writing and other forms of composition often drastically misalign with the ways in which students actually write and compose in their everyday lives (Rowsell, 2020).

Under these circumstances, it is unsurprising that Page and Thorsteinsson's (2018) research revealed students' resistance to learning a craft if they perceived the result as unworthy of the time they would invest in the learning process; in other words, any use of their time must yield a justifiable end. Students who consider themselves creative, however, willingly engage in crafting for the emotional reward and, therefore, may have a different understanding of what makes an activity worthwhile (Page & Thorsteinsson, 2018).

Futterman Collier and Wayment (2018) gave 465 first-year undergraduates enrolled in a psychology course a list of 18 activities divided into three groups: domestic activities (such as baking, cooking, scrapbooking, gardening, and hunting and fishing), DIY activities (such as woodworking and working with electronics), and arts and crafts activities (such as quilting, drawing, painting, making jewelry and other art forms, and engaging in photography and film-making). Their research revealed that students engaged less in maker activities and more in domestic activities (followed by arts and working with electronics), perhaps because of limitations on time and lack of exposure to DIY and arts and crafts activities given their age (Futterman Collier & Wayment, 2018). Still, most students reported benefits of their maker activities as being more present or "in the moment," improving mood, and engaging socially, while some students reported benefits such as "[gaining or asserting] individuality, recycling, and engag[ing] in life" (Futterman Collier & Wayment, 2018, p. 1232).

Perhaps with these benefits in mind, Boon and Pentney (2017) incorporated knitting into their upper-division undergraduate course about feminist praxis, with knitting taking place during class discussion and between classes. Boon and Pentney (2017) posed questions to students such as:

> How would [you] determine the success of an activist project? [Can] success be quantified or measured?...What [is] political about the process? The product? The installation? What might resistance to knitting as activism be founded upon?...Is craftivism inclusive? Can it be exclusive? How? (p. 29)

Students in the course reported that knitting aided listening and allowing for, and engaging in, conversations about difficult, emotion-laden topics, while Boon and Pentney (2017) point out that it allowed for accommodation of various learning types.

Moreover (as discussed in Chapter 1), in Bex Lempert's (2003) "Family Violence" course, she tasked students with creating tee shirts in tribute to a victim or survivor of violence (themselves, someone they knew personally, or someone in the news); the assignment required a one-page narrative explaining their choice of woman to feature and their design choices. Bex Lempert (2003) asserts that the assignment allowed students to gain awareness of their own narratives and how cultural narratives shape them. Furthermore, allowing students to compose anonymously permitted disclosure with some control over how they subjected themselves to responses, and shed light on the possibility of choosing to not disclose as an assertion of agency (Bex Lempert, 2003). Students meanwhile reported that creating the tee shirts helped them "catalyze personal and emotional reactions to course content" (Bex Lempert, 2003, p. 481). As Roswell and Shillitoe (2019) articulate, the act of making draws from emotion to yield stories.

Bex Lempert (2003) additionally points to the use of the tee shirt project as a means to help students reconceptualize "objective and subjective knowledge" (p. 483). I began my teaching career eight years after Bex Lempert published her article, and in the decade since, I have found that, regardless of institution, my students have problematic notions of objectivity and subjectivity. In my experience with students, such notions come from (1) their understanding of composing as consisting of rules rather than conventions and (2) their overvaluing of STEM fields and undervaluing of non-STEM fields (noted by other professors as well, such as Zaloom, 2019). For instance, students often denounce the use of "I" in research papers, when in reality choosing to use "I" in a research-based composition would depend on the rhetorical situation—the discipline; the audience; the purpose of the text; the social context in which it was produced and will be read or viewed; and the conventions of specific journals, programs, etcetera. Also, many of my students report being drawn to STEM fields because of these fields' "objective" nature—much unlike writing, according to them. In reality, subjective experiences of scientists and social demands for certain kinds of scientific research inform work carried out in the sciences. Likewise, the types of evidence necessary to make and support claims depends on the research question; some research questions demand personal accounts in order to draw reasonable and ethical conclusions or responses.

To this end, Cipolla (2019) writes of "feminist maker pedagogy" whereby students learn through doing in laboratory and other contexts, aiming to understand how they "fit into" those contexts (p. 262). Specifically, students "consider the radical potential of building from scratch in a digital age, the ethical imperative to re-write the world around us, and the philosophical experience of tinkering with knowledge itself" (p. 262). Like some researchers cited earlier in the chapter, Cipolla (2019) values the role of frustration in having students make, particularly as it relates to resilience. She advocates for students to "sit within this paralysis" of frustration in order to devote appropriate time to figuring out their dilemma and moving forward (Cipolla, 2019, p. 278).

Encompassing new understandings and moving forward, the Social Justice Sewing Academy, founded by Sara Trail in 2017, brings the art of patchwork to schools, prisons, and community centers across the United States, with the goal of allowing young people the opportunity to create and share personal stories (McGovern, 2019). Volunteers sew the patch work created by participants into quilts that get displayed in galleries; an artist statement accompanies each patchwork block (McGovern, 2019). Of course, engaging students via materiality does not have to occur on such a large scale or within a specific context such as the Social Justice Sewing Academy.

In my own writing classes, I allow for digital and non-digital composing in the forms of "mini makerspaces" and larger assignments. Adopted from T Passwater at Syracuse University, the mini makerspaces work by giving students "scenarios" to which they respond with a variety of materials (Play-Doh, Legos, paint and markers, pipe cleaners, personal cell phones, computers, etc.) that I have set up in stations around the classroom (see Appendix A for a list of sample scenarios). Compositions created in mini makerspaces are temporary, often deconstructed for the next group within a matter of ten minutes. Rather than grading the work, I ask students to reflect (in a free-write, small-group discussion, or large-group discussion) on the challenges and affordances of communicating in various forms. For larger assignments that ask students to compose with materials outside of Word documents, paper, and writing utensils, I grade the process rather than the product. Similar to Bex Lempert's (2003) one-page reflective paper, I have students compose an informal 2–3-page paper detailing the rhetorical decisions they made, and sometimes, connecting the arguments made in their compositions to course readings (see Appendix B for a sample assignment sheet).

In response to a public scholarship assignment, one of my students, Amber Smith, sewed an outfit that advocated for awareness of stereotypes of, and discrimination against, people with schizophrenia. An interactive website that explained the meaning behind each design feature accompanied the outfit (see Appendix C for Amber's full write-up). The course in which Amber completed her work had a theme of "Psychology of Being an Undergrad," partially described on the syllabus per the following:

> By examining common cultural narratives of undergraduate identity (in terms of psychological concepts like self-actualization, archetypes, mental health and mindfulness, and the psychology of technology), we will explore the following questions: How are notions of 'humanity' constructed rhetorically in relation to understandings of mental health, mindfulness, well-being, and technology? How does the 'undergraduate student' identity align or not align with these notions? To respond to these questions, we will read, listen to, and analyze a variety of texts (e.g. book chapters, journal articles, essays, social media posts, podcasts, and TED Talks), and produce texts such as personal and research-based essays and multimedia.

Amber actually wore her final creation on campus, and in a later reflection, she wrote:

> My favorite form of art is sewing clothes and I had not previously considered the idea of using components of clothing to make a statement. Without yet knowing what my project was going to be, I spent

the following weeks brainstorming what I could sew that is related to a course on mental health and wellbeing. My brain instantly gravitated toward working with denim (for the symbolism of its strength, the colors, versatility, and for something different from what I have typically sewed before...I made deliberate choices about the fabric, the colors utilized, the asymmetry and imperfection in style, the placement of each item (example: covering my head), and even the font...[L]ike writing, I found the project difficult since I found there to never be a true 'ending'... When I wore the outfit, I received quite a few comments, mostly directed at the hat or the coordination of the outfit. In response to most of the compliments, I said "thank you" and shyly, trying to be as modest as possible, exclaimed that I made the outfit. I told a few of my friends the significance—that the outfit symbolizes mental illnesses and aims to reduce stigma... but I wonder if the stigma of mental illnesses, the very essence of the issue that I am trying to dismantle with my project, held me back from sharing more.

Her work exemplifies what can come from giving students opportunities to think differently through the work we assign.

While Amber was a sewer prior to enrolling in the course, the course taught her about the potential rhetorical implications of her creations. Furthermore, we can see from her discussion about thinking through different materials, and ultimately choosing denim, that she considers the affordances and limitations of materials, rather than gravitating toward more familiar materials. Even if her product had never materialized—literally—into something viewed outside of the course, she would have thought critically about rhetorical situations and how to meet their demands, and about *how* to transfer knowledge about writing and rhetoric to other courses and to contexts outside of the academy altogether. Forcing her to work with digital materials would address some of the same goals, but would have failed to show Amber how to utilize her talents and hobbies for particular purposes. It may have also implicitly sent the message to Amber that her sewing is less valuable than what she can do with digital technology alone.

Intersections Between Materiality, Activism, Silence, and Pedagogy

Just as all materials or tools have their affordances and limitations, so do teaching practices. Making, especially in the presence of others, involves self-expression and experimentation, which may leave students feeling vulnerable and intimidated (Huotilainen et al., 2018), despite benefits such as trust-building and the unity that can come from multiple perspectives and ideas while making together (Hackney et al., 2016). Any act of making can yield frustration and unplanned difficulties that require time, patience, and problem-solving skills (Futterman Collier & Wayment, 2018), despite the benefits of increased cognition, liberation, and relaxation. In fact, some research has associated high arousal brought on by negative emotions with increased creativity (Tidikis, 2012). In other words, we must remain mindful of how attempts to empower students actually strip them of their agency, of how what we hope they gain comes with great sacrifice, and of how asking (or demanding) them to use their voice in some ways (or with particular tools/materials) silences them in others—or silences their silence. We can strive to create safe spaces for students to be who they are while asking them to explore what they are not.

As I wrote in my article, "Beyond Digital: What Women's Activism Reveals About Material Multimodal Composition Pedagogy" (2017), my work with the CP raises questions about the importance of visual communication in our society as it pertains to communicators and audiences. To reiterate what I state earlier in the chapter, though technology has allowed people to engage in visual communication more often, technology may fail to motivate people to create with other materials (Corey, 2017). The tee shirts in the archive I analyzed suggest that creators may struggle with such a task or not work to their full creative potential, therefore having implications for activist and pedagogical practices (Corey, 2017). The CP seems to foster "writing [as] a way of learning, a way of looking for allies who are looking for us, a way of winning recognition and resources vital to changing minds and changing social relations" (Tomlinson, 2010, p. 25 in Corey, 2017, para. 29). Also as I argued in 2017, for students to gain "a rich understanding of how writing and multimodal composition achieve... rhetorical goals, they need to have not only the broad understanding and redefining of 'composition' but a broader understanding of 'multimedia' and its function in relation to audience and purpose (para. 29).

Moreover, the role of silence in activism, mediated through a variety of 'composed engagements' with people, ideas, and the physical world, demonstrates ways in which the use of silence in our classrooms can foster meaningful engagement with ourselves and the world in which we live.

Materiality offers one way of mediating the interaction between silence, intellectual growth, and social engagement.

Again, the aim here is not to demonize digital or electronic technologies in favor of romanticizing materiality, but rather to speak to the importance of thinking ethically about any tools and materials we use, and the creations that they yield. I aim, furthermore, to remind readers of the affordances of materials in a society that seems to privilege digital and electronic technology. Many of our students remain familiar with digital tools, even when some of them still lack access to those tools. Challenging students to think through ideas not only in relation to theories presented in class, but in relation to the practicality of developing and communicating ideas through a variety of available materials, also offers a small lesson in the necessity of flexibility and creativity to solve problems. In other words, thinking about rhetorical situations (audience, purpose, text, and context) means thinking critically and ethically, and maybe even resiliently.

Discussion Questions

1. Drawing on Corbett's (2019) notion of "crafterthought," think about subject positions that may be involved in a cause you care about. What kinds of "crafterthought" questions can you construct for those subject positions? What kinds of material compositions could you create to advocate for your cause? How would you make those compositions rhetorically effective? (Think about context, audience, subject positions, Kairos, ethos, pathos, and logos.)
2. Think of a cause you care about. What movements or projects have circulated regarding that cause, and how have attempts for inclusion regarding that cause inadvertently enacted exclusion?
3. Think of a multimodal composition you've created in the past or might create in the future. How do empathy and intellect intersect with content and form (genre/product)?

References

Addison, J. (2010). Researching literacy as a lived experience. In E. E. Schell & K. J. Rawson (Eds.), *Rhetorica in motion: Feminist rhetorical methods & methodologies* (pp. 136–151). University of Pittsburgh Press.

Andersson, U., Edgren, M., Karlsson, L., & Nilsson, G. (2019). Introductory chapter: Rape narratives in motion. In U. Andersson, M. Edgren, L. Karlsson, & G. Nilsson (Eds.), *Rape Narratives in Motion* (pp. 1–16). Palgrave Macmillan. https://doi.org/10.1007/978-3-030-13852-3

Ann, F. C., & Wayment, H. A. (2018). Psychological benefits of the "Maker" or do-it-yourself movement in young adults: A pathway towards subjective well-being. *Journal of Happiness Studies, 19*(4), 1217–1239. https://doi.org/10.1007/s10902-017-9866-x

Ault, A. (2019, March 19). These haunting red dresses memorialize murdered and missing Indigenous women. *Smithsonian Magazine*. https://www.smithsonianmag.com/smithsonian-institution/these-haunting-red-dresses-memorialize-murdered-and-missing-indigenous-women-180971730/

Baker, C. N. & Bevacqua, M. (2018). Challenging narratives of the anti-rape movement's decline. *Violence Against Women, 24*(3), 350–376. https://doi.org/10.1177/1077801216689164

Baumstark, M. C. (2019). Social utopia: Craft and progress. In E. Garber, L. Hochtritt, & M. Sharma (Eds.) *Makers, crafters, educators: Working for cultural change* (pp. 212–215). Routledge. https://doi.org/10.4324/9781315179254

Bex Lempert, L. (2003). The clothesline project as student production: Creativity, voice, and action. *Teaching Sociology, 31*(4), 478–484. https://doi.org/10.2307/3211371

Bezemer, J., & Kress, G. (2008). Writing in multimodal texts: A social semiotic account of designs for learning. *Written Communication, 25*(2), 166–195. https://doi.org/10.1177/0741088307313177

Boon, S., & Pentney, B. (2017). Knitting the feminist self: Craftivism, yarn bombing and the navigation of feminist spaces. In G. Bonifacio (Ed.), *Global currents in gender and feminisms: Canadian and international perspectives* (pp. 21–34). Emerald Publishing Limited. https://doi.org/10.1108/9781787144835

Brandt, D. (2001). Sponsors of literacy. In E. Cushman, E. R. Kintgen, B. M. Kroll, & M. Rose (Eds.), *Literacy: A critical sourcebook* (pp. 555–571). Bedford/St. Martin's.

Bratich, J. Z., & Brush, H. M. (2011). Fabricating activism: Craft-work, popular culture, gender. *Utopian Studies, 22*(2), 233–260. https://doi.org/10.5325/utopianstudies.22.2.0233

Breaux, C. (2017). Why making? *Computers and Composition, 44*, 27–35. https://doi:10.1016

Cipolla, C. (2019). Build it better: Tinkering in feminist maker pedagogy. *Women's Studies, 48*(3), 261–282. https://doi.org/10.1080/00497878.2019.1593842

Coogan, D. J. (2010). Sophists for social change. In J. M. Ackerman & D. J. Coogan (Eds.), *The public work of rhetoric: Citizen-scholars and civic engagement* (pp. 157–174). University of South Carolina Press.

Cook, K. (2019). EmboDIYing disruption: Queer, feminist and inclusive digital archaeologies. *European Journal of Archaeology, 22*(3), 398–414. https://doi.org/10.1017/eaa.2019.23

Cope, B., & Kalantzis, M. (2009). "Multiliteracies": New literacies, new learning. *Pedagogies: An International Journal, 4,* 164–195. https://doi.org/10.1080/15544800903076044

Corbett, S. (2019, January 29). How a gentle protest with hand-embroidered hankies helped bring higher wages for retail employees. Ideas.Ted.Com. https://ideas.ted.com/how-a-gentle-protest-with-hand-embroidered-hankies-helped-bring-higher-wages-for-retail-employees/

Corey, J. R. (2017). Beyond 'digital': What women's activism reveals about material multimodal composition pedagogy. *The Journal of Multimodal Rhetorics, 1*(1).

Cushman, E. (1996). The rhetorician as an agent of social change. *College Composition and Communication, 47*(1), 7–28. https://doi.org/10.2307/358271

Dehoff, S., & Swiencicki, J. (2019). "Consent Trumps Everything": The Clothesline art project and the election politics of sexual assault. In H. Mandell (Ed.), *Crafting dissent: Handicraft as protest from the American Revolution to the Pussyhats* (pp. 201–211). Rowman & Littlefield Publishers.

Elsley, J. (1992). The rhetoric of the NAMES Project AIDS quilt: Reading the text(ile). In E. S. Nelson (Ed.), *AIDS: The literary response* (pp. 187–196). Twayne.

Exhibition put up clothes from women to prove they were NOT "Asking For It." (2019, July 3). Femalista. Retrieved January 25, 2020, from https://www.femalista.com/exhibition-put-up-clothes-from-women-to-prove-they-were-not-asking-for-it/?fbclid=IwAR2DZw7FZDDTdB-T0qzFdQLG1_P-UIoJHOjmC0zlxrko-932CUy_eWQ_qp0

Ey, M. (2019). Purling politics: Crafting resistance with the Knitting Nannas Against Gas. *International Journal for Critical Geographies, 18*(4), 957–976.

Fileborn, B. (2017). Justice 2.0: Street harassment victims' use of social media and online activism as sites of informal justice. *British Journal of Criminology, 57*(6) 1482–1501. https://doi.org/10.1093/bjc/azw093

Futterman Collier, A., & Wayment, H. A. (2018). Psychological benefits of the "Maker" or do-it-yourself movement in young adults: A pathway towards subjective well- being. *Journal of Happiness Studies, 19*(4), 1217–1239. http://dx.doi.org/10.1007/s10902-017-9866-x

Gallucci, N. (2020, May 23). *Sidewalk chalk is having a real moment during the pandemic*. Mashable. https://mashable.com/article/sidewalk-chalk-art-murals-coronavirus-pandemic/

Garber, E., Hochtritt, L., & Sharma, M. (2019). Introduction: Makers, crafters, educators: Working for cultural change. In E. Garber, L. Hochtritt, & M. Sharma (Eds.) *Makers, Crafters, Educators: Working for Cultural Change* (pp. 1–14). Routledge. https://doi.org/10.4324/9781315179254

Gee, J. P. (2001). Literacy, discourse, and linguistics: Introduction and what is literacy? In E. Cushman, E. R. Kintgen, B. M. Kroll, & M. Rose (Eds.), *Literacy: A critical sourcebook* (pp. 525–544). Bedford/St. Martin's.

George, D. (2002). The word on the street: Public discourse in a culture of disconnect. *Reflections, 2*(2), 5–18.

Gollihue, K. N. (2019). Re-making the makerspace: Body, power, and identity in critical making practices. *Computers and Composition, 53*, 21–33. https://doi.org/10.1016/j.compcom.2019.05.002

Grabill, J. T. (2010). On being useful: Rhetoric and the work of engagement. In J. Ackerman & D. Coogan (Eds.), *The public work of rhetoric: Citizen-scholars and civic engagement* (pp. 193–208). University of South Carolina Press. https://doi.org/10.2307/j.ctv6wghr9

Greer, B. (2011). Craftivist history. In M. E. Buszek (Ed.), *Extra/ordinary: Craft and Contemporary Art* (pp. 175–183). Duke University Press. https://doi.org/10.1215/9780822392873

Gries, L. (2015). *Still life with rhetoric: A new materialist approach for visual rhetorics*. Utah State University Press.

Hackney, F., Maughan, H., & Desmarais, S. (2016). The power of quiet: Re-making affective amateur and professional textiles agencies. *Journal of Textile Design Research and Practice, 4*(1), 33–62. https://doi.org/10.1080/20511787.2016.1256139

Hatch, M. (2014). *The maker movement manifesto: Rules for innovation in the new world of crafters, hackers, and tinkerers*. McGraw-Hill.

Heath, S. B. (2001). Protean shapes in literacy events: Ever-shifting oral and literate traditions. In E. Cushman, E. R. Kintgen, B. M. Kroll, & M. Rose (Eds.), *Literacy: A critical sourcebook* (pp. 443–466). Bedford/St. Martin's.

Higgins, L., Long, E., & Flower, L. (2006). Community literacy: A rhetorical model for personal and public inquiry. *Community Literacy Journal, 1*(1), 9–43.

Hipple, P. C. (2000). Clothing their resistance in hegemonic dress: The Clothesline Project's response to violence against women. *Clothing and Textiles Research Journal, 18*(3), 163–177. https://doi.org/10.1177/0887302X0001800305

Hira, A., & Hynes, M. M. (2018). People, means, and activities: A conceptual framework for realizing the educational potential of makerspaces. *Education Research International, 2018*, 1–10. https://doi.org/10.1155/2018/6923617

Hocks, M. E., & Balsamo, A. (2003). Women making multimedia: Possibilities for feminist activism. In B. E. Kolko (Ed.), *Virtual publics: Policy and community in an electronic age* (pp. 192–214). Columbia University Press.

Huang, S. (2015). The intersection of multimodality and critical perspective: Multimodality as subversion. *Language Learning & Technology, 19*(2), 21–37. https://doi.org/10125/44428

Huotilainen, M., Rankanen, M., Groth, C., Seitamaa-Hakkarainen, P., & Mäkelä, M. (2018). Why our brains love arts and crafts. *FormAkademisk, 11*(2), 1–18. https://doi.org/10.7577/formakademisk.1908

Jefferies, J. (2001). Textiles. In F. Carson & C. Pajaczkowska (Eds.), *Feminist visual culture* (pp. 189–205). Routledge.

Julier, L. (1994). Private texts and social activism: Reading the Clothesline Project. *English Education, 26*(4), 249–259.

Keller, J., Mendes, K., & Ringrose, J. (2016). Speaking 'unspeakable things': Documenting digital feminist responses to rape culture. *Journal of Gender Studies, 27*(1), 22–36. https://doi.org/10.1080/09589236.2016.1211511

Kellner, D., & Share, J. (2009). Critical media literacy, democracy, and the reconstruction of education. In D. Macedo & S. R. Steinberg (Eds.), *Media literacy: A reader* (pp. 3–23). Peter Lang.

Kim, Y. E., Edouard, K., Alderfer, K., & Smith, B. K. (2018). *Report: Making culture: A national study of education makerspaces*. Drexel University ExCITe Center. https://drexel.edu/excite/engagement/learning-innovation/making-culture-report/

Kock, C., & Villadsen, L. S. (2012). Introduction: Citizenship as a rhetorical practice. In C. Kock & L. S. Villadsen (Eds.), *Rhetorical citizenship and public deliberation* (pp. 1–10). Pennsylvania State University Press.

Kress, G. (2005). Gains and losses: New forms of text, knowledge and learning. *Computers and Composition, 22*, 5–22. https://doi.org/10.1016/j.compcom.2004.12.004

Kress, G. (2010). *Multimodality: A social semiotic approach to contemporary communication*. Routledge. https://doi.org/10.4324/9780203970034

Kress, G. R. (2003). *Literacy in the new media age*. Routledge. https://doi.org/10.4324/9780203299234

Kress, G. R., & van Leeuwen, T. V. (2006). *Reading images: The grammar of visual design* (2nd ed.). Routledge.

Lashgari, D. (1995). *Violence, silence, and anger: Women's writing as transgression*. University Press of Virginia.

Lieblich, A. (2013). Healing plots: Writing and reading in life-stories groups. *Qualitative Inquiry*, *19*(1), 46–52. https://doi.org/10.1177/107780041 2462982

Loizou, N. (2019, September 26). Online activism is dismantling barriers, but not for everyone. Raconteur. https://www.raconteur.net/technology/online-activism-pro-con

Long, E. (2008). *Community literacy and the rhetoric of local publics*. Parlor Press.

Macedo, D. (2006). *Literacies of power: What Americans are not allowed to know*. Westview Press.

Machin, D., & van Leeuwen, T. (2016). Multimodality, politics and ideology. *Journal of Language and Politics Multimodality, Politics and Ideology*, *15*(3), 243–258. https://doi.org/10.1075/jlp.15.3.01mac

Malema, D. R., & Naidoo, S. (2017). The role of community arts and crafts in the empowerment of women living in a rural environment. *World Leisure Journal*, *6*(2), 54–60. https://doi.org/10.1080/16078055.2017.1393878

Mandell, H. (2019). Introduction: Yarn, thread, scissors, fabric: A crafter's toolkit for mending democracy as engaged citizens. In H. Mandell (Ed.), *Crafting dissent: Handicraft as protest from the American Revolution to the Pussyhats* (pp. 1–11). Rowman & Littlefield Publishers.

Markus, S. (2019). Craftivism from Philomena to the Pussyhat. In H. Mandell (Ed.), *Crafting dissent: Handicraft as protest from the American Revolution to the Pussyhats* (pp. 15–32). Rowman & Littlefield Publishers.

Marsh, J., Kumpulainen, K., Nisha, B., Velicu, A., Blum-Ross, A., Hyatt, D., Jónsdóttir, S. R., Levy, R., Little, S., Marusteru, G., Ólafsdóttir, M. E., Sandvik, K., Scott, F., Thestrup, K., Arnseth, H. C., Dýrfjörð, K., Jornet, A., Kjartansdóttir, S. H., Pahl, K., … Thorsteinsson, G. (2017). *Makerspaces in the early years: A literature review*. University of Sheffield.

McGovern, A. (2019). *Craftivism and yarn bombing: A criminological exploration*. Palgrave Macmillan. https://doi.org/10.1057/978-1-137-57991-1

Naím, M. (2014, April 7). Why street protests don't work: How can so many demonstrations accomplish so little? *The Atlantic*. https://www.theatlantic.com/international/archive/2014/04/why-street-protests-dont-work/360264/

New London Group. (1996). A pedagogy of multiliteracies: Designing social futures. *Harvard Educational Review*, *66*(1), 60–93. https://doi.org/10.17763/haer.66.1.17370n67v22j160u

Page, T., & Thorsteinsson, G. (2018). The significance of practicing craft in the modern society. *i-Manager's Journal on Educational Psychology*, *12*(3), 1–12. https://doi.org/10.26634/jpsy.12.3.14662

Pahl, K. & Escott, H. (2015). Materialising literacies. In J. Rowsell & K. Pahl (Eds.), *The Routledge Handbook of Literacy Studies* (pp. 489–503). Routledge. https://doi.org/10.4324/9781315717647

Palmeri, J. (2012). *Remixing composition: A history of multimodal writing pedagogy.* Southern Illinois University Press. https://doi.org/10.1080/07350198.2013.828553

Parker, R. (1984). *The subversive stitch: Embroidery and the making of the feminine.* Routledge

Pottinger, L. (2016). Planting the seeds of a quiet activism. *Area, 49*(2), 215–222. https://doi.org/10.1111/area.12318

Powell, A. (2015). Seeking rape justice: Formal and informal responses to sexual violence through technosocial counter-publics. *Theoretical Criminology, 19*(4), 571–588. https://doi.org/10.1177/1362480615576271

Pratte, A. (2019, September 7). Trump 2020 plan: New threats to press freedom and trust in media, pillars of our democracy. *USA Today.* https://www.usatoday.com/story/opinion/2019/09/07/trump-2020-plan-new-risks-press-freedom-trust-in-media-column/2231149001/

Riley, J., Corkhill, B., & Morris, C. (2013). The benefits of Knitting for personal and social wellbeing in adulthood: Findings from an international survey. *British Journal of Occupational Therapy, 76*(2), 50–57. https://doi.org/10.4276/030802213x13603244419077

Robertson, K. (2011). Rebellious doilies and subversive stitches: Writing a craftivist history. In M.E. Buszek (Ed.), *Extra/ordinary: Craft and Contemporary Art* (pp. 184–203). Duke University Press. https://doi.org/10.1215/9780822392873

Rosenwald, G. C., & Ochberg, R. L. (1992). Introduction: Life stories, cultural politics, and self-understanding. In G. C. Rosenwald (Author) & R. L. Ochberg (Ed.), *Storied lives: The cultural politics of self-understanding* (pp. 1–18). Yale University Press.

Rowsell, J. (2020). "How emotional do I make it?": Making a stance in multimodal compositions. *Journal of Adolescent & Adult Literacy, 63*(6), 627–637. https://doi.org/10.1002/jaal.1034

Rowsell, J., & Shillitoe, M. (2019). The craftivists: Pushing for affective, materially informed pedagogy. *British Journal of Educational Technology, 50*(4), 1544–1559. https://doi.org/10.1111/bjet.12773

Salter, M. (2013). Justice and revenge in online counter-publics: Emerging responses to sexual violence in the age of social media. *Crime Media Culture, 9*(3), 225–242. https://doi.org/10.1177/1741659013493918

Serafini, F. (2010). Reading multimodal texts: Perceptual, structural and ideological perspectives. *Children's Literature in Education, 41*(2), 85–104. https://doi.org/10.1007/s10583-010-9100-5

Shipka, J. (2011). *Toward a composition made whole*. University of Pittsburgh Press. https://doi.org/10.2307/j.ctt5hjqkk

Short, A. (2018, December 9). Benefits of sewing and crafting for mental health. Your Coffee Break. https://www.yourcoffeebreak.co.uk/whats-on-health-fitness/26338782155/benefits-of-sewing-and-crafting-for-mental-health/

Street, B. V. (1984). *Literacy in theory and practice*. Cambridge University Press.

The Center for Artistic Activism. (2018). *Report: Assessing the impact of artistic activism*. The Center for Artistic Activism. https://c4aa.org/wp-content/uploads/2018/03/Assessing-the-Impact-of-Artistic-Activism.pdf

Tidikis, V. (2012). *Mood and creativity: The mediating role of attention*. Old Dominion University. https://doi.org/10.25777/4kr8-w293

Tomlinson, B. (2010). *Feminism and affect at the scene of argument: Beyond the trope of the angry feminist*. Temple University Press.

Warshauer Freedman, S. & Ball, A. F. (2004). Ideological becoming: Bakhtinian concepts to guide the study of language, literacy, and learning. In A. F. Ball & S. Warshauer Freedman (Eds.), *Bakhtinian perspectives on language, literacy, and learning* (pp. 3–33). Cambridge University Press. https://doi.org/10.1017/CBO9780511755002

Willett, R. (2016). Making, makers, and makerspaces: A discourse analysis of professional journal articles and blog posts about makerspaces in public libraries. *Library Quarterly: Information, Community, Policy, 86*(3), 313–329. https://doi.org/10.1086/686676

Willingham, A. (2018, March 24). Why you'll see a lot of 'evil eye' gloves at the March for Our Lives. CNN. https://www.cnn.com/2018/03/23/us/evil-eye-gloves-march-for-our-lives-trnd/index.html

Wolf, M., & McQuitty, S. (2011). Understanding the do-it-yourself consumer: DIY motivations and outcomes. *AMS Review, 1*(3), 154–170. https://doi.org/10.1007/s13162-011-0021-2

Wysocki, A. (2005). awaywithwords: On the possibilities in unavailable designs. *Computers & Composition, 22*(1), 55–62. https://doi.org/10.1016/j.compcom.2004.12.011

Zaloom, C. (2019). STEM is overrated: College is not just job prep, and the job market changes constantly. *The Atlantic*. https://www.theatlantic.com/ideas/archive/2019/09/college-not-job-prep/597487/

Zarrelli, N. (2017, June 1). *The wartime spies who used knitting as an espionage tool*. Atlas Obscura. https://www.atlasobscura.com/articles/knitting-spies-wwi-wwii

Zweiman, J. (2019). Forward: Reflections on craft—And craft-makers—As change agents. In H. Mandell (Ed.), *Crafting dissent: Handicraft as protest from the American Revolution to the Pussyhats* (pp. xii–xiv). Rowman & Littlefield Publishers.

CHAPTER 5

Future Directions

Like all research, the scope of my study addresses certain variables while neglecting others and, therefore, responds to some questions while raising others. First, as more briefly discussed in Chapter 3, this work does not account for CP participants' explanations of their design decisions. While such information would, of course, prove valuable in making additional sense of the data, it would only account for what participants notice and understand about their own involvement. Looking at the data without participants' accounts shows us the narratives implicated in tee shirts, which may or may not veer from what participants *intended* or from what participants recognize about their work. Similarly, without volunteers for interviews, this study cannot account for subject positions like race, gender identity, or sexual orientation. Future researchers may wish to examine the composing practices of specific populations, given that the cultural narratives that influence their identity and their communication practices may yield different results and have different implications for the fields of rhetoric and composition, political science, women's and activist studies, psychology, social work, and criminology.

Second, an initial analysis of this data was completed near the end of Barack Obama's presidency (through December 2015). The social upheaval that took place during Donald Trump's presidency could have altered decisions regarding the content and design of CP shirts created and contributed to the archive during that time. With Trump's presidency having ended in January 2021, researchers may wish to, if possible, examine activist materials created between 2016 and 2020 and compare them to those that precede and proceed them. Still, the archive from which this data emerged remains on display at the time of this writing (when the CP event is held), and many of the cultural narratives that existed at the time of analysis remain prevalent narratives today (such as those pertaining to re-victimization discussed in Chapter 3). Moreover, tee shirts in the "Consent Trumps Everything" CP, held after I completed my analysis, displayed messages similar to those in the archive I examined—such as calls for people to stand up and messages condemning silence (Dehoff & Swiencicki, 2019). The "Consent Trumps Everything" CP also showed the use of the tee shirt as a symbol of embodiment, as "the shirt can talk back to Trump's comments in a way that women can't" (Dehoff & Swiencicki, 2019, p. 209). Perhaps most compelling, Julier's (2000) study of CP tee shirts revealed results similar to those revealed in my study with regards to "abbreviated elliptical forms" of messages (p. 378)—despite the fact that they were conducted fifteen years apart—therefore suggesting the relevancy of these results today.

Finally, in regards to pedagogy, my work consists of theorizing the relationship between findings regarding material approaches to activism and composition pedagogy. My work contains a composition and reflection from one of my students, along with practical pedagogical tools. But future work may wish to examine experiences with material composing on a much larger scale and with marginalized populations in particular. For example, Tardy (2005) notes that opportunities to compose outside of linguistic or alphabetic texts may lessen anxiety about communicating in another language and enhance expression of individuality for multilingual writers or those who generally struggle in writing and English courses. Tardy (2005) makes clear that such an assertion is not meant to suggest that composing primarily via visual modes is "easier" but that it offers "different possibilities" from which at least some students may benefit (p. 19).

References

Dehoff, S., & Swiencicki, J. (2019). "Consent Trumps Everything": The Clothesline art project and the election politics of sexual assault. In H.

Mandell (Ed.), *Crafting dissent: Handicraft as protest from the American Revolution to the Pussyhats* (pp. 201–211). Rowman & Littlefield Publishers.

Julier, L. (2000). Voices from the line: The Clothesline Project as healing text. In C. M. Anderson & M. M. MacCurdy (Eds.), *Writing and healing: Toward an informed practice* (pp. 357–384). National Council of Teachers of English.

Tardy, C. M. (2005). Expressions of disciplinarity and individuality in multimodal genre. *Computers and Composition, 22*, 319–336. https://doi.org/10.1016/j.compcom.2005.05.00

Appendix A: Mini Makerspace Scenarios (From T Passwater)

1. Reflect on your first semester at college. Compose a response that touches on the highlights or low spots in the semester.
2. You're going to be late for class! Compose something for your instructor to either let them know or apologize.
3. You want to break up with your significant other. Compose something to let them know.
4. Your best friend just went through a rough break up. Compose something to console them or respond to that situation.
5. Two celebrities have gotten into a Twitter war and made #NoTeaNoShade a trending hashtag as more people get involved. How might you enter or respond to that conversation?
6. The Student Government is having a fundraiser to support next year's homecoming. Compose some form of advertising for the fundraiser.
7. Oh no! Your next paper/project has been lost! Quickly rewrite your project as best you can from memory with the material or technology in front of you.
8. The university president needs to be aware of one thing (your choice). How will you address/explain this to him/her/them?
9. Good golly your instructor's swell! How might you write him/her/them a thank you note?
10. You are about to attend a student protest regarding the social issue you are most passionate about. Create an expressive or persuasive

composition to communicate your thoughts or feelings to protest viewers.
11. You've decided to begin branding yourself for your desired post-college career. Create an artifact for your brand.
12. You're trying to explain to your writing teacher just how much you love/hate writing. But the teacher just isn't getting it. Try explaining it in a different form.
13. Ahhh! You just had an amazing experience. But the pictures you took were accidentally deleted from your phone and there was no room in the cloud. Create something to replace your photographs.
14. Give advice about this class to future students.
15. Your teacher is making you participate in this weird thing called a "Maker Space." You have a lot of thoughts about this—but you don't want to express them verbally. Either your enthusiasm for the activity will appear as sucking up or your annoyance will upset the teacher. Communicate your feelings by creating something.

Appendix B: Public Scholarship Assignment Sheet

Points:

Due Date:

Purpose:
Your Cultural Analysis & Argument assignment required you to rhetorically analyze a cultural artifact and draw from that analysis a research question. To respond to the question, you found, evaluated, and integrated a variety of scholarly and popular sources into an academic paper that made and supported an argument. You will now take an idea/argument from that work and present it to an audience of your choosing. To do this, you will draw on class discussions and readings from *Understanding Rhetoric*. The assignment addresses the following course objectives:

(1) Situate writing for specific audiences (In order to effectively advance their position within their fields of inquiry, scholarly writers need to be aware of disciplinary conventions and expectations.)
(2) Transfer writing knowledge into situations beyond WRT 101 (Even as scholarly writers situate their writing for specific audiences, they also need to transfer knowledge and practices across disciplines and contexts.)

Audience:
You will determine your audience. You will need to consider how the audience influences the content you present and the genre in which you present it. Therefore, you will consider relationships between alphabetic text and visual representations of concepts; advantages and limitations of different types of media; and rhetorically appropriate uses of language, citations, color, layout, sound, and other elements involved in composing.

Assignment:
This assignment has two components: (1) a composition that communicates an idea/argument from your Cultural Analysis & Argument paper and (2) a brief write-up (2–3 pages) that explains the choices you made in creating the composition.

First, you will choose one of the following ways to present your research/argument:

- an infographic in which you display your research as a data-rich visualization (digital or material)
- a visual argument for which you choose a medium to display your research (slide show, puppet show, video, play, TED Talk, sculpture, series of memes, painting, something you build, etc.)
- a tee shirt (You can purchase a tee shirt at a thrift store and use materials from my office.)
- a blog or website (Tumblr, Wordpress, Expressions, Wix, etc.) in which you write about your research, drawing on links, visuals, and other multimodal elements
- a podcast
- a comic that aims to create awareness of an issue or educate a particular audience (You may draw this or use a free digital program.)
- a draft of a submission to an undergraduate research journal (You need to actually find an undergraduate research journal and write according to its submission guidelines.)
- a proposal and presentation for an undergraduate research conference (You need to actually find a "call for proposals" (CFP) for an undergraduate conference and write according to its submission guidelines. I expect you to do the presentation, either via video or poster board).

Then, in a brief write-up, you will discuss the purpose of the form in which you present your research (what are you trying to communicate and why are you communicating it in that genre/form?), the rhetorical choices you made in regards to the elements listed in the Evaluation Criteria, and your experiences communicating your results in your chosen form.

Evaluation Criteria:
Public Scholarship

- Appropriate response to the assignment
- Evidence of critical thinking and reflection
- Awareness of the specified audience, which includes consideration of content and genre; relationships between alphabetic text and visual representations of concepts; advantages and limitations of different types of media; rhetorically appropriate uses of language, citations, color, layout, sound, and other elements involved in composing; ethos, pathos, logos, and Kairos
- Presentation of error-free texts (as rhetorically appropriate)
- Completion of a professional-grade communicative product

Helpful Resources (not an Exhaustive List):

- Google.com (Google is a great place to find samples of the genres you wish to compose. Make sure, however, that the samples are provided by credible sources.)
- Local craft stores (can be used for infographics, comics, tee shirts, or other works of art): Michaels Arts & Crafts, JoAnn Fabrics, Hancock Fabrics, Hobby Lobby, Binders Discount Art, Pearl Art & Craft, Utrecht Art Supplies
- YouTube.com (YouTube is full of tutorials for how to create videos and other multimodal compositions.)
- https://www.canva.com/create/infographics/ (infographics)
- http://piktochart.com/ (infographics)
- https://www.figma.com/ (infographics and other design products)
- https://www.oberlo.com/blog/best-free-video-editing-software (video)
- https://wordpress.com/ (blogs)
- https://www.tumblr.com/ (blogs)
- https://www.wix.com/ (website)
- http://www.makebeliefscomix.com/Comix/ (comics)

- http://www.toondoo.com/ (comics)
- https://www.cur.org/ (undergrad research conferences and journals)
- https://undergraduatecommons.com/open_to_submit.html (undergrad research journals)

Appendix C: Amber Smith's Material Project Write-Up

We SEW Need to Break Mental Health Stigma

The artist, Amber C. Smith, *sew* wants to break mental health stigma. She designed and sewed fashion pieces that support the rhetorical argument that augmenting knowledge on schizophrenia is imperative to diminish the stigma around this mental illness in order to improve the quality of, and the adherence to, treatment. The artist utilized various aspects of her artwork to symbolize the numerous characteristics of schizophrenia. With deliberate consideration of the items created, the colors utilized, the asymmetry and imperfection in style, the utilization of patches and a zipper, and even the font selected, each attribute offers a plethora of arguments regarding schizophrenia specifically, and mental illnesses in general.

The interactive link makes this message accessible to anyone with internet access. Kids, adolescents, and adults can all benefit from learning about the themes addressed through the fashion pieces. Specifically, though, these pieces draw the attention of the fashion industry. It has not been uncommon to hear designers describe their style as "schizophrenic" (Ducksworth et al., 2003), a comment that can heighten the stigma surrounding the disorder. The symbolism throughout this outfit serves to draw attention to how the stigma around mental illnesses is problematic to the well-being of those with schizophrenia. Additionally, it urges the fashion industry to use designs to raise awareness of the issue, instead of further perpetuating the stigma. This product could be marketed and sold on a large scale to reach a broader community with the message.

First, the types of clothing items were carefully selected. A skirt is a clothing item that is more frequently worn by female-identifying individuals in the United States. Similarly, mental illnesses are often more likely to be discussed by women rather than men. Toxic masculinity often hinders conversations about mental health between men. Nevertheless, mental illnesses—particularly schizophrenia—affect every demographic. Additionally, the hat serves a purpose. Hats cover your head and, therefore, your brain—the epicenter for hallucinations. Just like Cecilia's mother told her not to tell the doctor about her hallucinations because she worried they would think she is crazy ("TedX Talks," 2017), many individuals choose not to share that they have schizophrenia due to the stigma. It is not going to be easy for people to take off their hat, and share about their experience with schizophrenia, until the stigma is reduced.

The colors also rhetorically demonstrate the desired message. Colors aside from just black and white denim were utilized to exemplify how eradicating the stigma around schizophrenia, and mental illnesses in general, does not have a simple 'black and white' answer. The process to end stigma, involving education and unlearning of myths, will take time and persistence. Furthermore, the outfit utilizes cool colors to represent that those with schizophrenia are predominately calm despite the media's portrayal of them as erratic and dangerous. Additionally, there exists juxtaposition of the different shades of blue. Blue represents sadness, an emotion often felt by the burden of a severe mental illness and stigma. On top of sadness, though, blue is the color of the ocean, which is vastly unexplored; likewise, there is an extensive amount of unknown information the public needs to learn about schizophrenia to eradicate the stigma.

Next, the asymmetry and imperfections serve to represent the imperfections within the lives of individuals with schizophrenia (and everyone else's lives). Despite the asymmetry, the hat functions well; this illustrates that even imperfections can be beautiful and help one accomplish a desired task, just like individuals with schizophrenia can still live flourishing lives. Additionally, the fraying represents the difficulties the stigma around schizophrenia poses for many individuals to keep their life looking "perfect" and keep from unraveling. With stigma—not to even mention the extremely high cost of treatment—treatment is not always feasible, or even seen as an option. In turn, the stigma interferes with adherence to treatment and better recovery and can even lead to people with schizophrenia "isolating [themselves] from society" (Vahabzadeh et al., 2011, p. 440). With social isolation and without treatment, schizophrenia can become very intrusive in someone's life and unravel their life, depicted by the unraveling skirt. Nevertheless, there is a seam sewed just above the edge to prohibit the skirt from fraying significantly; it represents that with the proper stigma-free treatment, individuals with schizophrenia can stop their lives from unraveling and live fulfilling lives. The shirt additionally reveals the theme of imperfection through the placement of the pocket. The pocket is placed askew on the shirt with the message on an angle. Even with the pocket slanted, though, the message can be read. These imperfections represent the reality of imperfect lives, even demonstrating that the goal is not to correct the imperfections but to persevere despite them—to be functionally imperfect (whereas some might say perfectly imperfect).

Additionally, the patches and coalescence of different denim colors on the skirt aim to represent that broken pieces can be put back together. Individuals with schizophrenia can be "sewn" with treatment that can help them return to a flourishing life. Just like you can still see the seams connecting the patches, this will not eradicate their mental illness or the hardships that come with it, but they will be able to function and flourish, just like the hat and skirt function with visible seams. Nevertheless, the seams could not have been sewed without some thought and care. Similarly, treatment will better improve the quality of life of people with schizophrenia when we take the care to thoughtfully consider those with mental health issues and end stigma. Furthermore, the two denim sides of the skirt express two facets of identities: the identity individuals show to the world and who they truly are. Just like Cecillia's mother urged her to not share her mental illness ("TedX Talks," 2017), many individuals feel shamed into keeping their mental illness to themselves and not share that 'side' with the world.

The means to close the skirt, the zipper, was also thoroughly thought through. First, the metal in the skirt represents the strength people with schizophrenia have to use to live through their days with hallucination, delusions, and more. Additionally, this skirt would fall down if the zipper was not closed, just like stigma can bring people down if they open up about having schizophrenia.

And last but not least, the font chosen on the shirt makes the "IMPERFECT" text stand out. The font appears "perfect," error-free, though all people have imperfections (defined differently by different people) and can still manage to live flourishing lives amidst the challenges thrown at them. The words were intentionally selected to denote that individuals are "perfect the way they are," not just in spite of their imperfections but because of how their imperfections shape them. Stigma-free means not changing the individual with mental illness but accepting them as the person they are: changing the world around them.

Overall, this piece is designed to appeal to pathos and instill empathy regarding the dangers of mental health stigma. The design elements throughout this outfit were carefully selected. Each aspect offers a rhetorical argument around the difficulties that people with schizophrenia face and emphasizes the need to end stigma. A fashion piece serves as a public medium for these messages to reach a broad audience. We *sew* need to eradicate the stigma to improve the treatment and ultimate quality of life for those with schizophrenia and all mental illnesses.

REFERENCES

Duckworth, K., Halperh, J., Schutt, R., & Gillespie, C. (2003). Use of schizophrenia as a metaphor in the U.S. newspapers. *Psychiatric Services, 54*(10), 1402–1404. https://doi.org/10.1176/appi.ps.54.10.1402

TedX Talks. (2017, March 27). *I am not a monster: schizophrenia*. [Video]. Youtube. https://www.youtube.com/watch?v=xbagFzcyNiM&vl=en

Vahabzadeh, A., Wittenauer, J., & Carr, E. (2011). Stigma, schizophrenia, and the media: Exploring changes in the reporting of schizophrenia in major U.S. newspapers. *Journal of Psychiatric Practice, 17*(6), 439–446. https://doi.org/10.1097/01.pra.0000407969.65098.35

Index

A
abuse, sexual, 133, 136
activism, quiet, 79, 164, 184
activist events, 1, 8–9, 12, 19, 20, 75, 76, 78, 93, 96, 114, 137
activists, 11–12, 14, 22–23, 39, 41, 90, 91, 96–102, 102–111, 111–118, 129–131
agency, 12, 28, 55, 64, 78, 80, 102–107, 125, 131, 132, 135, 169
  covert assertions of, 91, 102–103, 104–105, 106–109, 125, 131
AIDS quilt, 14, 160
alphabetic text, 13–14, 16, 17, 41, 91, 109–113, 148, 184, 190
androgyny, 15, 146
apartheid, 57, 59
appeals
  ethical, 92–94, 105
  logical, 92, 93, 98, 105
archives, 25, 28–33, 34, 35, 36–39, 41, 114, 114–116, 133, 150, 172–174

archiving, 29, 31–34, 34–37, 90, 133
art, 12, 15–16, 51–53, 57, 58, 127, 130–131, 134, 151–152, 158–159, 159, 163, 168
  fabric, 16, 114, 115, 131, 133
artifacts, 23, 30, 35, 36, 67, 90, 132
artistic activism, 164–166
artists, 12, 15, 31, 58, 93, 132–134, 165, 193
art therapy, 160
assault, 24, 35, 37, 38, 97, 98–103, 104, 115, 126, 129
audience, 11, 12, 14, 16, 36, 91, 94–95, 97–98, 109–111, 113–114, 119, 151, 165, 169–171
audience members, 26, 93, 94, 98, 101, 103, 121, 122, 134, 136
authority, 30, 58, 64, 65, 71, 105, 107, 123, 164

B
Black lives Matter hats, 160

body, 19–21, 23, 90–91, 100–104, 106–109, 125, 132, 149
bumper sticker messages, 105, 123, 135

C
campus, 9, 24–25, 30, 31, 37, 99, 171
 sexual assaults on, 24, 37
censorship, 12, 42, 73, 131
characters, 92, 93–95, 98–99, 99–101, 103, 116
Charlottesville, 161
classrooms, 67–72, 145, 165–167, 171, 173
Clothesline Project. *See* CP
clothing, 15, 18–19, 20–22, 25, 97, 99, 146, 161, 162, 171
community, 21, 25, 34, 129–130, 145, 154, 163, 164, 166, 170, 194
community literacy, 146–148
composing practices, 13, 15, 16, 36–39, 115, 145, 148, 183
composition pedagogy, 29, 41, 173
compositions, 17, 36, 39–41, 148, 150–153, 155, 168–169, 171–172, 173, 174, 183, 184
Confucian silence, 64
consciousness-raising (CR), 26
CP activists, 103, 105, 107, 117, 118–119
CP (Clothesline Project), 4, 5, 7–10, 12–14, 18–20, 23–24, 25–26, 30–33, 34–40, 78, 89–91, 93, 110–112, 113–117, 119, 122–125, 126–129, 130–131, 134–135, 161–162, 172–174
CP events, 8, 26, 36, 37, 41, 120, 184
CP participants, 19–21, 38–39, 89–92, 98–99, 101, 103, 105–107, 110, 111, 114, 121–123, 129, 130–132
CP shirts, 19–21, 30, 89, 96, 123, 131–132, 183–184
crafters, 156, 163
crafting, 157–161, 163, 164, 166–168
craftivism, 158–159, 161, 164, 165, 169–170
craftivists, 159–161, 162, 165
crafts, 156, 157–160, 163–164, 168
creativity, 31, 57, 122, 155, 173, 174
criminology, 39, 154, 183
culture, 2, 5, 29–30, 40, 41, 61–63, 79, 109–110, 115–116, 117, 118, 133

D
Davis protest, 75
Deaf President Now, 78
democracy, 61
design decisions, 13, 89–90, 111–112, 131, 148, 183
designs, 13, 38–42, 111, 118, 124, 148–150, 169, 183, 184
deviance, 121
digital compositions, 13, 148, 150–152, 155
Disability Clothesline Project, 160
disclosure, 15, 16, 74, 80, 92–94, 95, 120–123, 131, 134, 135
discourse, 2, 11, 17, 35, 60, 69, 118, 123, 126, 131, 146–148
Discussion Questions, 39–41, 80, 137, 174

E
education, 20, 64, 67–70, 72–73, 76, 78, 111, 137, 168
embodiment, 90, 116, 164, 166, 184

emotional appeals, 92–95, 104, 123, 135, 137, 148
emotional experiences, 59, 92–94, 124
emotions, 54, 57–58, 60–63, 65–67, 93, 104, 105, 109, 114, 123–124, 129, 130, 135, 156, 160, 173
empathy, 40, 67, 165–166, 174, 196
empowerment, 12, 28, 53, 66, 74, 100, 124, 132
engagement, civic, 2, 57, 148, 173
ethos, 8, 65, 71, 80, 92–96, 98, 116, 164, 174
evil eye gloves, 161
exclusion, 8–9, 69, 94, 156, 158, 167, 174

F
Fab Labs, 156
failure, 61, 158, 167
feminism, 37, 39–40, 67, 151, 159
feminist, 25, 51, 56, 92, 133, 151, 169, 170
feminist activism, 5, 7, 10, 12, 24, 51, 92, 133, 149, 151
feminist activist work, 6–8, 12
fraternities, 9, 37, 99
freedom, 127, 166

G
Gallaudet University, 78–79
Gay, Lesbian, and Straight Education Network (GLSEN), 77
gender, 7–9, 15, 34, 39, 96, 110, 154, 160
gender violence, 19–21, 91, 93–95, 96, 99, 101, 102, 104–105, 115, 119, 120–123, 125, 126, 132–134
genres, 13, 77, 153, 174

gestures, 52, 58, 123, 127
governments, 37, 77, 121, 132, 161
graffiti, 20, 159
groups, marginalized, 12, 74, 154, 161

H
hackerspaces, 156–157
Handmaid Coalition, 161
happiness, 65, 109–110, 163
healing, 25, 102, 104–105, 106–109, 119, 126–129, 130, 135
hearts, 28, 96, 109–110, 110–112
hearts of cville, 161
Herstory, Brooklyn, 29, 30
history, 22, 40, 41, 64, 119, 149, 158, 159

I
identities, 3, 4, 8–9, 15, 18–22, 26, 27, 34–36, 38–40, 62, 109, 116, 119, 121, 127, 132, 136–137
ideologies, 2, 3, 11–12, 14, 36, 54, 90, 115, 117, 145, 146, 148, 150, 155, 167
images, 12–14, 16, 18–20, 21, 27–28, 91–92, 95–97, 104–105, 109–110, 148–151, 153
Immigrant Yarn Project, 160
inclusivity, 9, 69, 76
industrialization, 156
informal justice, 154
information literacy, 79–80
injustice, 27, 80, 102, 127, 136
innovation, 122, 152, 153
instructors, 67, 69, 157, 166
Interactive Silence, 54–55
introverts, 70, 120

J
Jeffco student protests, 53

justice, 6–8, 16, 19, 30–34, 39, 71–73, 154

K

knitting, 158–159, 163, 167, 169

L

language, 2, 4, 13–15, 26, 56–57, 78, 79, 122, 127, 129, 133, 134, 147–148, 183–184
law, 75, 95, 120
learning, 63, 67, 70, 156, 157, 160, 166–167, 173
legend of cautions, 130
LGBTQIA community, 8, 10, 129
LGBTQ's National Day of Silence (DOS), 75
liberation, 25, 101, 108, 121, 135, 173
linguistics, 54, 147, 148, 184
listening, 23, 53, 54, 56, 61, 65, 67, 68, 75, 101–102, 127
literacy, 10–12, 15–16, 20–23, 102, 117, 118, 135–137, 146, 147, 165–167
literacy sponsors, 146
literate artifacts, 2, 4, 10, 11, 16, 36, 90, 118
literate practices, 2–3, 10–11, 16–18, 24, 91, 101, 111–112, 119, 132, 146, 148
local publics, 147
logos, 92, 98, 174
Long Walk Home, 160

M

makerspaces, 156–159, 171–172
March for our Lives, 76
marginalization, 5–8, 64, 70, 90, 129

Marjory Stoneman Douglas High School, 76
mass shootings, 76, 168
materiality, 1, 18, 28–30, 39–41, 68–69, 122, 133, 148–149, 150–152, 156–160, 164–166
material multimodality, 24, 39, 148–149, 166
materials, digital, 149, 152, 172
Matter movements, 75, 122
media, 80, 90, 114, 158, 171, 194
  new, 149, 153, 158–159
media literacy, 166
medium, 5, 36, 41, 115, 190
memory, 29–30, 58, 167
mental health, 163, 171–172, 192–195
MeToo, 122
microcollecting, 30
modes, 12–14, 114, 121–122, 131, 132, 137, 146, 148–149, 160
Monument Quilt, 162
movements, 9, 14–15, 17, 101, 122, 130, 132, 148, 153, 156, 160, 165, 174
multiliteracies, 23
multimedia, making, 173
multimodal composition, 13, 39–41, 90, 152, 173, 174
multimodality, 12, 42, 145, 148, 151–152, 166

N

NAMES Project, 25
Names Quilt, 14
narratives
  ideological, 115, 146
  normative, 109, 111
  patriarchal, 90, 109, 120
non-binary individuals, 8

O

Obama, President, 24
objectification, 19–20, 161
objects, literate, 20, 21, 23
Occupy Wall Street, 156
online activism, 38, 155, 159
opposition, 20, 22, 28, 67, 71, 136, 146
oppression, 7–8, 10, 20, 25, 28, 52–56, 65–66, 127–128, 130, 134–135

P

pain, 16, 29, 59, 61, 127, 129
pandemic, 163, 164, 168
paralinguistic, 54
participation requirements, 2, 72, 100
pathos, 8, 92–94, 98, 123, 137, 174, 196
patterns, 9, 36, 38–40, 57, 90, 92–94, 111, 115, 120
pedagogy, 3, 39, 41, 51, 166, 170, 172, 184
personal experiences, 94, 98, 99, 101, 104, 105, 109, 115, 123, 130
Perspectives on Silence, 62
persuasion, 11, 148
photographs, 5, 20–22, 29–30, 114, 160, 166, 168
Pink Tank Project, 160
politics, 16, 20, 25, 40–41, 51–52, 59–60, 73, 117–119, 124, 136–137, 169
power, 27, 34, 35, 41, 52, 56, 58, 67–68, 73–76, 78–79, 98, 117–118, 123–124, 131–132, 166–168
  faces of, 27, 132
prisons, 126, 170
process, 2–3, 16, 17, 22, 31, 33, 38, 69, 107, 109, 134–135, 145–147, 149, 157–158
composing, 11, 152
protection, 18, 19, 26, 57, 74, 77, 105, 126
protests, 20, 22, 73–77, 124, 127, 131–132, 158–159, 161, 164, 165
  silent, 70–72
psychogeography, 128
psychology, 3, 18–20, 39, 40, 95, 168, 171
psychosocial
  composing/compositions, 1–3, 17–18, 22–25, 36–38, 40, 95, 107–119, 131–133, 145
Pussyhat Project, 160

Q

questions, crafterthought, 162, 174
Quietists, 59

R

race, 8, 9, 34, 62, 79, 99, 130, 166, 183
rape, 27, 99, 103, 116–118, 128, 136–137, 155
rape culture, 117, 118, 135–137
REDress project, 161
refugees, 160
refusal, silent, 52
relationships, 13, 16–19, 24, 26–28, 40, 91–95, 111–113, 117, 118, 151, 183–184
religion/faith, 107
remembrance, 12, 54, 57
representations, constructed, 91, 107, 124–126, 149, 167
resilience, 89, 170
resistance, 7, 58, 71, 116, 118, 119, 124, 128, 155, 158, 168, 169
re-victimization, 19–20, 39, 99, 104, 105, 119, 184

rhetoric, 10–12, 26, 39–41, 51, 53, 65, 76–77, 79–80, 107, 133
  visual, 16, 25–29, 89–91, 95, 133, 148, 151, 190
rhetorical analysis, 28, 91, 92, 95
rhetorical appeals, 92
rhetorical citizenship, 11, 148
rhetorical situations, 11, 69, 166, 170, 172, 174
rhetorical strategy, 11, 103, 113
rhetoric and composition, 3, 145, 148, 183
risk, 8, 9, 61, 65, 122

S
Saturday Mothers, 76, 77
Saturday People vigils, 75
scene, 28, 78, 98, 108, 110
scrapbooking, 149, 168
semiotic analysis, 91–92, 95–96, 149
semiotics, 90, 148
settings, 92–95, 97–99, 104, 113, 115
sexism, 7, 10, 34, 39, 161, 168
sexual assault, 15–16, 37, 115, 126, 154, 161, 162
sexual identity, 22, 74, 77
sexuality, 119, 166
sexual violence, 10, 16, 24–26, 73, 74, 98–99, 101, 105–107, 118, 120, 122
shirts, 4, 5, 8–10, 21–26, 27–30, 77–80, 89–98, 122, 169–171
silence, 12, 16, 40, 41, 51–80, 90, 116–118, 122, 125–129, 132, 153, 164–166
  administrative, 65–66, 75
  breaking, 53, 56, 79, 101, 124
  breaking the, 77, 128
  categorizations of, 51
  ceremonial, 63
  complexities of, 62, 78
  consumptive, 55
  deliberative, 52
  democratic, 124, 125
  eloquent, 53, 54
  expectations for, 65, 66
  expectations of, 65, 74
  fast-time, 54
  functions of, 52, 62
  insubordinate, 74
  mental, 54
  notions of, 25, 77
  power of, 52, 75
  rhetorics of, 16, 40, 41, 51, 90–91, 122, 151, 164
  role of, 52, 59, 65
  selective, 54
  social construction of, 80
  speaking, 77, 128
  student, 75
  tactical, 52–53
  tolerance of, 68
  transformation of, 117
  use of, 16, 57, 60–63, 65, 67, 72, 173
  women's, 59, 74, 115, 122, 130
silence and listening, 61, 67, 75–76
silencing, 8–9, 26, 52, 64, 69, 73, 74, 105, 121–124, 127
silent responsive understanding, 53
Slow-time psycholinguistic silences, 54
Slut Walk, 122, 128
social action, 91, 126, 127, 147
social change, 8, 102, 118, 127, 132, 148, 151
Social Justice Sewing Academy, 170
social media spaces, 155
social narratives, 2, 3, 25, 35, 36, 90, 91, 96, 115, 117, 118, 164
social structures, 10, 13, 28, 73, 123, 146
social systems, 24, 56, 95
Sociocultural Silence, 54

spaces
  public, 22, 27, 120, 128, 147, 148
  safe, 4, 173
speech, 53–54, 56, 61, 62, 64, 67–68, 69, 71, 72, 74–77, 123–124, 153
standing man protest, 76
Steubenville rape case, 117
stigma, 64–65, 78, 172, 193–196
students, 23, 24, 26–30, 64, 67–71, 75–76, 78, 79, 89, 153–155, 165–167
  deaf, 78, 79
  identifying, 33–35
  quiet, silent, 63, 68–71
subject positions, 9, 10, 40, 52, 99–100, 118, 119, 129, 134, 147, 167, 174, 183
subversion, 22, 123, 125, 135
suffragettes, 158
support systems, 34, 126, 163
survivors, 4, 7, 15–16, 28, 34–36, 72–74, 77, 78, 89–90, 93–95, 98–99, 102–104, 117–118, 120–124, 126

T
Take Back the Night (TBTN), 9, 12, 15, 16, 112, 122, 128
TBTN. *See* Take Back the Night
teachers, 23, 67–69, 71, 166, 168. *See also* education
technology, 39, 114, 149–157, 163, 166, 167, 171–174
tee shirt literacy, 130, 135
tee shirts, 4, 5, 12, 18–26, 34–36, 77–79, 89–90, 93–96, 98, 101–105, 107–109, 111–112, 117–118, 121–123, 169, 173–174, 183–184
text and images, 14, 91–92, 95, 111–113, 151
themes, 20, 21, 28–29, 94–95, 131–132, 171, 193, 195

therapy, 3, 136
Title IX, 23
Toxic masculinity, 194
trauma, 31, 37, 59, 73, 89, 121–122, 126, 127, 129, 134–135, 136–137
Trump, Donald, 24, 159–161, 166

U
UC Davis protest, 75
Unite the Right Rally, 161
use silence, 60, 62, 65, 67, 69–70, 74, 78, 125, 126

V
victim blaming, 39, 73, 93–95, 128, 136
violence
  interpersonal, 27
  police, 75, 76
  politically-associated, 73
  racial, 160
visual communication, 111–114, 173
visual representations, 14, 39–40, 107, 111–112
visuals, 15, 17, 28, 89, 90–91, 107–110, 167
vulnerability, 16, 28, 38, 102, 129

W
Western cultures, 65–67, 152
women's activism, 12, 173
women's experiences, 28–30, 78, 93, 103
Women's March, 161
work, public, 41, 131, 167, 168, 170
worldviews, 2, 3, 8, 28, 121
writers, multilingual, 184

Y
yarn bombing, 164

The manufacturer's authorised representative in the EU is Springer Nature Customer Service Centre GmbH, Europaplatz 3, 69115 Heidelberg, Germany. If you have any concerns regarding our products, please contact ProductSafety@springernature.com

Printed and bound by CPI Group (UK) Ltd, Croydon, CR0 4YY
25/03/2026
02078175-0003